CRASH INTO ME

The World of Roswell

CRASH INTO ME

The World of Roswell

ROBYN BURNETT

ECW

Published by ECW PRESS
2120 Queen Street East, Suite 200, Toronto, Ontario, Canada M4E 1E2

NATIONAL LIBRARY OF CANADA CATALOGUING IN PUBLICATION DATA

Burnett, (Robyn S.)
Crash into me: the world of Roswell / Robyn Burnett.

ISBN 1-55022-539-1

1.Roswell (Television program) I. Title

PN1992.77.R64B87 2002   791.45'72   C2002-902175-8

Editing: Jen Hale
Cover and Text Design: Tania Craan
Typesetting: Tannice Goddard
Production: Mary Bowness
Printing: Transcontinental
Front cover image: Chip Simons/Getty Images
Front Cover Actor Photos: Shiri Appleby – Christina Radish; Brendan Fehr – Christina Radish; Katherine Heigl – Harry Langdon/Shooting Star; Jason Behr – Albert L. Ortega; Majandra Delfino – Christina Radish
Colour section, in order: Paul Fenton/Shooting Star; Christina Radish; Christina Radish; Christina Radish; Christina Radish; Fionna; Photo by William Sadler, courtesy Fionna; Christina Radish; Christina Radish; Dale Josephson; Dale Josephson

This book is set in AGaramond and Imago

The publication of *Crash Into Me* has been generously supported by the Canada Council, the Ontario Arts Council, and the Government of Canada through the Book Publishing Industry Development Program. **Canada**

DISTRIBUTION
CANADA: Jaguar Book Group, 100 Armstrong Avenue, Georgetown, ON L7G 5S4

UNITED STATES: Independent Publishers Group, 814 North Franklin Street,
Chicago, Illinois 60610

EUROPE: Turnaround Publisher Services, Unit 3, Olympia Trading Estate,
Coburg Road, Wood Green, London N2Z 6T2

AUSTRALIA AND NEW ZEALAND: Wakefield Press, 1 The Parade Way West (Box 2066),
Kent Town, South Australia 5071

PRINTED AND BOUND IN CANADA

ECW PRESS
ecwpress.com

Thanks

Acknowledgments

Many, many people helped me on my *Roswell* writing journey, and I would like to take this moment to acknowledge them for their support, time, effort, patience, and encouragement. This book has been a collaborative effort, and I cannot thank them enough for being integral part in this process.

First, I have to say thank you to the Crashdown Web site, the Webmasters, and all of the contributors. Without your amazing site, I have no idea what I would have done. A special thank you to Kenn Gold for his constant support, his generous nature, and for being such a great cheerleader. Thank you, also, to Fan Forum's *Roswell* posting board. Thanks must go to Fionna Boyle, Michelle Woolley, Kristi Bergman, Lena, Kim, Wisty, and all the other members of the Charity Crew who generously dedicated their time and efforts for various worthy causes over the past few years: your work has been inspirational. Thank you to all of the contributors of the Crashdown Yearbooks, to the Web Master and contributors of *Roswell* MP3's site, and Garn's Guides, and to Nancy Billows and Shirley Ozment for their help on the Rosquilters information. Also, thanks to Gregory Schwartz, Christina Radish, Albert L. Ortega, and Dale Josephson for providing some amazing photos. All of Dale's proceeds have been donated to Families of Spinal Muscular Atrophy.

This is my second opportunity working with ECW Press, and I would like very much to thank Jack David for giving me a chance, and Jen Hale for being the best editor a girl could have. I also owe my eternal gratitude to: Robert, Kelly and Jay Burnett, Christopher Giardino, Cathey Kilner, Debbie Barton-Moore, Katie Mead, Barb Gibbins, the Parker family, Margot Massie, Lindsay Stephens, Kasia Puhacz, and everyone else who put up with me in February 2002.

Finally, there are two people who have been a vital part of this project and without whom I would be completely lost: Fionna, and my agent, Sanjay Burman. Thank you, Fionna, for your unconditional generosity, your incredible work with the campaigns, and for your monumental efforts in helping me through this process. Thank you, Sanjay, for believing in me from the very start, for your constant dedication and support, and for our daily chat sessions.

This book is dedicated to the fans of *Roswell.* The spirit of the show lives on.

Contents

Contents

Acknowledgments v

Introduction 1

1 The Roswell Incident 3

2 The Cast of Roswell 17

3 The Roswell Fan Phenomenon 71

4 Roswell on the Internet 111

5 Leaving Normal. . . . The Roswell Quiz 123

6 Answers 131

7 Off the Menu. . . . The Roswell Chicken Jokes 135

8 Roswell Episode Guide 141

Bibliography 297

Introduction

"How do we know that they're not three feet tall, green, and slimy?"

A show about teenage alienation. Literally.

The idea seemed absurd to many at the start, but it didn't take long for viewers to be won over by this little show with big potential. The history of the television show *Roswell* is almost as dramatic and unique as that of the famous incident on which it was based. After all, how many shows start off attached to one network, are saved by Tabasco sauce, end up on a second network, and are finally bought out by a third — and can boast a fan base that has raised over $250,000 U.S. for charity? Who would have thought that a show about teenage aliens could touch so many different lives?

The first major organized fan campaign involved *Star Trek* in 1968. The *Star Trek* fans banded together, arranging a letter-writing campaign in order to convince NBC to film another season of the low-rated show. *Cagney and Lacey*, the CBS female police series, was rescued in 1983 by a letter-writing campaign, and lasted five more seasons! In *Roswell's* case, a new twist was thrown into the mix. That twist involved the spicy sauce known as Tabasco.

Jason Behr, Katherine Heigl, Shiri Appleby, Majandra Delfino, and Brendan Fehr at the Teen Choice Awards (Photo by Christina Radish)

The Tabasco campaign helped to spark new trends for fans everywhere who are determined to make sure the networks hear what they have to say.

The show revolves around the lives of three teenage human/alien hybrids, who are living with the secret of their identity in Roswell, New Mexico. Descendants of the crash victims of 1947, Max, Isabel, and Michael know nothing of their other home, and long for answers. Max, however, risks exposing them all when Liz, the girl he has adored for years, is shot, and he uses his powers to heal her. The show has been described as *The X-Files* meets *Dawson's Creek*, as well as an alien/human version of *Romeo and Juliet*. The *Roswell* saga began on October 6, 1999, on The WB following *Dawson's Creek*, and has caused quite a stir ever since.

Chapter 1

The Roswell Incident

In 1947, a series of strange events occurred in the region of Roswell, New Mexico, that rocked not only the United States of America, but other nations as well. Not since Orson Welles's famous broadcast of *War of the Worlds* had the concept of aliens invading the planet seemed so real. Unlike the broadcast, however, this incident *was* very much a reality, or so many would like to believe. Did the small town of Roswell witness a massive military cover-up operation, or were overactive imaginations at work? After all, Roswell was the home of the U.S. Air Force's 509 bombardment group, which was storing nuclear warheads. Was the explosion and debris truly a top-secret military operation gone wrong? While the military still denies that there was an alien crash, many individuals came forward after years had passed in order to reveal a different version of the events of 1947. This is their story.

JUNE 24, 1947

Kenneth Arnold had reached an altitude of 9,200 feet as he flew his single-engine plane over the Cascade Mountain Range in Washington State. The

32-year-old resident of Boise, Idaho was suddenly stunned by a brilliant flash lighting up the sky around him, even reflecting off his own aircraft. Arnold scanned the sky, then noticed something coming from the vicinity of Mt. Baker at a tremendous speed. It appeared to be a number of aircraft, all without tails, and unlike anything he had ever seen. Not only were they unfamiliar but their flight pattern was in complete reverse of the standard pattern: the first craft flew at a higher altitude than the ones following. Coasting near Mt. Adams, Kenneth decided to try to clock the speed of these unusual craft as they approached.

As they drew near, Kenneth got a better look at one of the nine disc-shaped aircraft. He noticed one in particular appeared slightly larger than the others. When it flashed and spun, it seemed almost circular. The fleet of ships flew erratically, skipping across the sky. The craft swooped by, past the southern ridge of Mt. Adams and out of sight. Quickly, Kenneth checked the second hand of his watch. They had covered a 50-mile distance in one minute and 42 seconds. Their speed: 1,700 miles per hour.

Kenneth reported this event to the Oregon press. While Kenneth's sighting was not the first, it was one of the first to gain widespread media attention. The military began to take more notice.

JULY 2, 1947

Mr. and Mrs. Dan Wilmot were well-respected, reliable citizens of Roswell, New Mexico. They did not like to tell stories, especially ones of strange flying objects; but on that summer night, that is exactly what they saw. Approximately 1,500 feet high in the sky, and flying at what seemed to be 500 miles per hour, the craft first came into view southeast of their home and disappeared over the trees in the area known as Six Mile Hill. While Mrs. Wilmot heard a swishing sound for the duration, Mr. Wilmot was struck by the appearance of the strange objects; like two bowls placed rim to rim, glowing from the inside.

Hoping someone else would step forward and report seeing the strange flying oval, Mr. and Mrs. Wilmot kept the strange experience to themselves.

It wasn't until six days later, when the Air Force announced that they had a flying saucer in their possession, that the couple came forward with their story.

JULY 4, 1947

It was 11:30 p.m. and at St. Mary's Hospital, two nuns were in the midst of their shift change on the third floor. Looking out of the window, they noticed a large flash just northwest of the town of Roswell. Believing it to be a crashed plane, they simply recorded it in their notebooks. No one knew of their observation until 30 years later.

Just south of St. Mary's at the military base, the control tower also noticed a bright explosion of light. The men working that night knew right away that it was a crash, and within a short period of time, it was confirmed that the craft was not one of theirs. This meant one thing to the men: the next day would involve a search for survivors, and identifying the aircraft.

It also meant a search for witnesses.

Jim Ragsdale was out for a good time that night. At a secluded campsite up on Boy Scout Mountain, about 50 miles from Roswell, Jim and his girlfriend Trudy were spending some time together away from work. Naked, stretched out in the back of his pick-up truck, they took a break from making out to enjoy a cold beer. The only threat they could see was a storm approaching, but even that appeared to be moving to the north.

Then suddenly, there was a huge flash followed by an explosion. A thundering BOOM filled the air. A moment later, a large object plowed towards the pick-up, chopping up the trees in its path. It missed them by about 60 yards, landing instead between two huge rocks.

Taking a moment to pull themselves together, Jim and Trudy grabbed a couple of flashlights and made their way over to the crash site. The saucer had been cracked open and Jim took a long look inside. There appeared to be four or five seats, and a Captain's seat that appeared similar to a throne with what looked like rubies and diamonds. The bodies inside were child-like, with large, balloon-shaped heads. Their skin had the same texture as a snake's, but Jim couldn't be certain if it was a uniform or not.

Jim and Trudy started to gather up some of the debris, returning to their truck. That next morning, as the military vehicles approached, the couple left the scene as quickly as they could. Taking their findings down to a local tavern, The Blue Moon, to show them off, Jim and Trudy split up the material and headed their separate ways. They had no idea how this event would drastically change their lives.

JULY 5, 1947

The military rushed in to recover what was left of the craft. It was hauled out by truck and taken off to the base in Carrizozo before it was separated and shipped off to a variety of different military bases. Carrizozo was a water stop in the 1940s on the road between Albuquerque and El Paso. Getting a craft out of the mountains and to the train without being seen was not an easy feat, but the military managed to deal with the issue without major public awareness.

Mr. R.E. Fresquez, a respected rancher, lived within the vicinity of the crash site, just northwest of Roswell. Suddenly, his life became one of military confinement. Fresquez was under orders not to leave his ranch unless the guard assigned to his property was present. As for checking the land and feeding the livestock, that was a different matter. The only way he could do so was in the company of military personnel. Even then, there were areas no one was allowed to cross, disturb, or trespass onto, even with a military escort. Whatever was happening, it was serious.

That same morning, W.W. Brazel, or "Mac" as he was known, saddled up his horse to check on his herd. Mac, the classic honest cowboy, worked as a cattle and sheep rancher, leasing the Foster Ranch 75 miles northwest of Roswell. He'd heard a fierce thunderstorm the night before. He'd also heard a strange thunderclap that was louder and different than the others. He asked Dee Proctor, the son of his neighbors Loretta and Floyd Proctor, to join him.

The first thing Mac noticed as he rode along was metal debris strewn over a large area of his land. Then he spotted a shallow trench dug into the earth that extended out for hundreds of feet. Noting the strange properties of the metal, he selected a few pieces to take back. Wanting to get another opinion on the bizarre debris, Mac Brazel took some to the Proctor ranch.

Loretta and her husband were also intrigued by the unique findings, and encouraged Mac to take it to the town sheriff. After all, the metal Brazel had found could have been a piece of wreckage from some secret government project, or even . . . a UFO. If that was the case, it should definitely be reported. And who knows what sort of profit could be made from that! Returning to the site with his truck, Mac dragged the largest piece back and stored it in his barn. He also collected a box of the debris. The next day, Mac would head into town to see Sheriff Wilcox.

JULY 6, 1947

Sheriff George Wilcox wasn't expecting Mac Brazel when he showed up with his box of metal. Brazel explained to Sheriff Wilcox that his ranch was covered with the stuff, and if the military was responsible, he wanted them to get out there and clear it up. The sheriff and his deputies didn't argue with Brazel. Whatever the debris was, it was . . . different. The sheriff suggested they call up the Roswell military base. Before that, however, he spoke with Frank Joyce, a cub news reporter. Frank had already heard from Brazel. Not believing the rancher, he suggested Brazel speak with the sheriff first. Now he listened as Sheriff Wilcox told him Mac Brazel's tale might be interesting after all.

Sheriff Wilcox picked up another line and called the Roswell Army Air Field. Colonel William Blanchard assigned Intelligence Officer Major Jesse Marcel of the 509 Bomb group to investigate Mac Brazel's story. The senior counter intelligence corps agent, Captain Sheridan Cavitt, would join him. They arranged to meet with Brazel at the sheriff's station, where they would follow him back to his ranch and discover exactly what he was talking about.

Each driving his own vehicle, they arrived at the Foster Ranch that evening. Brazel took them to the barn and showed them the largest piece he had found. The material was a dull silver color and extremely lightweight. Maj. Marcel immediately pulled out a Geiger counter and checked it for radiation. There was only a normal amount. It was too late to go out and check the rest of the debris, so Maj. Marcel and Cpt. Cavitt stayed over at the

Foster Ranch, feasting on a dinner of cold beans and crashing on the bunkhouse floor.

JULY 7, 1947

The next morning, Maj. Marcel, Cpt. Cavitt, and Brazel headed out to the field. Three-quarters of a mile of land was covered with chunks of debris, most pieces being only the size of a man's hand. Brazel grumbled to them, complaining his sheep refused to cross the land, which made it all the more difficult for him. He had to herd them around it so they could get their water. If this was the army's debris, he wanted it cleaned up *now*.

Maj. Marcel was in awe of the sight. The whole area was covered with the stuff! It was clear to him immediately that this was no ordinary aircraft. Whatever this material was, it wasn't from planet Earth. There was no apparent impact point, which suggested to Maj. Marcel that the craft had exploded above ground, showering the debris over the earth. Based on the pattern of the debris, he was able to determine what direction it came from, and where it was heading.

The weightless, I-beam pieces were around one-quarter inch thick and fairly short in length. Unbreakable and unbendable, some had cryptic glyphs along them in two different colors. It felt like indestructable tinfoil. Maj. Marcel attempted to ignite a piece with his cigarette lighter. The stuff didn't burn. Excited, the three men began to collect as much of the debris as they could, loading it into their vehicles. The two officers took off towards Roswell.

At KGFL Roswell, the local radio station, Frank Joyce relayed Mac Brazel's story to the station owner, Walt Whitmore. Whitmore loved the idea and wanted the exclusive so he drove to the Foster Ranch and picked up Brazel. Returning to town, they headed to the station with the intent to wire-record an interview. Mac spoke of the debris, and its unique properties: aluminum-like, it would resume its shape after being crushed, and some pieces had pinkish/violet glyph writing on them. The station closed at 10:00 that evening, so it was too late to broadcast immediately. Whitmore invited Brazel back to his home, hoping to keep the other media away from the story. Then he stored the wire recording away in a safe place.

Cpt. Cavitt made his way straight to the base. Meanwhile, Maj. Marcel took a detour home before returning. Maj. Marcel had wracked his brain analyzing what the debris could have come from. It wasn't from a weather balloon; he'd seen debris from that. It certainly wasn't a rocket, missile, or aircraft. No, this was something he'd never seen before, and as he was not under orders to keep his findings secret, he wanted to share the discovery with his loved ones.

Rushing into the house, he woke his young son, Jesse Jr., and his wife, Vy. He spoke of flying saucers to the sleepy boy, who didn't even know what one was. Together with his son, they unloaded boxes from his father's '42 Buick and took them into the kitchen. Spilling out the material onto the floor, he told his son, "This is something you'll never see again but that's why I want to show it to you now."

They spread the debris out over the kitchen floor, sorted through it, then attempted to piece things together, as though working on a giant puzzle. Small purple metallic symbols similar to Egyptian hieroglyphs but more geometric in form shone on several pieces. The family separated the debris into three differ-ent categories: metal fragments similar to dull aluminum foil; pieces similar to a plastic metal, still light, but heavier than the foil; and finally, the I-beams.

They sorted through, fascinated, for 15 to 20 minutes before packing it all up again. Maj. Marcel then made his way back to the base, knowing they had made the discovery of a lifetime.

JULY 8, 1947

At dawn, Walter Whitmore Jr., who was home from college for the weekend, met Mac Brazel. As they sipped on their morning coffee, Brazel relayed his tale to Walter Jr., and he showed the young man some of the debris, then sketched out a map. As Walter Jr. headed out to see for himself, the phone rang. Whitmore Sr. answered.

A high powered Washington official was on the other line. He carefully reminded Whitmore that his station ran under a federally granted license, and should Whitmore decide to air any interviews with Mr. Mac Brazel, KGFL

Roswell's F.C.C. license would be withdrawn, and Whitmore's career would be over for good. Moments later, military vehicles arrived at Whitmore's home. Brazel was immediately escorted to Roswell's military base. His wire-recorded interview disappeared.

Maj. Marcel reported what he had found to Col. Blanchard that morning. He took the opportunity to show the Colonel the unique wreckage and the Colonel agreed that it was unlike anything he had ever seen. He instructed Maj. Marcel to accompany the boxes of debris to the Fort Worth Army Air Field in Carswell. Brigadier-General Roger Ramey, the Commanding Officer of the Eighth Air Force, would meet him there.

That same morning, Col. Blanchard found himself in a difficult position. He certainly did not want the public searching high and low in the desert for debris. At the same time, he knew enough of the townspeople were aware of the situation that it wouldn't take long before they started heading to Brazel's field. The craft that had been retrieved in the mountains was someone else's responsibility; the debris in Brazel's field, that was his. It was time to clean up the field, and fast.

Col. Blanchard made his decision. He instructed his public relations officer, Lt. Walter Haut, to issue a statement to the media, saying that the army had found, and now possessed, a flying saucer. He believed that if the general public believed that, then they would feel the army had already collected all the debris, and therefore would not search themselves. At 11:00 a.m., Lt. Walter Haut finished writing his statement, and it was released to two radio stations and several newspapers. At 2:26 p.m., the story got out on the AP wire. It was the only admission ever given by the U.S. Government that a UFO existed, and they had it.

Once the press release got out, pandemonium ensued. Calls flooded the offices of Sheriff Wilcox and Col. Blanchard. The attention was placed on Roswell Army Air Field, allowing Brazel's field to be cleared quickly and efficiently. Col. Blanchard left the base mid-afternoon and made his way to the Foster Ranch. Sheriff Wilcox, on the other hand, was having difficulty with the new celebrity status. He fielded calls from all over the U.S. as well as

Mexico. Even England was calling the small town, filled with questions about the discoveries in Roswell.

Meanwhile, as chaos ensued in town, Mac Brazel was held at the army air force base, unable to return to his ranch. Kept in the guest house, he was held incommunicado for a week. No one knows for sure what occurred, whether he was threatened, bribed, or whether the army appealed to his patriotic duty. Whatever happened, Mac Brazel never spoke a word about the experience at the air force base. He went to his grave with it.

Maj. Marcel arrived in Ft. Worth, taking some of the debris with him into General Ramey's office and carefully spreading it out on the desk for the General to inspect. Gen. Ramey returned to his office, took a quick look at the material, then asked Maj. Marcel to show him on a New Mexico map the exact location of the debris field. The two men headed straight to the map room down the hall. Before returning to the office, the General informed Maj. Marcel that reporters would be coming in to join them for a press conference. He also made sure that Maj. Marcel understood that Gen. Ramey would be doing all of the talking. Maj. Marcel agreed, having no idea what lay ahead.

The first thing Maj. Marcel noticed when he re-entered the office was the mangled remains of a weather balloon spread out on the floor. The Roswell debris was nowhere in sight. Camera bulbs flashed all through the room, then silence as Gen. Ramey gave his statement to the press: it had been an error in judgment. Officer Irving Newton then informed the press that the infamous debris was simply a weather balloon. Unable to argue, Maj. Marcel could only comply when a reporter asked him to kneel down by the balloon and hold it for the camera. That famous photo was hung in Gen. Ramey's office.

Col. Thomas DuBose, Ramey's chief of staff, knew the General's story was only a cover. He was told to get rid of the original material, and keep the whole thing top secret. And as he was under orders, that was exactly what he did.

JULY 9, 1947

The debris continued to be crated and stored in an airplane hangar before being shipped off to various different bases. Oliver "Pappy" Henderson was one of the many pilots taking off with large, lightweight boxes marked "TOP SECRET." He respected those words, and kept his missions to himself. On July 9, Pappy was scheduled to fly the B-29, flight #3 to headquarters. This time, however, he had a new cargo, something he had never seen before in his life, and would probably never see again.

Pappy Henderson was transporting the bodies. They were smaller than humans, with large heads and slanted eyes that had sunk into their heads. The clothing they wore was not of any earthly material. It was very apparent that these beings were not of this planet. And for 34 years, Pappy kept his observations to himself.

There was an issue, however, regarding the preservation of the alien bodies. The mortuary officer was unsure of the most effective way of dealing with the situation. So, he called up Glenn Dennis, a mortician in Roswell. He told Glenn he was looking for any three by six or four-foot baby caskets that could be hermetically sealed. A strange request, but Glenn did not ask questions.

Later that day, the same officer phoned, wondering about the chemical composition of embalming fluid and what it might do to tissue or blood. Again, it was an odd phone call, but Glenn did not inquire further. After all, even if he had, he would not have gotten an answer.

JULY 10, 1947

Glenn Dennis's funeral home provided ambulance services for the Roswell military base. Early in the morning, Glenn was called in to take an injured airman over to the military infirmary. As Glenn took the patient into the building, he spied some strange debris. Appearing like stainless steel, some pieces were pink, some black, and all the pieces were being stored in three of the old RAAF ambulances.

As soon as he got there, the M.P.'s went to work on escorting him out of the infirmary immediately. Annoyed, he started on his way out, until he spied a young army nurse that he knew. She had just left the supply room, her eyes red from crying. She covered her mouth with a towel, coughing heavily.

Following behind her were two pathologists, who also covered their mouths with towels, coughing. She looked up, spying Glenn, her eyes widening. Suddenly, she screamed at Glenn, "Get away! Get out now!" Before he could respond, however, the M.P.'s hustled him out of the infirmary.

Later, Glenn Dennis received an urgent phone call from that same nurse. She wanted to meet him at the officer's club. Glenn agreed. When he got there, the young woman was a mess. She was still crying and it was very apparent that she was incredibly shaken up. Glenn sat down with her, and within moments, she was relaying a fantastic tale.

Two pathologists had been brought in to make some observations on some corpses, and she had been asked to take notes. On one gurney lay a crash bag, and inside were two small, mutilated bodies. With large heads, they appeared almost ancient, with Chinese features. The other gurney only held one body. The torso, arms, and head remained intact, but the legs had been cut off. As they relayed the details to her, she worked to keep herself together.

She handed Glenn a small sketch that she had made on the back of a prescription pad of the creatures she had seen. The heads were oval, with slanted eyes, and the fingertips appeared to have small suction cup-type pads. Glenn kept the sketch, and offered her a ride back to the nurse's quarters. It was noon when he left her. Two hours later, she was shipped out to an unknown destination. Glenn never saw her again.

THE AFTERMATH

Mac Brazel was released from the base after a week of detention, but was a changed man. He started to ignore his friends and kept his distance. Escorted by military personnel, Mac returned to KGFL Roswell and retracted his story. Speaking again with Frank Joyce, Mac claimed that the debris had been on his field since mid-June, and in fact was simply the remains of a crashed weather balloon. He still stuck with the fact that the material was unlike any he'd seen before. When Joyce confronted him about the radical difference in this story from the previous one involving little green men, Mac had only one comment: "Well, they're not green."

Later on in the afternoon, an officer went by the various radio stations and newspaper offices to collect all the copies of Lt. Walter Haut's press release.

After that, Mac stayed quiet about the incident. Within a year, he and his family moved to another town. There was some speculation about whether or not he was bribed financially. His neighbors saw a man who had been used and was afraid to talk. Even his children were kept in the dark.

Jim Ragsdale's girlfriend Trudy died in an accident soon after their discovery on Boy Scout Mountain. Jim's home was broken into, but the only things stolen were debris collected from the crash site. He, too, was afraid of the military, for himself and for his family. Later, his daughter Judy came to understand her father's paranoia. He would keep a loaded gun by his bed in case of intruders. It wasn't until Jim knew he was terminally ill years later, that he spoke out in a video interview. Five days later, he died.

When Maj. Marcel returned from Ft. Worth, he told both his wife and son that the experience had been a "non-event" and they were not to speak of it ever again to friends or to anyone else. In 1978, however, Maj. Marcel came forward and shared his strange tale on *Eyewitness News*. In 1990 Dr. Jesse Marcel Jr. went under hypnosis to remember everything he experienced that night, years ago, when his father came home with the boxes of debris.

Years later, Sheriff Wilcox's wife Inez told their granddaughter, Barbara, that the Military Police had threatened to kill their whole family if any of them ever spoke of the incident.

In December 1984, Jamie Shaderay, a Hollywood film producer with a fascination for UFOs, received a strange, lumpy envelope. The postmark was Albuquerque. An undeveloped roll of black and white, 35mm film was the only thing inside. The final pictures turned out to be of a top secret military document surrounding the Roswell incident. And if the document proved to be authentic, it meant that indeed, extra-terrestrials had landed on Earth.

The document was meant for the highest office, namely, for President Elect Dwight D. Eisenhower. Prepared on November 18, 1952, it was used as a preliminary briefing. It spoke of a development intelligence operation named MAJESTIC-12 (the group was established by President Truman in

September of 1947, and was comprised of 12 high-ranking officials). It begins with a brief description of Kenneth Arnold's flight over Washington State, confirming also that hundreds of reports of similar sightings followed Mr. Arnold's. Then, it refers to Mac Brazel's discovery of debris on his ranch.

It speaks of a secret operation put into motion on July 7, 1947. The purpose was to recover the wreckage in order to commence scientific studies. Four beings were discovered as well. Apparently, they had ejected from their ship before the explosion, and were discovered two miles east of the wreck. All four were dead. The bodies had decomposed due to environmental exposure and animal acts. The craft was removed and sent to different locations along with the victims. Any witnesses to the event were debriefed and given a cover story to relay to others.

The final analysis on the report was that the ship must have been a short-range reconnaissance craft. The reason for this conclusion was due to the size of the craft and the lack of provisions (at least identifiable ones). The analysis of the "aliens" led to the possible conclusion that while they had human-like features, they had very different biological and evolutionary processes to human beings. Thus, the term "Extra-Terrestrial Entities" (ETEs) was created.

There was little success in deciphering the codes on the debris. Also, the efforts to discover exactly how the ship propelled itself failed. No conventional methods of propulsion were discovered in the crash. As to the point of origin, no definite conclusions were ever drawn.

In the early 1990s, the Pentagon stepped forward with another story. The Roswell incident was actually the result of Project Mogul, a highly classified military operation working with radiation detection. Still other theories on the incident surfaced, but none were conclusive.

The truth has yet to be uncovered.

The Roswell incident has fascinated and frightened many for years. Movies, books, and television shows have been made, all inspired by this mystery. There have been subsequent reports suggesting the entire event was a hoax, and that the events in Roswell have been blown completely out of proportion by the media, scientists, and most certainly, the public. That doesn't stop hard core believers from flocking to Roswell in the hopes of discovering more about the apparent "crash."

Movies like Stephen Spielberg's *Close Encounters of the Third Kind* depict similar-looking aliens to the ones described in the incident. The television series *Dark Skies* was inspired by the MAJESTIC-12 document, and, of course, *The X-Files* touches upon aliens and government conspiracy.

In 1994, Walter Haut, Glenn Dennis, and Max Littell created the International UFO Museum and Research Centre (IUFOMRC) in Roswell, New Mexico, a non-profit organization designed to provide information to those seeking the truth about what happened in July of 1947. Their site offers a whole range of different accounts of the event including audio coverage with the original witnesses.

In 1994, Showtime aired a film based on the true events of 1947. *Roswell*, starring Kyle McLachlan as Maj. Jesse Marcel, sticks fairly close to the original breakdown of the events. The alien bodies used in the film were later donated to the IUFOMRC. On an interesting note, in 1996, Penthouse published photographs they claimed were originals of one of the 1947 alien victims. Paul Davids, the producer of the movie *Roswell*, came forward and confirmed that the photographs were, indeed, of his props. On the August 3, 1996, episode of *The Today Show*, it was stated that one in every three adults believe an alien spaceship did land in Roswell.

Since 1994, six other films about the incident have been made. Then, in 1999, the television series *Roswell* debuted, and offered a whole new spin on the events of 1947. Now, a whole new generation of believers has surfaced.

Chapter 2

The Cast of Roswell

"I'm Liz Parker and five days ago I died.
After that, things got really weird . . ."

THE POD SQUAD

JASON BEHR
(Max Evans)

As sensitive, troubled teen alien Max Evans, Jason Nathaniel Behr has garnered a lot of attention for himself. Born on December 30, 1973, in Minneapolis, Minnesota, Jason describes himself as a "Heinz 57" in reference to his cultural background. He spent his early years living in eight different cities, primarily in Minnesota and Arizona. Once his mother Patricia split up from his father, she took Jason and his three brothers and settled in Richfield, near Minneapolis. Very private about his personal life, Jason doesn't speak of his father much, but claims his father's restlessness was the reason for the frequent relocations.

His first taste of acting was on stage at age five. With his mother's encouragement, he participated in the school play as a sunflower. Then, at age six,

Jason Behr at the 2001 TV Guide Awards (Photo by Christina Radish)

another opportunity presented itself. After an audition, Jason was cast in a Season's Greetings spot on one of the local Minneapolis channels. Jason recalls being on a horse-drawn sleigh singing "We Wish You A Merry Christmas" with three other children. That wasn't the best part, however. "I got out of school, they gave me McDonald's Happy Meals, and I thought, 'This is the life.'" That was the start of Jason's love of acting.

Due to the constant upheavals, Behr was always dealing with the difficulties of being the new kid. It was tough to make friends when the odds were the family would soon be moving again. Therefore, his family's importance in his life grew even stronger.

Despite his family's nomadic lifestyle, he kept pursuing his newfound love. At age eight, he landed a Stomper Trucks toy commercial, and was modeling for local department stores. "It was great because my mom was a single mother raising four boys and it was nice to have another income."

Meanwhile, Jason was living a normal life. His older brother John and his two younger brothers Aaron and Andrew would quibble over their shared *Star Wars* action figures. Jason would volunteer to do extra chores as long as he could play with Chewbacca. Aside from *Star Wars*, other movies played an important part in Jason's youth. His parents were both fans of older films, giving Jason a lot of exposure to the classics. In fact, his first crush was on actress Audrey Hepburn.

At this time, Jason was also making impressions on his classmates at St. Richard's Elementary, a small private school with no more than 20 children per grade. Known for pulling harmless pranks and joking with everyone, he was an actor at heart. While he kept modeling and acting in commercials, it didn't help quash one major insecurity: his height. "I was always an outsider as a small kid. I was 4'11" in the eighth grade and all my friends were twice my size. I didn't grow until high school." That insecurity would later help him to identify with the insecurities of Max Evans in *Roswell*.

In high school, however, Jason finally grew to just under six feet tall. Behr put his time into intramural sports instead of getting involved with the school teams. Active in afterschool basketball, football, and softball, Jason participated in several different activities, including the school yearbook. In 1992, Jason graduated from Richfield High School having been voted by his classmates as the one "most destined for fame." Looking back on it now, Jason notes that high school "is such an important part of a lot of people's lives, either good or bad." It helped Jason to reflect on those times while living the life of a high-school student once more — on television.

After high school, Behr made the decision to head to Los Angeles in order to pursue his career. While in Minneapolis, he met a manager who told him to give him a call when he got down to L.A. His mother supported his decision completely, and encouraged him to follow his dream. So, with $200 in his pocket, Jason made his way to Hollywood in the hopes of becoming a success.

Once there, Jason hooked up with manager Marv Dauer, who in turn referred him to an agent. The day after that meeting, he was out auditioning. At this point, he was living in Santa Monica in a barrio near the beach. For three months he lived there, then found himself moving around L.A. He had sporadic work in the beginning, but he struggled on, paying the bills by doing commercials and waiting on tables. Being away from his family was also tough on him, but he kept going.

In 1991, Jason won roles on *Step by Step* and *JAG*. Then, in 1995, he was cast in the short-lived Showtime comedy *Sherman Oaks*. Behr played Tyler, the son of a wealthy plastic surgeon who believed he was an oppressed black man. The show lasted two seasons.

In 1996, Jason found himself landing more parts. Aside from a role in the made-for-television movie *Alien Nation: Millennium* (which might have been a sign of things to come), Jason appeared in *Profiler*, *7th Heaven*, and *Pacific Blue*. Then, in '97, he found himself on *Cracker*, then on *Buffy the Vampire Slayer* where he played Billy "Ford" Fordham in the episode "Lie to Me." Jason portrayed a teenager with a fatal brain tumor who hoped to receive the gift of immortality from the vampires in turn for handing over Buffy. His experience working with *Buffy* creator Joss Whedon was very positive, and again, it was another step closer to the world of *Roswell*.

The next year was a big one for Behr. After *Buffy*, Jason was cast as

Dempsey Easton in *Push*, an ABC television series following college athletes training for the Olympics. The show lasted only four episodes, much to the disappointment of the cast, who had undergone extensive physical training for the roles. On a positive note, however, it was at this time that Jason's family started making their way to California, drawn to the warmer climate. Having his family close by was a great comfort to him.

Pleasantville, starring Reese Witherspoon and Tobey Maguire, was Jason's film debut. The role may have been small (Jason was cast as "Mark Davis's lackey"), but it was still a beginning. Soon afterwards, he landed the plum role of Chris Wolfe on the popular show *Dawson's Creek*. He was nervous at first about joining an established group, but he found himself quickly invited into the fold.

Chris Wolfe was described as a "bad boy" or a "lady-killer," and Jason played him for six episodes. "*Dawson's Creek* was an opportunity to work with a great bunch of people and that character was more on the evil side. He was kind of the antithesis of Dawson, but I had a lot of fun with him." Jason's previous characters were a far cry from the sensitive character Max Evans. "When I was starting out, I was playing all these jerks. After I was on *Dawson's*, [my 11-year-old half-sister] called me up and asked, 'When are you ever *not* going to play a creep?' I thought that was hilarious."

Of course, it was there that Behr first read the *Roswell* script, and the character of Max Evans was definitely not a jerk. The series was originally entitled *Roswell High*, after the book series by Melinda Metz. Jason immediately understood what it was about. "I related to Max's search for the truth about himself, about life, about his place in the world, which I think everybody goes through."

It also helped that David Nutter (*X-Files*), Jason Katims (*My So-Called Life*), and Jonathan Frakes (*Star Trek: The Next Generation*) were attached. Know-ing the story was in safe hands cemented Jason's interest. And as far as Jason was concerned, Max's strength was a message in itself. "There are a lot of young people who have had really tough situations and grow up really quickly and take the burden onto themselves. It's good they're finally putting that on TV, because a lot of people can relate to it."

One choice for the role of Max Evans was actor Heath Ledger, but Fox went with Jason instead. David Nutter explains why Behr won the part. "Jason is one of the most naturally gifted actors I've ever worked with. We talked a lot about this character during the show's early stages. Even in the audition process we talked about him, and he totally got the guy. He understood Max's humility, he understood that that was Max's strength. There's also a wonderful calmness, maturity, and wisdom about the guy that I thought was very important. All three of the aliens needed to [convey a sense of] wisdom that was something other than what you would expect in a young person, and he was perfect at that." The show brought all of its young stars into the limelight, and fast. Their popularity grew, putting Jason and others on many top 10 lists.

In 1999, along with *Roswell*, Jason was cast in the film *Rites of Passage*, also starring Dean Stockwell. The movie was a stretch for Jason, who was cast as Campbell, the homosexual son of Dean Stockwell's character. The story surrounds a father and his two sons who are forced to put their issues aside when two escaped convicts show up and endanger them all. "I found Jason wonderfully hard-working and ego free," said director Victor Salva. "He's one of those rare actors that rivals your own dedication and enthusiasm for making the movie the best that it could be." *Rites of Passage* won the Grand Jury prize at the Santa Monica Film Festival, and Jason was nominated for Best Actor. It was a chance for Jason to expand his acting range, and it worked.

Behr's most recent project has been *The Shipping News* with Kevin Spacey, Cate Blanchett, Julianne Moore, and Judi Dench. Jason's latest challenge was mastering the Newfoundlander accent while playing Dennis Buggit, son of the editor of the local paper. To be in the company of such stars was a little intimidating at first, but before long, Jason was hanging out with the cast. "I actually got the chance to play pool with Judi Dench."

PERSONAL FACTS

Jason lives in a Spanish-style gated home with two bedrooms and a fireplace. With a city view, it is one of about six built in 1940 and recently refurbished. He resides with his dog, Ronin. In his spare time, he loves to hike with Ronin, play basketball, or watch movies. Jason is also an aspiring painter. He loves fast German cars yet he's quite content to spend a day with Cocoa Pebbles, watching *Thundercats* or *Robotech* on the cartoon network. Either that or munch on his weakness — Krispy Kreme donuts.

Jason Behr with girlfriend Katherine Heigl at the premiere for Windtalkers

(Photo by Christina Radish)

He has grown to love his new home in L.A. and the wide variety of activities it provides. It also helps that his current girlfriend, co-star Katherine Heigl, is around to join him.

His multi-faceted nature allows him to be serious one moment, then breaking into wacky impressions the next. On set, he's known for them. And while he'll do something crazy like use real Tabasco on the food as they film an episode (" . . . our eyes started watering and our noses started plugging up, but we just kept going. As soon as they yelled 'Cut!,' we all ran for water"), he'll turn off the humor just as fast. "He's a professional," says co-star Brendan Fehr, "Even when he doesn't like something he goes about it in a very diplomatic way. There's this old kind of soul to him."

Jason has come a long way, but fame hasn't yet swallowed him up. Hanging out in his trailer with reporter Neal Justin, Jason reflected on a childhood memory where he was engulfed by a wave while he wasn't paying attention. "Maybe that's why I'm always watching my back — or I'm just aware of what's behind me." As for fame, "You don't want to put up walls and you don't want to alienate anybody — no pun intended — but you have to be aware; you have to be careful, or it will eat you alive." After all, Jason knows that fame isn't what it's all about. "For people to tell you nice things or compliment you is rewarding, but if you allow yourself to buy into the notion you are now a star, then you stop being an actor."

KATHERINE HEIGL
(Isabel Evans)

Born on November 24, 1978, in Washington, D.C., Katherine Marie Heigl is of Irish/German descent. Soon after her birth, her parents, Nancy and Paul (a banker), moved Katherine and her older siblings Jason, Meg, and Holt, to a large old farm house in a wealthy neighborhood in New Canaan, Connecticut.

Katherine's family was classic in many ways. Christmases were always large events filled with her mother's wonderful cooking and elegant decorations. Katherine got on the creative bandwagon by making her family gifts from bookmarks to scarves to personalized poetry. All holidays were celebrated with flair in the Heigl household.

In 1986, a tragedy rocked the family. Katherine's 15-year-old brother, Jason, was thrown from the back of a pick-up truck and killed. Katherine was seven. After an eight-hour operation, Jason was declared brain-dead. Jason's organs were donated to help save others, and the Heigl family continues to support the cause: "Organ donation is the most honorable way to preserve the memory of someone you love," Katherine said. "I learned through difficult experience that this is the right and humanitarian thing to do." Nancy described him as a good-natured son, who liked to play fun jokes on Katherine. It was a dark, difficult time for Katherine and her family and in some ways, Katherine believes her mother became more involved with her career "[to] take us away from the heaviness."

At age nine, Heigl's aunt sent a photograph of Katherine to the Wilhemina Modeling Agency in New York City. With striking features, she was an immediate hit. Soon after, Katherine was traveling to New York for various catalog photo shoots and occasional commercials. Her mother was Katherine's biggest supporter, and her encouragement led Katherine to a new path: the world of movies.

At 11 years old, Katherine was cast in *That Night* starring Juliette Lewis, Eliza Dushku, and C. Thomas Howell. While it was a small role, it would soon

*Heigl with her mother Nancy at
the 2001 ACE Eddie Awards*
(Photo by Christina Radish)

lead to bigger things. In 1993, Heigl won another role, this time in Steven Soderbergh's depression era drama *King of the Hill*. Things were moving quickly for Katherine.

Katherine had only a small amount of acting training, and her father always wanted her to pursue more. Heigl, however, now has a different viewpoint. "[Acting is] like a foreign language. When you learn it young, you just know it. It becomes a part of you. Acting is just a part of me." Obviously, directors agreed, because the roles kept coming.

At 14, Katherine snagged her first lead role in a film: *My Father the Hero* with Gerard Depardieu. Beating out Alicia Silverstone for the role, she portrayed Nicole, a young girl desperate to grow up quickly. On holiday with her father, Nicole tells people that her father (Depardieu) is actually her older lover. It was not only her first lead, but her first *real* kiss! Nervous about kissing her co-star, Dalton James, she was even more embarrassed when the young man asked if she could French kiss!

Around that time, she attempted a long-distance relationship with *Blossom* actor Joey Lawrence. The two had met at a *Seventeen* magazine party, but the distance was too much, and the relationship only lasted three months.

Balancing school and work was difficult for Katherine. In many ways, she longed to be a normal teenager and to fit in with the popular crowd at high school in New Canaan. Due to her busy schedule, it was hard for her to make friends and the situation bothered her enough to prompt a change. During her sophomore year, Katherine kept her career on hold so that she could spend time at school, and she discovered that being herself was more important than trying to be what other people want. And that year, she made some of the closest friends of her life.

Her career wasn't on hiatus for long, however. In 1995, Heigl found herself acting opposite Steven Seagal in *Under Siege 2: Dark Territory*. Being in an action film was a new experience for Heigl, especially working with Steven. She found she was constantly having to resort to improvisation as Steven veered away from the script. "Eventually, the director took me aside and said, 'Look — don't worry. If I have to, I'll edit it word for word.'" The popularity of the movie brought Katherine to a new level of stardom. She soon found herself appearing on *Letterman* and the *Tonight Show*, and on the cover of *Seventeen* magazine. She was on her way, and she hadn't even finished high school.

Katherine's next film, *Wish Upon A Star*, followed the *Freaky Friday* concept of longing to trade lives. The premise: two sisters make a wish on the same star that they could trade places. Of course, once they do, chaos ensues. However, while Katherine's professional life was taking off, she was having problems in her family. In 1996, not only did Katherine's parents divorce, but her mother battled cancer. Even though it had been Katherine's dream to go to college, she felt it was more important to pursue her career. "I was a good student, but I had found my niche as an actress and I was already looking to the future." So, after she graduated from New Canaan High School in 1996, Katherine and her mother (now her manager) made their way to Los Angeles, and to a new life.

Once in Hollywood, Heigl got straight to work. In 1997, she completed *Prince Valiant*, a UK/Irish/German production, and *Stand-ins*, where she portrayed Rita Hayworth look-alike "Taffy." While neither production was a major success, Katherine kept going. Then, 1998 offered her the campy horror *Bug Buster*, followed by *Bride of Chucky*.

She had just finished with *Bride of Chucky* and was in Connecticut visiting her sister when she got the call about *The Tempest*. Katherine was excited about the opportunity to work in the television movie version opposite Peter Fonda. The American Civil War was the new setting for this Shakespearean drama. Heigl, playing 16-year-old Miranda, was torn between her father

(Fonda), and a young Union soldier. While the southern accent was tough to grasp, Katherine was glad for a chance to try out a very different role.

Katherine was a self-confessed television snob, and when she was given the pilot script to *Roswell*, she read it hesitantly. Yet, she found herself warming up to the story. She tested for all three female leads, but in the end, Isabel was the one she wanted. The commitment was huge, however. She would have to agree to a seven-year contract. Before her audition, she thought, "This is what I've avoided all of these years, because I was so afraid of getting stuck on a show and playing a character I would eventually get so bored with." And yet, after two grueling auditions — one in front of producers, and the other in front of network executives — Katherine discovered she really *did* want the part. Looking back, she realizes how much you can explore character growth when you work with the same story for a long period of time.

"Katie Heigl's character really needed someone with a lot of beauty and stature," David Nutter claimed, "as well as someone with depth, heart, and soul beneath the hair and body. She had to be someone much more there than you would expect, and Katie will be able to show that more and more as the series goes on."

Isabel has become her favorite role "just because she is the most complex character I've played so far." Part of the reason she feels that way is due to the amount of time she has had to get to know the character. "She's the girl who wants to be like everyone else. So, she wants to fit in, but she's really different, and she's fighting between these two sides of herself." It seems as though Katherine's high school experiences parallel those of her character!

The new challenge involved working on a television show. *Roswell*, being very much an ensemble piece, was unlike working on a movie. "When I started *Roswell*, I had to humble myself a bit and realize the show wouldn't be carried by me, that it's carried by everybody. And now I'm so grateful that it's an ensemble show." Working 12- to 14-hour days, with a myriad of different directors, can be draining. Katherine recognized the difficulties, but then, once in front of the camera, everything else disappeared, and "that makes up for all the hours of working, all the tedium, and I think, 'This is why I love acting. This is why I'm here.'"

Since *Roswell*, Katherine and her castmates have shot to fame. While the fate of the show had been questionable more than once, the fans have remained dedicated. Katherine has been spotlighted in several magazines, as well as creating a sex-symbol status for herself. She found it strange to think that she was on TV every week. Even her family were watching actively. When talking with her sister, Katherine found "she would get into it and discuss things about the show and ask me questions. It was really weird that my sister, who lives across the country, was watching me on *Roswell*. And going into the show, I didn't think it would feel that different from doing film. But it is."

Katherine's new career didn't stop her from pursuing film, however. In 2000, she was part of the film *100 Girls*, about a college freshman trying to identify his mystery dream girl from a whole dormitory of women. Then, in 2001, Heigl could be seen in *Valentine*, with David Boreanaz of *Angel* fame. Back in the horror genre, Katherine plays one of four girls hunted down by a killer seeking revenge for past rejection. Heigl wasn't the only Roswellian involved with this project. Writers Gretchen J. Berg and Aaron Harberts (who wrote a variety of second and third season episodes) were responsible for the screenplay.

In November 2001, Katherine's NBC film *Ground Zero* was shelved for an indefinite period due to the terrorist attacks of September 11. Not only was the name of the film unsuitable, but the film itself involved terrorists stealing a homemade nuclear bomb, with Heigl playing a nuclear physicist. Katherine was disappointed by the decision. "It's a different story because the terrorists are Americans who are part of the KKK or militia." She still hopes the project will be revived.

Ground Zero wasn't her only disappointment. *Sorority Rule*, the directing debut of actress Ileana Douglas, was postponed due to lack of funding. Featuring actresses including Heigl, Gretchen Mol, Amy Smart, Selma Blair, and more, it appeared to be a great vehicle for a group of actresses just on the brink of major success. While Katherine's last two projects seem to have been

Katherine Heigl, looking as radiant as ever (Photo by Albert L. Ortega)

a bit rough getting off the ground, she has a strong philosophy that pulls her through. "It takes a lot of commitment and faith and belief in yourself. You can't let anybody tell you that you can't."

PERSONAL FACTS

Katherine spends her spare time writing, drawing, reading, hiking, or just relaxing and watching movies. She also has her schnauzer, Romeo, to take care of. As for her personal life, she continues to date co-star Jason Behr. In fact, rumors abound about the Claddagh (Irish wedding band) ring Jason gave to her. Katherine spends her time between Jason's home and the four-bedroom home she shares in L.A. with her mother.

As for the rest of the cast, Heigl finds herself laughing at Jason's and Brendan's antics. She has also become very close with Majandra Delfino. Family continues to play an important role in her life. Whenever she can, she loves to get back east to visit with her father (also her accountant), her sister Meg, and her young nephew.

In the future? Katherine would like to explore the world of producing. "Whenever I'm watching previews for movies in the theaters, these inspirational trailers make me want to make greatness. They reach people and I want to be part of developing projects, not just be in them. I'd like to be in them too, though."

BRENDAN FEHR
(Michael Guerin)

Brendan Jacob Joel Fehr is a true Canadian. Born on October 29, 1977, in New Westminster, British Columbia, Brendan was the first and only boy born to the Fehrs. He has two older sisters, Angela and Shana. His parents divorced when he was six, and in 1990 his mother took Brendan and his two sisters to live in Winnipeg, Manitoba. There, she worked as a case manager for the Stony Mountain Correctional Institute. His father, a yacht manufacturer, stayed out west, but remained close with his children.

Fehr grew up loving hockey and working hard at school. He wasn't a saint,

Brendan Fehr arrives at the Teen Choice Awards
(Photo by Albert L. Ortega)

however. Discipline came in a rather prophetic form for Brendan and his sisters: instead of spankings, his mother would put drops of Tabasco sauce on their tongues. Who could know that years later, he would be playing a character who consumes Tabasco sauce regularly, and in mass quantities!

As Brendan's family is of the Mennonite faith, he attended the Mennonite Bretheren Collegiate Institute in Winnipeg. A small Christian private school, it taught strong values along with providing biblical studies and chapel services. Brendan was a strong student, and in grades 11 and 12, he geared his educational path towards either accounting or teaching math. "I like math, because there's only one right answer." Fehr had no alienation issues in high school; it was actually a positive experience for him. As it was a small school, everyone knew one another, and the entire group were friends. As for himself, he admits, "I was a smartass more than anything, making jokes and speaking out of turn. Didn't break the rules, however."

Growing up in Winnipeg was a far cry from life in L.A. "In Winnipeg, you go to the bar and if you want to look real spiffy, like if you're with a chick, you tuck in the flannel shirt." Brendan was growing up with fashion fads of tight jeans, white high tops, mullets, and Metallica. "When Metallica is there, the town just goes nuts." Good thing for Brendan that he's one of Metallica's biggest fans.

In 1995, Fehr graduated with honors. The graduation ceremony took place in a church. Following that was a dinner celebration with parents at a large hotel. Brendan's school did not condone dancing, however, so a post-graduation party was arranged independently. He had given up on the idea of accounting, and was prepared to attend the University of Manitoba's education program. That, however, required money, which his family did not have. So, Brendan took two years off to raise some.

Brendan got to work, alternating between a lawn care company and Mat Master, delivering floor mats to different businesses in Winnipeg. The idea of modeling came up one day with his lawn care co-workers. He first began modeling for the grocery store chain Super Store in Winnipeg. Modeling was an easy way to make good money, and Brendan had no problems with that.

After registering for U of M, Brendan headed out west to a family wedding. While in Vancouver, he made the decision to check out Look Management in the hopes of possibly getting some modeling gigs to help out with his tuition payments. He walked in and met Jim Sheasgreen, his future manager. "He had just come back from lunch," recalls Fehr. "He took a look at me and for whatever reason thought that I could be on television." Acting had never been in Brendan's plans. As far as he was concerned, he was supposed to go to U of M and become a teacher. He thought the idea of acting was crazy, but then had a talk with his mother about it. At 19, with his mother's support, Brendan made the decision to give acting a try for a month. "It was going to be a good ride," he remarks in hindsight, "and I could afford to get bucked off."

Brendan was sent out to his first audition — a small role on the television show *Breaker High*. The show was about a high school on an ocean liner, where students learned aboard, as well as traveled the world. Brendan's mom flew out to Vancouver, and one month of acting turned into six, and so on. Brendan never took acting lessons, preferring to look upon his life experience as theatrical education. Nervous about an audition for the film *Mystery, Alaska*, Brendan took a one-hour preparatory lesson, but didn't get the part. He found himself looking to the words of Anthony Hopkins after that. Hopkins had said in an interview, "If you memorize the lines and say them in a way that should be said, in a natural way, that's all you can do."

Television seemed to like Brendan Fehr. He found himself getting roles on *Millennium* (twice), and on *Night Man* and *The New Addams Family*. Then, in 1998, Brendan found himself in the made-for-television movies *Every*

Mother's Worst Fear and *Perfect Little Angels*, both starring Cheryl Ladd. He was also cast in a small role in the film *Final Destination*. It was after that film that Brendan was cast in *Disturbing Behavior*, a horror film about creating "perfect" teenagers, a twist on the film concept *The Stepford Wives*. *Disturbing Behavior*, starring Katie Holmes, also showcased another *Roswell* talent: William Sadler (a.k.a. Sheriff Valenti).

While Brendan calls *Disturbing Behavior* "his least favorite acting experience," it would be his first experience working with director David Nutter. Apparently, David had told Brendan he would have a line, which Brendan never got. "Acting's not fun when you don't speak." In the end, however, the experience was to Brendan's benefit. David remembered him.

When David Nutter became attached to *Roswell*, he was the one to suggest to FOX that they look to Vancouver for talent. When they did, Brendan was brought down to L.A. to test for the show. "Brendan Fehr has such charisma and such natural ability. He hasn't been doing this for a very long time at all, but he has wonderful instincts. He's from Vancouver, and looks a little like David Duchovny, so that can't hurt, especially when you're talking about aliens."

Fehr wasn't immediately sold on the idea of *Roswell*, however. He didn't see the show as offering serious acting roles. "I didn't like it, I didn't want to do it, I mean teenagers and aliens, you know." Once he read the script, however, he started to change his mind. Originally reading for the part of Max Evans, Brendan found he was much more interested in the Michael Guerin role. It was edgier and different than his own personality.

Brendan made the move down to Los Angeles, but it wasn't easy for him at first. "When I moved to L.A. there was such a negative vibe. Being in Hollywood sucked the life out of me." The fast-paced party scene was not to Fehr's taste. For a young man who has "never been drunk, never done drugs," it's no wonder he would crave normalcy. When questioned about his value system, Brendan says "that's just common sense to me. I think it's an obviously healthier way to be. I'm not here to impress anyone with how I live my life. I'm here to impress them with what I do on screen."

Brendan began to adjust to his new world, even though the weather was tough at first. On set, Brendan was craving the colder weather of Winnipeg over the intense heat of California. His enthusiasm for the show was heating up, however. Living with two roommates in West Los Angeles, and his Rottweiler, Opa, he started to enjoy the new environment.

It helped that he had already bonded with his two "alien" counterparts, Jason Behr and Katherine Heigl. He equates his relationship with Jason to that of two little boys: "Our sense of humor is so immature, we find absolutely anything funny." As for Katherine, he's quick to tease her as often as possible. While he did not get along with co-star Majandra Delfino initially, that soon changed. In fact, they have had an on-again, off-again romantic relationship for almost two years.

Roswell's success soon brought Fehr into the spotlight. He was one of *Teen People's* Top 25 under 25 in 2000, and one of *E! Online's* "Sizzling Sixteen." His acting has even been compared to that of James Dean. *Roswell* was certainly a big step forward for Brendan. His attitude was simple: "I signed with *Roswell* with the hopes it would be something. I figured if it was terrible, it never would have gotten picked up, and it would have nonetheless gotten me a little bit of exposure and I could build up from there." A little bit of exposure was an understatement!

While Brendan still missed his friends in Winnipeg, he found buddies in Wilmer Valderrama and Topher Grace from *That 70's Show*. None of the actors are big "bar hoppers." Instead, they prefer bowling, dinner at a diner, playing video games, or just chilling out. His friend Valderrama states that "[Brendan's] one of the few very down-to-earth guys in Hollywood; I think it's probably because he comes from Canada that he's such a nice guy."

The *Roswell* schedule may have been draining — working over 2,500 hours for over nine months could take its toll — but it didn't stop him from pursuing other projects. In 2001, two films of Fehr's came out. The first, *Kill Me Later*, starred Selma Blair, and the second, *The Forsaken* showcases Brendan and Kerr Smith (of *Dawson's Creek*) as vampire hunters. While Brendan didn't feel the film was terribly brilliant, he did believe it put him on the map, which is exactly what he wanted.

Brendan and Majandra goof around at the 2000 Teen Choice Awards
(Photo by Christina Radish)

Fehr also got some exposure in U2's recent video "Stuck In A Moment." The director compiled a list of up-and-coming actors, and Brendan got the offer. Rumors have also floated around that Brendan is being considered for the title role in *Mad Max 4*. His most recent project, however, has been a film entitled *Wilderness Station*. Taking on the challenge of playing a cruel frontiersman, Brendan describes the film as "a good, character-driven story with a murder mystery twist." In 2003 he'll star in *Biker Boyz* with Laurence Fishburne.

Brendan's career may be growing steadily, but he remains level-headed. "The person I want to be . . . I'm going to get there, whether I go back to Winnipeg or whether I'm here doing this. And I'm going to make mistakes along the way, and I'm going to fall. It's just a matter of how quickly I get back up. And I just need to be able to make those mistakes without anyone blaming it on Hollywood."

PERSONAL FACTS

Brendan calls himself a "mama's boy." Whenever he's confused, he takes a moment to ask himself what mom would do, then finds the answer. It helps him keep on track. After a long chat with his mother about the Hollywood value system, he insists that his "personal growth won't be dependent on his environment." Still very religious, Fehr is active in many different charitable causes, including Habitat for Humanity. In 2000, Brendan was the Canadian spokesperson for World Vision's 30-Hour Famine.

An avid *Spider-Man* fan, Brendan collects the action figures, along with other *Spider-Man* memorabilia. He auditioned for the film, but lost out to Tobey Maguire. Brendan also has a fascination with Monopoly, owning several versions including the Marvel Comics, NHL, *X-Men* and NFL editions. And of course, there is his favorite band, Metallica. He even has two Metallica-style tattoos. He also claims to have a "thing" about his hair, fixing it constantly, and is a "laundry freak." Clean clothes are an absolute must. He recently had to give up his dog, Opa, but has taken on a cat, named "Dog" due to its affectionate licking.

Brendan's unique personality makes him even more appealing to his fans. Honest and upfront, Fehr is not afraid to speak his mind. While *Roswell* has been a good experience for him, he has had his fill of the world of television. He wants to venture into the film world, and try his hand there.

Acting may be his passion, but his integrity has remained intact. On his official Web site, Fehr sent out the following message to his fans: "Don't let yourselves be led to believe that actors/actresses are more important than anyone else. There are a lot of people out there busting their ass trying to make this world a better place and doing it and we just make TV shows and movies. Me, along with other celebrities will never ever make or break this world through acting, that'll never really determine our importance. It's what a person does to better his or her world that determines that. And that's as easy as simply being nice, ethical, and at the very least living by the golden rule. Just be sure not to underestimate the importance of your classmates, friends, family and MOST IMPORTANTLY YOURSELVES as a result of perhaps never being famous, well known, or wealthy. You all know in your hearts what importance should be based on. Thank you for reading this and feel free to comment. By the way, Metallica on NYEVE rocked!!!"

THE CRASHDOWN WAITRESSES

SHIRI APPLEBY
(Liz Parker)

Shiri Appleby is no stranger to Hollywood. She was raised 20 miles north of there in Calabasas, California. Born on December 7, 1978, to Dena, a school teacher, and Jerry, a telecommunications executive, Shiri's Hebrew name means "my song." Shiri has one brother, Evan, who was born a couple of years later. Her mother is a native of Israel, and her father is American. Embracing their Jewish religion, Shiri and her family go to Temple regularly.

Shiri entered the acting world very early on in her life: she was only four years old. Neither of her parents were in the business, but she wanted to explore it. She managed to get a commercial for Raisin Bran cereal, but it never aired. The auditions continued, but as far as Shiri was concerned, they seemed more like games than work. She hadn't quite grasped the concept that acting was something through which you could make a living.

Shiri continued to do commercials of all sorts, including ones for Cheerios, M&M's, and Taco Bell. Then, when she was seven, she landed the role of Katie on the soap opera *Santa Barbara*. Shiri found herself learning how to balance school, homework, ballet lessons and acting. Living in Los Angeles, however, Shiri wasn't an anomaly; there were other kids at her school doing the exact same thing as she was.

Her acting career continued to grow, and from 1986 to 1989, Shiri had small roles on the television shows *thirtysomething*, *The Bronx Zoo*, *Doogie Howser M.D.*, *Baywatch*, and *Knight & Daye*. As well, Shiri landed roles in the television movies *Mystery Magical Special*, *Blood Vows: The Story of a Mafia Wife* with Melissa Gilbert, and *Go Toward the Light* with Linda Hamilton. She also made appearances in the films *The Killing Time* with Kiefer Sutherland and *Curse II: The Bite*.

It was in 1990 when Shiri won a role that took her to the big screen. Cast as Millie in *I Love You To Death*, Shiri found herself working with actors like Kevin Kline, Keanu Reeves, and Tracey Ullman. The success didn't get to her head, however. Her parents made sure Appleby led a normal life, keeping her away from Hollywood parties. Shiri's acting was no more special than her brother playing soccer. It just was something she did for fun.

When Shiri entered her teenage years, however, she started to long for something she did not have: a normal school experience. High school was extremely important to her, and she wanted the opportunity to experience it like her friends were — hanging out after school, joining clubs, working at part-time jobs. These things suddenly seemed more important than they had been before. "I just wanted to experience high school. I knew it was the one time in my life I wouldn't want to miss, so I didn't work at all for those four years." Shiri put acting on the back burner. She joined the yearbook commit-tee, which spawned her interest in photography. For two years in a row, Shiri

Shiri Appleby on the set of Roswell *(Photo by Dale Josephson)*

took on the responsibility of yearbook editor. She also got involved with various committees, and in her sophomore year, Appleby joined the Calabasas Coyotes' cheerleading squad. She was a model student as well.

Shiri also broke into the teen job market. She worked part-time at a local pizzeria and had a blast. In the summers, Shiri worked as a hostess for a gourmet restaurant one year, and as a camp counsellor another. She was only making a fraction of the money she could get from acting, but it didn't matter to her. "I wanted to have those experiences because all of my friends were having them."

And yet, she continued to go to the occasional audition, and land some pretty nice roles. She had small guest roles on *ER*; *Xena: Warrior Princess* (twice); *Beverly Hills, 90210*; *Sunday Dinner*; and The WB show *7th Heaven*. She also managed to find the time to be in the film *Family Prayers*, with Joe Mantegna, and the television movie *Perfect Family*, starring Bruce Boxleitner. It was the latter that secured her first acting nomination: Best Young Actress in a cable movie at the Young Artist Awards.

Shiri graduated from Calabasas High School in 1996, and was voted "Most Spirited" by her fellow classmates. She was not planning on pursuing acting full-time, however. Her friends were all applying for Santa Barbara State, but the distance was too great for Shiri. "I decided I was going to go by myself without any of my friends to the University of Southern California, and I was in theater for a while."

In the second semester of her freshman year, Appleby switched her major to English. While Shiri enjoyed the educational aspects of her new school, it was tough for her to be without her friends. She found herself motivated once more to pursue work. She managed to get a larger role in a straight-to-video film called *Deal of a Lifetime* starring Kevin Pollack. In the film, an agent for the Devil tries to swing a 17-year-old boy over to the dark side by tempting him with what he does not have . . . one of those things being Laurie (Appleby). The movie was not a huge success, yet one benefit for Shiri, which she would find out later, was meeting actor A.J. Buckley.

She was also cast in small roles in the feature films *The Other Sister* with

Diane Keaton, and *The Thirteenth Floor* with Vincent D'Onofrio, but neither was significant enough to postpone her university career. At times, she wasn't sure if she should even continue with theater.

And then *Roswell* came into the picture.
When Shiri first discovered that a search was on for actors for the television pilot *Roswell*, she was eager to get an audition. It wasn't that easy, however. The casting directors wouldn't even look at her resumé at first, and Shiri was losing hope until she got a lucky break. "A friend of mine knew the executive producer and gave him my picture and resumé. I was really embarrassed because I felt like I was cheating."

Casting Liz had turned out to be more difficult than the producers had thought. When A.J. Buckley (who worked with David Nutter in *Disturbing Behavior*) came in to audition for the role of Kyle Valenti, he also suggested to David that they look at Shiri. "A.J. had worked with her on a low-budget feature and said, 'Why don't you see this girl? She's quite good!' We were at the stage where we were trying to find the right Liz, so I said sure, and bang, that was it." When Appleby auditioned, she read for all three of the female roles. She did not read for the part of Liz until her fifth call-back "because I wasn't what they envisioned for the part. They kept bringing me back and finally, they said, 'Why don't we just have her read Liz?' Eventually, when they realized I wasn't right for Isabel, it was down to Maria and Liz. The last two times I went in, I was still reading both parts." Ironically, Appleby landed the role of Liz, while the role of Kyle was given to Nick Wechsler over Buckley.

Part of the appeal of *Roswell* was the writing. "[Jason Katims] really is capable of expressing how teenagers feel by writing in a way that is very realistic and easy to understand. That's probably the biggest thing that attracted me to the show." Shiri still wasn't confident that she would get the part, however. She was brought back seven times to read. Returning for her fifth audition, Shiri was sure the network was interested in someone else. Now a sophomore, Appleby still had her studies to consider. "I had my schoolbooks with me because I had a final the next day. I was studying in the waiting room and I didn't think I was going to be a part of the show at all."

On her seventh call-back, she was asked to read with Jason Behr, who had already been cast. While she had never met Jason before, she recognized him from his role on *Dawson's Creek*. As they read, it became very apparent that Jason and Shiri had amazing chemistry. On the drive home, Shiri finally got the call that she had been hoping for. The part of Liz Parker was hers. "I just hung up and called my parents right away. Had to call the parents."

The pilot episode was filmed during Shiri's winter break. By the end of her sophomore year, the show was picked up by The WB, and in August, Shiri and the *Roswell* gang were shooting full-time. As she'd been on television before, adjusting to the pacing wasn't so difficult. There were other difficulties for Shiri, however. "In the first season, I was really fighting everything. I was like, 'This is not happening to me — I'm still in college.' So it takes a little while to accept what is happening and say, 'Okay, I can't be ashamed or embarrassed, or feel like I owe other people things because I've gotten lucky.'"

Appleby, along with the other members of the *Roswell* cast, quickly shot to fame. In fact, during the second season, her fans felt that she was not getting enough air time, so they took out an advertisement in *Daily Variety* magazine to thank Shiri for her acting, causing her to be "incredibly touched and shocked." As for how Shiri deals with her fame: "You just wanna make sure that you are safe. It's not something I'm really thinking about. It's not my goal: I'm not hoping to be noticed on the street."

Like her fellow castmates, Shiri also pursued other roles during her hiatus from the show. She appeared in the Bon Jovi video "It's My Life." Another one of her adventures involved getting over her fear of animals. When she was around nine, while petting the new puppies of a Chow, the mother Chow bit Shiri just above her eye. The experience shook her up so much she was afraid of animals from that point on. Since all of her castmates from *Roswell* were bringing their dogs with them to work, Shiri started to notice the bonds between pets and owners. So, she took on the challenge of reporting for *Teen* magazine and acted as a veterinary assistant for a day in Denver, on a program called Emergency Vets. Detailing her whole experience for the magazine, Shiri finally managed to conquer her fear. Afterwards, she ended up adopting a tabby kitten from the pound.

Shiri's first major movie experience was in the film *A Time For Dancing*. The story revolves around Samantha and Jules, best friends and dancers, who are forced to cope with Jules's diagnosis of cancer. Shiri cried after reading the script, and while driving home, suddenly connected to the character. Once home, she wrote it all out, and kept it with her. At her audition, she grew surprisingly nervous, and almost froze up. Then, she found herself pulling out her notes and reading her thoughts to the director. "While I was reading, my nerves went away and I just felt anger, my character's anger. It was such a weird thing to do at an audition, but for some reason I didn't care. I still have that piece of paper." Not only did Shiri get the part, but she had an amazing experience.

Her latest project, *Swimfan*, was released in September 2002. Following in the footsteps of *Fatal Attraction*, *Swimfan* stars Erika Christensen (*Traffic*), and Shiri. Shiri plays the girlfriend, while Erika is the obsessive other woman who comes to town to shake things up. Appleby also took the time off to backpack through Europe with a close friend. It was "the most positively profound experience of my entire life."

As for the future, Shiri hasn't ruled out the idea of returning to school. If she did, she would switch her major to psychology. For now, however, Shiri is happy to be an actor, and a working one at that. She's still adjusting to the fame. "This kind of stuff [interviews by the press] is fun when it comes to me, but I always feel awkward sitting here talking about myself, and saying, 'Yes, I'd like to be famous' — well, that's just not me. I just feel so pretentious sitting here. It gives me a headache afterwards; then I sit in my car, thinking, did I say anything I shouldn't have?"

PERSONAL FACTS

Shiri lives with a friend she has known since junior high. Since most of her friends attend Santa Barbara State, Shiri goes out there as often as she can. In her spare time, she reads, knits, crochets, and plays backgammon, and is also learning how to play the guitar.

Still single, Shiri keeps active with charity work and spends time with her family. Her brother, now a computer science major at UCLA, thinks his sister's

Shiri working for Habitat for Humanity, building a home for a less fortunate family
(Photo by Christina Radish)

work is "pretty cool." Her parents, while proud of her accomplishments, are also very protective of their daughter.

Of the *Roswell* cast, Shiri is closest to Majandra. Shiri takes as many photos as possible with a digital camera, lots of which are of Majandra hamming it up for her. Shiri reaffirms that the cast and crew of *Roswell* are quite hilarious when they want to be.

She does feel that the public has a very different idea about her personality. "People think I'm a shy, really sensitive, quiet girl, but I'm a lot more outgoing than that." And yet, she admits to being very introspective at times. As for her impact on the public, Shiri feels she is no different than anyone else. "I don't feel that I'm a role model, but I do know that in some way I'm in the public eye. So I just try to make smart choices, but I don't put any more pressure on myself than if I were in any other job."

MAJANDRA DELFINO
(Maria DeLuca)

Maria Alejandra Delfino was born in Caracas, Venezuela, on February 20, 1981, to father Enrique (Venezuelan) and mother Mary (Cuban-American). Her parents split up soon afterwards, and in 1984 Mary moved to the U.S., taking three-year-old Maria, and her older sister Marieh, with her. Her father continues to reside in Venezuela. Maria Alejandra became Majandra thanks to her sister Marieh. Having difficulties pronouncing her full name, Marieh combined the two names, and thus "Majandra" stuck. Majandra and her sister grew up in a very family-oriented, Catholic household in Miami, Florida.

Close to her mother and her step-father Leopoldo, Majandra had a positive childhood, embracing her new country but keeping her Latin roots. Her sister Marieh would pick on her as a child, as older siblings do, but when Majandra turned 16, they became close. As a young child, Majandra was a natural performer. Her singing and dancing prompted her mother to enroll her in ballet classes, and later piano and vocal lessons. At 10 years of age, Majandra performed in the Miami Ballet's production of *The Nutcracker*. She also found herself in local community productions of shows like *Grease!* and *Oliver!* While she thrived on stage, however, her scholastic life was suffering and her parents hired tutors to help her bring her grades up. In fact, Majandra would later say her tutors were an inspiration to her throughout her life.

At an early age, Delfino had become close friends with Samantha Gibb, the daughter of Bee Gee Maurice Gibb. As they shared a love of songwriting and singing, the two girls decided to form a band, China Doll. China Doll, the all-female quartet, embraced the Latin pop sound. They were invited to open for the Bee Gees at a benefit concert at Miami Beach, and in 1995, China Doll recorded a demo with Polygram. A few years later, however, both Majandra and Samantha left the group.

In her pre-tattoo days, when she was 13, she got her boyfriend's older brother to pierce her belly button. It had to remain hidden, however. Sure enough, two years later, her parents gave her the ultimatum — lose the belly button ring or go to boarding school. The piercing was soon gone.

Acting entered Majandra's life at 14 when she auditioned for musical theater at the New World School of the Arts in Miami. Suddenly, she wanted to try her hand as an actress. Her mother was against it, concerned that the Hollywood scene would have a negative impact on Majandra, but people told Mary what a wonderful actress her daughter would make. So, she compro-

*Majandra and her sister Marieh
at the season one wrap party
for* Roswell

(Photo by Christina Radish)

mised. She gave Majandra six months to test the waters and find herself something significant. Otherwise, she would concentrate all her efforts on school.

Delfino found a local talent agency in Miami and was sent out to a whole slew of commercial auditions. "[I] was told terrible things about myself and my looks and then I actually booked something and they started being nicer." The agency sent her out to everything, sometimes when the role wasn't even appropriate for someone her age! It didn't take long for Majandra to secure an agent, however, and within two months, she was cast in the feature film *Zeus and Roxanne.*

In accepting the role of Judith in *Zeus and Roxanne*, Majandra had to choose between the film and going to New World School of the Arts. After careful thought, she made the decision to stick with her present school, Ransom Everglades, and work with a tutor while filming in the Bahamas. Starring Steve Guttenberg and Kathleen Quinlan, *Zeus and Roxanne* followed the friendship of a dog and a dolphin, and the romance formed between their owners. Acting in a movie wasn't exactly what Majandra had expected, however. The hard work and early hours took away her glamorous image of what making movies was all about. Still, Majandra continued to pursue the craft.

Delfino was soon asked to come to Los Angeles and audition for different roles in television productions. In 1997, right after working on *Zeus and Roxanne*, Majandra was cast as Tina DiMeo on *The Tony Danza Show*. It inspired the family to set up a house in Los Angeles. Working with Tony Danza was a great experience for Majandra. "He was just the nicest, most polite and fun man to work with ever. He was honestly like a dad to me in such a short period of time." The character of Tina, however, was challenging. "It is actually a lot easier for me to be dramatic than light, bubbly, and loud and funny. In TV drama-wise, light and bubbly is a different story from a sitcom. On a sitcom, it's so overdone. . . . And that was really hard for me because it was going against all my acting. You know — all the understanding that I had of acting, which was all the subtleties and showing what you were thinking and stuff like that." While 13 episodes of *The Tony Danza Show* were filmed for NBC, only seven aired. Majandra was a free agent once more.

School was still a factor, however, as Delfino split her time between Miami and Los Angeles. "I guess when I started acting, I'd go back to high school and it was a kinda weird freakish thing. People would stare a lot and you'd feel like an alien." And yet, of all her accomplishments, one she is proudest of is academic. "In the tenth grade, I was in Calculus and I had missed so much school because of acting. I had to come back to school and take six tests. Six calculus tests in like one day and I was 'I'll do it, I'll do it!' So, I studied. I got A's on all six of the tests and that was like my proudest moment . . . Just getting it, like that [snaps fingers]." Now, Majandra loves math.

Majandra finished up high school in Los Angeles. In 1999, a film Majandra had worked on, *The Secret Life of Girls*, starring Linda Hamilton, was released direct-to-video. Majandra was one of the leads. Natalie Sanford (Majandra) is a 15-year-old girl who decides to reveal her father's affair with one of his students. Playing Natalie was a treat for her, simply because she liked the fact the film was based on a true story. In 1999, Majandra was also involved with another television series called *Katie Joplin*. The WB show aired only five episodes from August to September of 1999. Majandra played the recurring character of Sara, a troublesome 16-year-old.

And then came *Roswell*. "When I read the script, I just loved it. When I finished reading it, I was like 'Woah, gotta do this.' I figured if I liked it, other kids my age will too." Delfino was initially brought in to audition for the role of Liz. The character didn't appeal to her, however. Liz, being serious and scientific reminded Majandra of "another Felicity. [Delfino] want[ed] to be the girl who's freaking out over there, the psycho best friend."

Majandra's audition for the part of Liz went well, but then an unexpected complication threw everything into a tailspin. "When you go in to test, you have to draw up the contract right then and there, so I asked for a studio teacher because I was only 17, but I had told them that I was 18 because I was going to be turning 18 by the time I did the pilot. They figured out I was 17 and they told me they never wanted to see me again. They told me not to ever go back to that casting office or even try to work for Regency or Fox. They hated me and wanted to blacklist me, so I wrote them all letters explaining, 'Listen, I'm going to be 18 by the time I do the pilot and, when you're six months away from your 18th birthday and you have a GED (General Educational Development),' which I had, 'then you are allowed to work as an adult.' Finally, they were like, 'Oh, okay,' and they brought me back in and said, 'Listen, in the process of you sending your letters, we already cast the Liz role. Would you be interested in coming in for Maria?' Maria only had two scenes in the pilot, but they said, 'We're totally turning it around. It's going to be different. It's going to be much bigger,' so they sent me the new script and I agreed. I went in and basically got the role the next day."

The character of Maria DeLuca was originally Latina, but when Majandra was cast, Maria's heritage was changed. There were concerns, Majandra says, that the Latin community would be upset that an "American-looking girl" was playing a Latina woman. Delfino was upset, being Latina herself, but the producers had made their decision. As for the positive side to Maria: " . . . my character's crazy, my argument is always, 'Oh, well, she's crazy, so I should be able to start screaming right now.' It's great because I have the ability to just experiment with her psychology. I can make up lines and I can say or do something, just as long as it's funny, even if it risks the seriousness of the situation."

Majandra's popularity grew as the public embraced her character. She enjoyed the colorful aspect of Maria's personality, along with her fearful reaction to the aliens — what she calls "normal." She was nominated for a Young Artist Award in 2000 for her portrayal of Maria DeLuca on *Roswell*, as well as being nominated for an ALMA Award (American Latino Media Arts). Her fans spoke out, wanting more "Maria" screentime on *Roswell*, and Majandra had "never been more flattered before in [her] life."

She continued to pursue other projects, and had a small role in the hit film *Traffic* directed by Steven Soderbergh. Majandra played Vanessa, a drugged-out teenager and friend to Erika Christensen's character, Caroline. While she was seriously considered for the role of Angela in *American Beauty*, she lost out to Mena Suvari in the end. She has a role in the independent thriller *The Learning Curve*, and plays Callie in the "Hitchcockian" horror/thriller *R.S.V.P.*, set to be released in 2002.

Delfino's first love, however, is singing. Over the previous year and a half, she had been working on her debut album, *The Sicks*. Writing song lyrics on whatever was available ("Napkins, call sheets, journals, hotel pads . . ."), Majandra not only sang, but did all the instrumentals herself. She hooked up with Art Martinez and Anthony Rodriguez of *Sci-Fi Lullaby* and they produced and released three of her songs ("Siren," "Bruised," "Tattoo") to the Web. As for the title, "When I wrote and recorded these songs I was overwhelmed with a general feeling of sickness, and on top of it a sickness with no remedy, a sickness I had to just cope with until it slowly disappeared."

Initially, Majandra was working with a record label on her album. With her *Roswell* schedule, she was only available to work on her music on Sundays. "To have to schedule creativity is tough, but we managed to do that. Every Sunday is not a lot when you think about it and you realize what a process music is." Soon, due to creative differences, Majandra left the label and hooked up with Anthony and Art. Her CD sells though the Internet on her Web site — Majandra.com.

Majandra acts in order to fund her musical career. She likes the idea of exploring different roles. "The whole point of acting, for me, was to channel the schizophrenia and that wouldn't be channeling anything if I continue to do the same thing." As for her advice to aspiring actors? "Find a good support group and strengthen your self-worth, because it's all pretty much a fight against constant rejection."

Majandra at the premiere for Original Sin *(Photo by Christina Radish)*

PERSONAL FACTS

Described as open, sweet, and bubbly, Majandra is very upfront and honest. Brendan Fehr jokes that "she always has the director yelling at her to be quiet because she's always yapping." Of the people on the show, Delfino is closest with Brendan. Their on-again, off-again relationship has not affected their friendship. "It is a joy to work with him. I am his mom and he is my dad, we are brother and sister and we are best friends, we are everything and it's just the ultimate relationship of pure unconditional love. It's pretty great BECAUSE of our history together. I have never had a love like this before, neither has he so . . ." At the time of writing, rumor has it that the relationship is on again.

She also has a good relationship with her other co-stars. "Shiri is kind of like a real high school sort of girl. Katie is proper and polite. Jason is real kooky and fun. Nick is hilarious. He's a genius. [Colin's] like real casual and calm and not the least bit dorky. William is like the most kiddish one on set." As she often says, they have become like family to each other.

Majandra, also a homebody, loves to paint as well as sing. Her CD features some of her artwork. She is a believer in astrology and sports four tattoos, one on the base of her spine, and one of which is her Chinese horoscope, located on her foot. She is actively involved with organizations supporting children and animals, and works to raise money for them. As far as she's concerned, "Children are our angels and should do nothing but have innocent fun and live in dreamland as long as possible. Such behavior in my opinion makes amazing and deep adults." She is also, at present, writing an Internet journal sharing her thoughts and viewpoints on the world. She lives in L.A. with her family and her royal standard poodle. Her family continues to be supportive, including her sister, Marieh, who has followed in Majandra's footsteps by pursuing an acting career.

As for where she sees herself in the future? "Probably married and with doggies and not leaving the house because I just want to spend time with my husband and dogs. Probably. Well, 10 years from now, that's not bad."

THE SUPPORTING CAST
"Welcome to the ever-burgeoning 'I know an alien' club."

WILLIAM SADLER
(Sheriff Jim Valenti)

On April 13, 1950, William Thomas Sadler was born in Buffalo, New York, to parents William and Jane. Bill grew up on a 13-acre farm in Orchard Park, a small town south of Buffalo. "I loved that place" says Sadler. "As kids my friends and I played endless make-believe games there, improvising wild elaborate stories and playing all the roles ourselves." One of his favorite games was *Star Trek*, where he and a friend would nail mayo jar lids to the wall to create dials for the space ship. "In a way, I feel like I've always been rehearsing for all the genre projects I've done since I was about eight years old." As a child Bill claims to have actually seen a UFO on his farm. The light apparently traveled across the sky at amazing speeds, making both a hard right and left-hand turn. "My friend and I just stood there in my backyard, dumbfounded."

When he was eight years old, a new passion emerged: a love for music. Bill would play the ukulele while his father played guitar, performing duets for family events. Sadler continued to perform folk music through junior high, and then switched to rock and roll once he discovered girls. Working hard over one summer allowed him to purchase an electric guitar, and with his friends he formed the band *The Knight Ryders*. Music helped Bill realize his love of performing, but he wanted to explore different veins. So, in 1967, he auditioned for the Orchard Park High variety show. Armed with his banjo and a handful of jokes, he not only won a spot in the show, but the role of MC. For two years following, Bill performed with his band, as well as doing his solo comedy banjo act around Buffalo.

In his senior year, his English teacher approached him about auditioning for the school play, *Harvey*. Following that, Sadler performed in a community theater production of *The Subject Was Roses*. He had found his niche. "It was more fun than doing stand up and more fulfilling than playing in the band. And I was good at it." Good enough to get him into the drama

William Sadler at the 2001 UPN All-Star summer party
(Photo by Christina Radish)

program at the State University of New York. In his four years of university, Bill acted in a wide variety of shows. Theater wasn't the only thing he studied, however. "My father insisted that I get my teaching certification. Something to fall back on. Not a bad idea given the odds against ever making a living as an actor."

He then went to Cornell University on scholarship to do his Masters of Fine Arts. Known for its rigorous two year training, the program involved mime, fencing, acting, theater history, yoga, voice, dialects, aikido (a martial art), tai chi, as well as rehearsals for whatever play they were performing. When finished, Bill felt prepared to take anything on.

Bill's first professional role was as Hamlet at the Colorado Shakespeare festival of 1973. "Playing one of the greatest roles ever written and getting paid for it was a fabulous revelation." Following that was a touring production of *End Game* by Samuel Beckett. Then, Sadler moved in with his sister, Cindy, in Situate Harbor. During the day he worked in a boat yard, and at night he would drive to Boston to the Street Theatre, where he was performing in *The Relations of Paul Le June.*

Sadler had not yet made the jump to the New York stage. "I knew I would end up there eventually, but the place scared me. I would come up to the city, see a show, and leave." On one trip, he ran into a friend who was directing a production of *Ivanov* and missing a lead! It was Bill's first opportunity to perform off-off-Broadway, and he took it. Soon after, he made New York his home.

Over 12 years, Bill performed in 75 different shows, in both small and large Broadway venues. He was honored with Villager and Obie awards, a Drama Desk Award nomination, the Dramalogue Award, and the Clarence Derwent Award. His best moment during this period of his life, however, was meeting his wife, artist Marni Bakst, while doing an outdoor version of *Henry V.* Bill was also in the original cast of the Neil Simon award-winning Broadway show *Biloxi Blues* as crazy drill sergeant Merwyn Toomey, acting opposite Matthew Broderick.

When Matthew went off to film *Project X*, Bill followed suit. *Project X* was his first film. "The film scared me to death. I had no experience in Hollywood before that, no experience to speak of acting in front of cameras. I didn't know the difference between playing a close-up and a wide shot." It didn't seem to hinder his career, however. He moved on to perform in a wide variety of films including *K-9*, *Die Hard 2*, *Bill & Ted's Bogus Journey* (as the Grim Reaper), *Rush*, and one of his favorites, *The Shawshank Redemption*. "We didn't know we were making something special," Bill says of *Shawshank*, "It was like playing tennis and suddenly you're on a court with the best players on the planet. Your game just gets better." As for his television credits, he guest-starred on *Tales From the Crypt*, *Murphy Brown*, *Dear John*, *Roseanne*, *The Outer Limits*, and *Star Trek: Deep Space Nine*. Being on *Star Trek* was a special experience for Bill, realizing a childhood dream.

It was during the filming of *Disturbing Behavior* that Bill met David Nutter. Nutter told him about *Roswell*. "We didn't know whether he would consider doing it. He had a very successful, steady film career going. But we needed somebody of his caliber because we wanted a three-dimensional character," says Jason Katims.

Roswell was Bill's first full-time job on television, even though he had filmed a number of pilots. Not only were the special effects different from what he had previously worked with, but he'd never had an on-screen romance before. He gets along well with the cast, especially with his on-screen son Nick Wechsler. Nick has a lot of respect for Sadler's talent. "I really admire his acting ability. He is always in control and I try to live up to him." It doesn't bother Bill at all that he's the oldest member of the cast. "I sometimes wonder what would have happened if I came out here 20 years ago when I was cute and stupid," he says. "These days, I think what would make me really, really happy as an actor is to find myself in that little circle of actors who are offered the great character actor roles. I think I'm getting there."

Sadler and his wife have a 16-year-old daughter. When they're not in L.A., they spend time at their antique farmhouse in upstate New York. In the third season, he tried directing an episode for the first time ("Four Aliens and a Baby"). "I've seen it from the other side of the camera for many years. It's fabulous to sit behind the camera and help 'steer the boat.' So, I'm totally jazzed!"

NICK WECHSLER
(Kyle Valenti)

If a sense of humor is genetic, then Nick Wechsler's family must be hilarious. Born to Janet, an administrative assistant for the U.S. Forest Service, and Joseph, a sheet-metal worker, on September 3, 1978, in Albuquerque, New Mexico, Nick Wechsler is the fifth of seven boys. It was no wonder then that Nick found he excelled in wrestling in high school — he had some extracurricular practice.

While Nick was shy in middle school, he grew out of it during his years at Highland High School. Wechsler first thought about acting after watching a school play. "I saw a play in high school and it was like my freshman year and everyone was so terrible in it. Afterwards, they all came out and everyone is applauding them and they were all bowing like 'thank you, yes, thank you' and I was just thinking, 'YOU SUCK! I can't believe that you have the balls.' I just thought to myself I would love to do that so I can prove to you that I am not just anyone and I can do better than you."

And prove it he did. Like his co-star William Sadler, Nick began his career on stage. He got involved with a variety of different shows at the Performing Arts Center in Albuquerque, acting in *Rebel Without a Cause*, *A Midsummer Night's Dream*, *One Flew Over The Cuckoo's Nest*, *Waiting for Godot*, *Pippin*, and *You Can't Take It With You*. Nick's teachers praised his acting talent, noticing how he inspired other students. He was also, at this time, with girlfriend Holly, who Nick said has inspired him the most. "She taught me what life is really about, how to be fair, and how to be a better person."

In 1996, Nick graduated from high school and made the decision to pursue an acting career in Los Angeles. He was the only one of his brothers to leave Albuquerque. When he first arrived in L.A., it wasn't an easy ride. "I didn't go through what a lot of people went through. I didn't wait for years and years. I guess in a way, part of the reason it was just miserable for me is

Nick Wechsler at the UPN All-Star winter party
(Photo by Christina Radish)

that everyone I knew and loved was back in Albuquerque and I came out here. I only knew one person out here and I stayed with him for like six months on his floor." Nick kept auditioning, however, in the hopes of getting work.

Nick's first break was landing a small role in the made-for-TV movie *Full Circle*, based on a Danielle Steel novel. Next, he was cast in the Robert Urich western TV series *The Lazarus Man*. Unfortunately, due to Urich being diagnosed with cancer, the show was cancelled. Nick then moved on to *Team Knight Rider*, playing 'Trek' Sanders. A spin-off of the original *Knight Rider* series, the show had five operatives, all driving state of the art "vocal" vehicles. Trek was "the one who can make a bomb out of a couple of pennies, a box of paper clips, and a Q-Tip to help his teammates break into an impenetrable fortress." Part technical genius, part slacker, Trek rode a motorcycle called "Plato." The show ran from 1997 to 1998, then Nick was once more looking for work.

In the meantime, Wechsler worked at a video store. He was almost cast in a small role in *American Beauty*, but unfortunately the budget was cut, and so was his role. Then, the role of Kyle Valenti came along. Nick wasn't concerned with what the series was actually about. "I had to get something because I was doing nothing. It sounded all right to me. I initially read for the role that Colin [Hanks] got. Then they called me back for the role that I ended up getting."

While Nick couldn't relate to the jock element of Kyle (Nick had trouble playing basketball), he found other ways to connect to his character. "He's so damn handsome, it drives me crazy! No, I guess I like that, contrary to what some people believe, he has a sense of humor, it just happens to be dry or dark, I guess. It can be goofy, too. People don't seem to think he has a sense of humor, but I can tell you he does."

Nick wasn't prepared for the success of the show, and wasn't even aware of it at first. It took some time to adjust to the world of Hollywood. "It's kind of strange. There are people who bring you water all the time. Why can't people get their own water? I don't get it," he said on set at Paramount. He's a perfectionist, however, and constantly puts down his own performances. "I know I'll be better. I know I'm mortal and I explore it constantly, and because of that I get down on myself. I'm excited about going to work. I love acting. But I have yet to like one of my own performances." It's not a question of modesty. It's just Nick.

Nick Wechsler's sense of humor is one thing that the cast would agree upon. Brendan Fehr is the first to vote him the funniest man on set. "He's got these little things, . . . You're like, from what part of the brain does this come from?" As for Nick's response to the question about the hardest thing he's had to do on *Roswell*? "Pretending I like Brendan." Bill Sadler agrees with Brendan about Nick: "[Nick]'s very gifted and, by the way, very funny. He has a dry, twisted sense of humor that you don't see right away when you meet him."

Aside from *Roswell*, Nick can be seen in his two most recent films, *The Chicks* and *Perfect Game*. Nick enjoys music and loves the ocean. He gets back to Albuquerque to visit with his family when he can. He's been described as everything from wacky to sweet and gentle. And while he loves acting, he has another passion. "My favorite thing to do, and this may sound ridiculous and obvious and it may even sound egotistical, I hope it doesn't, but it's to make people laugh. It's the only thing I know I can make people do."

COLIN HANKS
(Alex Whitman)

The first child of actor Tom Hanks and Samantha Lewes, Colin was born in New York City on November 24, 1977. At the time, Tom was still struggling with his career, and the family lived in a rough area of the city. In 1980, when Tom landed the role of Kip Wilson in the television series *Bosom Buddies*, he moved the family out to Los Angeles. At this point, Colin was two, and now had a baby sister, Elizabeth. Living out in the land of sunshine was a far cry from the apartment in New York. As his father launched into a successful movie career, his marriage started to suffer. Samantha and Tom split up in 1985, and Samantha and the children moved to Sacramento, California.

Colin grew up away from the Hollywood scene, living the life of a "normal" teenager. He had the acting bug, however, getting involved in various productions in junior high and high school. "For me, it's always been sort of like playing with toys. Playing with my Transformers growing up. It was always make-believe. And when they started offering classes in it in middle school and high school, I did that." Tom could already see that Colin had what it took to be an actor, if he chose to pursue it.

From grade three through to his high school graduation, Colin attended a small private school. On a whole, the experience was a positive one. "I'm pretty outgoing, so I was kinda the class clown. But we all have our teen angst periods. I wore the black pants and black shirt, so I had some instances when I was a bit alien. And I went to a small school so that was kinda alienating in itself, because I saw kids going to other schools with football teams." In 1996, Hanks graduated in a class of 35 students. His next step was Loyola Marymount University in Los Angeles.

During his breaks from school, Colin would visit with his father. He had the opportunity to get into some hands-on behind-the-scenes work for *Apollo 13*, and then stepped in front of the camera for his father's feature directorial debut, *That Thing You Do*. It was a tiny role (a male page), but it was Colin's first official movie credit. His sister, Elizabeth, was also cast in a small role.

Colin took some time to think about what his next steps would be in university. He finally decided upon theater, knowing how unhappy he would be if he wasn't performing. While he was featured in a few of the LMU productions (including *Noises Off!*), it wasn't exactly what he wanted. So, again he made a serious decision: to leave school and dive into the professional acting world. Colin's parents didn't object. "[My father] stayed pretty much away and let me make my own decision. He said, 'You're good at it. You're very talented. And you could definitely do it if that's what you want to do. But if you're going to do it you have to go full force. You can't stick your toe in the water and then decide you don't want to do it.'" So, Colin took the plunge.

The "Hanks" name may have got Colin in the door of a few different places, but it wasn't always a bonus to have the "Hanks" name. "People are always so quick to judge me in terms of, 'Well, he's so-and-so's son. That's probably why he got the job,' which is so far from the truth. If I couldn't act, if I couldn't make the grade, no one would hire me. No one's stupid enough

Colin Hanks at the premiere for Scream 3 *(Photo by Christina Radish)*

to cast someone on name recognition alone." And in 1998, Colin proved acting was his calling. In one weekend, he landed two roles: the comedic role of Cosmo in *Whatever it Takes*, and the role of Alex Whitman in the television series *Roswell*. "The pilot [of *Roswell*] was the first thing I was ever cast in." Apparently, he had managed to get the role without the producers discovering who his father actually was. Not that it would have made a difference — it was his skill that earned him the role of Alex, Liz and Maria's best pal. "I went through 18 million callbacks. I had to do the final testing just like everyone else." Like his father, Colin would be getting his start on television.

Colin liked the fact that *Roswell* wasn't a "classic" teen show, that it had a science fiction edge to it. He also valued the opportunity to show the teenage audience that "'just because a kid wears baggy pants and a wallet chain doesn't mean that he's not a nice kid,' because ultimately Alex really is one of the nicest kids on the show." Initially, Colin didn't get a lot of screen time. It wasn't an issue for him, however. "I'm just happy to work. The first two months I only worked, like, seven days, but I was the happiest kid on the face of the planet." That changed quickly, however, as Colin's popularity on the show grew. Even his father is a fan, calling occasionally to comment on Colin's performance in particular scenes.

Like his co-stars, Colin continued to audition for films while working on *Roswell*. He filmed the comedy *Get Over It* with Kirsten Dunst, and had a small role in the award-winning TV miniseries *Band of Brothers* (produced by Tom Hanks). He was offered the lead role in the film *Orange County*, directed by Jake Kasdan, but the film schedule conflicted with *Roswell*'s production schedule. So, Colin approached Jason Katims, telling him if it meant working seven days a week, he would do it in order to work on both projects. Jason asked Hanks to let him think about it.

"Two weeks later, I got a call from Carol Trussell, who's also one of the producers on the show. She said, 'I'm going to give you a head's-up here of what we're thinking about doing. We think we're going to kill you.'" And sure enough, Alex's demise was planned and executed. Not only did Alex's death mean Colin's departure from the show, it also tied into Emilie de Ravin's

(Tess) exit. Grateful to Jason Katims for his first major acting experience, Colin left *Roswell* and took the role of Shaun Brumder in *Orange County*.

While Colin's film career is taking off, he would rather avoid the fame. More comfortable staying at home than heading out to clubs, Colin keeps his personal life to himself. He can't hide his famous family name, though. While on the press tour for *Orange County*, he had to deal with constant questions about his father and comments about their similarities. "And to be honest, I totally understand that. If I wasn't in this situation, I'd do the same thing. My hope is that eventually, with the next movie I do, it won't be that big of a deal. I will have sort of gotten through the initiation. We're all inevitably somewhat like our parents. And I'm not ashamed of it. That's who I am."

ADAM RODRIGUEZ
(Jesse Ramirez)

Adam was new to *Roswell*, having joined the cast for the third season. Born August 31, 1971, near Yonkers, New York, he is the oldest of the "teen" crew. His younger sister, Vanessa, is a mutual funds analyst. His father has a military background, and he describes his mother as "strong, with a love of family." Of Puerto-Rican descent, he grew up with dreams of playing baseball and wasn't particularily focused when it came to school. When he graduated from high school, he started at community college, but that didn't pan out.

His baseball dream was shattered when a spinal injury prevented him from pursuing the sport professionally. During his rehabilitation, he was forced to reassess his life path. In the meantime, he found work as a janitor, a bellman, working in construction, and delivering pizza. Then, at 19, Adam began working at a brokerage house. In the back of his mind, however, he had begun to realize that acting was something he'd like to explore. It wasn't until Adam was just about to get his stockbrokers' license that he realized he wasn't interested in being a broker. He had some head shots taken and began working as an extra, hoping it would lead to something greater.

In 1996, his father stepped in to give Adam a hand. A friend from his father's military days was now working on *NYPD Blue* as a technical consultant. Rodriguez was given a one-liner role which helped him to win a regular spot on the television series *Brooklyn South*, created by Steven Bochco. The show cast Adam as Officer Hector Villanueva, a young, eager cop. The show only lasted a year, however, moving Adam onto his next project, *Felicity*. Adam played Eric Kidd, the sleazy record executive, for three episodes. Adam was in the pilot episode of *Ryan Caulfield: Year One*, and has appeared in *Resurrection Blvd.*, and *Law & Order*.

Then, Adam blew off four auditions for the television series *All Souls*, because he was up for a part in the short-lived TV series *The $treet*. The producers of *All Souls* were insistent, however, and kept calling back. Adam read for two roles: Patrick Fortado and Bradley Sterling. "My payback for blowing [the audition] off so many times was that I had to read five times. On my last experience I only had to read twice. I'm like, 'Man, how many times do I have to go in? This is getting crazy already.'" Since auditions are Adam's least favorite part of acting, it was an even more painful process. He lost the role on *The $treet*, but at this point, he wanted to be a part of the *All Souls* cast. "I had to go in for Aaron Spelling, that was the most surreal part of everything, 'cause I was a TV addict as a kid. *Charlie's Angels*, *T.J. Hooker*, *Love Boat*, *Fantasy Island* — that was like a staple for me. So, I go in and meet him and he's cool as can be."

Adam was eventually cast as Patrick Fortado, a paraplegic computer expert, and the best friend of Dr. Mitchell Grace. Working in a wheelchair was an important experience for Adam. "I get to do my wheelies and roll around," he jokes. "In all seriousness, it opened my eyes to being more aware of people in wheelchairs. A lot of people don't acknowledge handicapped people, I find. Now, when I see somebody in a wheelchair, I make sure to make eye contact and say hello." The series was dubbed as a paranormal hospital drama on UPN, but only aired for six episodes. While it was pulled from the network's schedule due to poor ratings, it wasn't cancelled, but rather put on hiatus. "I think that the problem with *All Souls* was that it was just a little ahead of its time. A year or two from now, I think people would eat it up."

Following that, Adam was cast in the role of Jesse Ramirez, a young attor-

Adam Rodriguez at Bogart Backstage (Photo by Christina Radish)

ney in love with Isabel. The only problem is, his character has no idea that she's half-alien. Adam had to do some homework before joining the show. "I had to learn about Skins and Antar and how the alien kids ended up on Earth and had their DNA mixed with human DNA and were put in these pods and then walked out of the desert 12 years ago and were adopted by human families. It's been an education. I really dig it."

Adam can be seen in the films *Details*, *Rikki the Pig*, and *Imposter*. He is also in the Jennifer Lopez music video *If You Had My Love*. He was most recently cast in the new series *CSI Miami*. As for future goals? "I'd like to bring the Adam Rodriguezes of the world to the forefront and just provide a positive example for people and a positive representation of the Adam Rodriguezes that are out there. Jesse wasn't written as a Hispanic character. None of the other actors who came in to the audition were Hispanic. I just happened to be, in the eyes of the producers, the best guy for the job. And that's great. That's the way it should be."

EMILIE DE RAVIN
(Tess Harding)

Emilie was born in Mount Eliza, Victoria, Australia, on December 27, 1981. Emilie's mother raised her as an only child, as there was a large age gap between Emilie and her two older sisters. She started taking ballet lessons at the age of nine, and at 10 was given a walk-on role in an Australian Ballet Company production, and has been involved with Danceworld 301. When she turned 15, she was accepted into a three-year training program at the prestigious Australian Ballet School. After her first year, however, she longed for a change, and acting was an intriguing possibility. So she left her dancing career behind and began her studies at Australia's National Institute of Dramatic Art.

Emilie followed her NIDA workshop with two courses at Swinburne University for Film and Television, and then a two-month stint in Los Angeles in 1998, where she studied under Australian director John Gauci at the Prime Time Actor's Studio. When she returned to Australia, Emilie was cast in the television series *Beastmaster* as the recurring character The Demon Curupira, who was responsible for the title character's ability to speak with the animals.

Emilie wanted to explore other roles, however. She made the decision to return to Los Angeles in order to find an agent. "I'm very into persevering. Nothing stops me. If I want to do something, I'll do it." She left Australia in the winter of 1999, and within a week, Emilie secured herself an agent and returned home for the holidays. At that time, a casting agent for 20th Century Fox, who had seen her on *Beastmaster*, called her to arrange an interview. It was enough to prompt her to move to Los Angeles permanently. The *Beastmaster* producers let her out of her contract early, and Emilie made L.A. her new home in February 2000.

She met up with the agents from FOX, and won them over. After only two call-backs, Emilie was cast in the role of Tess Harding, the fourth alien. Tess debuted on *Roswell* in April 2000, and continued on for the remainder of the season. "When I read the script, even before I shot anything, I thought [Tess] was interesting. She had no human side to her at first, none whatsoever. She had been raised by this cold-blooded alien, and had no human contact until she met up with Max, Isabel, and Michael."

Playing an alien was a challenge at first, if only because she had to quickly catch up with the *Roswell* storyline. She soon fit in with her fellow cast members, however. When it came to working with the other aliens, "We get along and we strategize well. When we have scenes together, we rehearse for a while and get it down, really working at the intricacies we find." As for her work with the Valenti duo: "Those two guys are crazy. It's so much fun working with them. I can't stop laughing, especially with Nick."

As far as the fans were concerned, Tess was trouble, and they were not happy. While the cast was friendly and accomodating to Emilie, the fans lashed out. "At first I got terrible mail. I wasn't welcome because Tess broke up a relationship between two other characters, Max and Liz. It was hard for the viewers to accept another girl in Max's life . . ." The Anti-Tess campaign spread throughout the Internet, but soon, things quieted down.

De Ravin found it challenging to portray Tess at the beginning. "I haven't had any alien experiences and I haven't had that many life experiences as a

Emilie de Ravin at the premiere of Get Carter

(Photo by Christina Radish)

human. So it's hard sometimes to draw on emotions and associate with something that's happened to me." Eventually, she settled into her character's skin, and the fans grew to enjoy her. "I was online the other day; it has actually gotten a lot better. There are so many pro-Tess sites now, which is really nice to know. It never bothered me personally, though, because Tess is a character."

Emilie's regular stint on *Roswell* ended at the climax of season two, when her character returned to Antar with Max's child. She still lives in Los Angeles, and enjoys hanging out with friends, shopping, exercising, and painting. While she misses dancing, she does not intend to return to it. "It's a wonderful way to express yourself, another form of acting, in a way. But if I were to [resume it], it would take me about five years to get back to the professional standard I was at."

While Emilie enjoys television work, she would like to pursue movies in the future. "I want to pursue as much of a serious acting career as I can, not just a flimsy overnight career. I take it very seriously."

Chapter 3

The Roswell
Fan Phenomenon

The Aliens Have Landed

The *Roswell* teenagers first appeared in the mind of Laura Burns at Pocket Books. She sent the idea to 17th Street Productions, a packaging company who are known for such properties as the best-selling series *Sweet Valley High*. One of the editors of 17th Street Productions then fleshed out the idea with author Melinda Metz, who became attached to the project. The *Roswell High* series was born. The first book was published in 1998. Liz Ortecho and Max Evans, star-crossed lovers in a more literal sense, were the focus of the first book, but soon the stories branched out to involve the others — aliens Isabel and Michael, and humans Maria, Alex, Kyle, and Sheriff Valenti. The *Roswell High* series ended at book 10.

The books came to the attention of producer Kevin Kelly Brown, who purchased the television rights and got to work by bringing Jonathan Frakes (*Star Trek: The Next Generation*) and producing partner Lisa J. Olin on board. Twentieth Century Fox was soon linked to the project, and Jason Katims (*My So-Called Life*, *Relativity*) was attached as the writer. When Jonathan Frakes got caught up in re-shoots for the feature film *Star Trek: Insurrection*, director David Nutter (*21 Jump St., The X-Files, Disturbing Behavior*) came onto the scene. It was a diverse group, but perfect to launch a television series incorporating high school angst with sci-fi elements. After all, Jason's high school coming-of-age series *My So-Called Life* continues to receive great critical acclaim, even though the show was cancelled in 1995. Also, David Nutter and Jonathan Frakes were obviously well-versed in the sci-fi genre. David had been one of the early collaborators with Chris Carter on *The X-Files*, while Jonathan had not only starred on *Star Trek: The Next Generation*, but had directed various episodes as well. The next step involved making the series believable, both on a story level, and a character level.

Originally, Jason was attracted to the unrequited love story element. "[I]f you want to do a contemporary love story about young people, it's hard to find a real obstacle. And I think that the fact that they are different life forms gives you a real obstacle. So that's what drew me to the thing before anything else." David Nutter also had a vision of what he wanted *Roswell* to be. "My biggest goal is to keep it smart. I'm very aware the audience for shows like *The X-Files* are the kind of audience that if they like the show, they'll embrace it, and they're the best fan base of all time. If they see they're being taken advantage of or taken for granted, as far as their intelligence, they'll turn on you, so I think they deserve a lot better." Jason Katims and David Nutter got to work shaping Katims's original draft, which incorporated many of the elements of the first *Roswell High* book — *The Outsider*. The plan was to work with the characters from the series, but break away from the plotlines and explore new stories.

There were a couple of elements from the book, however, that executive producer Kevin Kelly Brown was sad to lose. "[T]he Isabel character was obsessed with order. When she'd get upset, she'd go up to her room and she would dump all of her lipsticks onto her bed and rearrange them. Because they were *all* in perfect order *all* of the time. I thought that was a really interesting character trait, and I'm sorry we lost that. Another big thing that got dropped that was really cool was that Liz had a sister who had died of a drug overdose, which is why her parents were so protective of her. I always thought that we should at least tease [that idea], so we could bring it in at some point." In the book series, Maria had a pesky younger brother, and Alex had three older brothers to contend with.

Once the script was ready, the producers began the tough task of finding the right actors for the roles. Both American and Canadian actors were considered. "If you don't have the right people to begin with, then all the directing in the world isn't going to save you," said Nutter. Originally, the character of Liz Ortecho was Hispanic, and there was an effort made to cast Latino actors and actresses. In the end, however, Shiri Appleby won the role of Liz. Concerned there would be backlash at casting Shiri in an obvious Latina role, Liz's last name was changed to "Parker" as it sounded more "WASPY." "You cast for parts, you look for the best actor, regardless of where they came from," David said. It was a tough choice, but in the end, Nutter and Katims agreed that diversity would be explored in other ways, namely, by moving the story into the Native American community for a few episodes.

Once the show was cast and the pilot filmed, problems with FOX arose. FOX was looking for more of a *Beverly Hills 90210* slant, and in the end, there were concerns that *Roswell* was "skewed too young for their audience." FOX also had difficulties fitting it into their fall line-up, so the producers took the show to The WB. The WB in turn, pulled an unprecedented maneuver by guaranteeing the show a full 22 episodes right at the start. Doug Herzog, president of FOX, claims that they did not reject *Roswell,* and were still considering the show for their mid-season slot, but couldn't offer the same episode guarantee as The WB. In the end, The WB won out, and the show was set to premiere October 6, 1999, after *Dawson's Creek.*

The actors got to work doing promotional photo shoots and interviews for various magazines. The words "teen alienation" were thrown about frequently as a witty catch phrase. There were hopes that an Internet fan base would get on board, and David Nutter commented, "I think [the Internet users are] a wonderful group of people to try to win over. And it's a very difficult group to win over." But win them over they did, and on a larger scale than anyone expected.

Roswell scored well with the critics, and kept steady ratings. It made many best-of-television lists of 1999 including *Wanda's E!Online* picks. The writing was intelligent, and the characters believable. The writers did not shy away from humor, nor were they afraid to delve into more serious storylines. While the premise of teen aliens in high school could have been construed as cheesy, it was no worse than a California girl named Buffy slaying vampires. In fact, many reviewers not only compared the two shows, but it was a universal expectation that the *Buffy the Vampire Slayer* fans would embrace the world of *Roswell*. The strong chemistry between actors Jason Behr and Shiri Appleby certainly increased the show's popularity as well. Also, *Roswell's* principal photographer was Emmy Award winner John Bartley. *Roswell* had all the right elements, and a bright future.

The show was already collecting fans after its first episode, and on October 9, 1999, fan Leif Alexander (Goldenboy), purchased the domain name Crashdown.com. Leif had already been active on the Web creating "Fan Forum," a non-profit venue for fans to voice their opinions and share thoughts with other fans on their favorite shows in a clean and friendly atmosphere. "Fan Forum" was already very popular with the *Dawson's Creek* audience. In the summer of 1999, Leif launched a Jason Behr site connected to "Fan Forum." Jason had been on *Dawson's Creek* and *7th Heaven*, and was known to both sets of fans. Now, he had been cast in a new show, *Roswell*, which also had Jonathan Frakes attached to it. Seeing as some of the administrators on "Fan Forum" were also Trekkers, Leif worked alongside Kenn Gold (NetRanger) and Darien Wilson (squanto) to create a site on *Roswell*. At this point, only a few other *Roswell* sites were available for fans, *Roswell Online*, created by Elyssah; and *Roswell*-High.com and Area-51, created by CourtneyGirl. In September, Area-51 was asked to join "Fan Forum."

Then, on September 19, the first *Roswell* Message board was launched. Darien became a co-Webmaster of Area-51. The three men took over Area-51, recreated it into Crashdown.com, and it was re-launched in December 1999. Crashdown.com not only provided information on the cast, but had news items, polls, strived to update their information on a daily basis, and obviously

Michelle, Bill Sadler, Kim, Kenn and Angela Gold, and Leif Alexander
at the Crashdown party (Courtesy Fionna)

linked to the "Fan Forum" message board. *Roswell*-High and Crashdown.com
later became sister sites, sticking together until *Roswell*-High closed during
season three. Another site called Not of This Earth was considered one of the
best *Roswell* sites by many different publications. Run by a 15-year-old girl
named Stephanie, it had problems due to activity and eventually merged with
Crashdown. Stephanie stayed on at Crashdown.com as a Webmaster until
school became too busy for her to continue.

On December 24, when *Roswell* Online, the largest and most popular
Roswell site, was hacked into, Elyssah made the choice to discontinue her site,
and a whole surge of fans rushed to Crashdown.com/"Fan Forum" to get their
Roswell fix. Two of her assistant Webmasters, Michec and Kenna, moved over
to Crashdown, and Elyssah handed over a large amount of the content related
to the first six episodes. Crashdown.com was growing fast. In a few months,

there were 20 people on the Web staff.

The cast was starting to take notice of the fan boards and the discussions. Their first brush with celebrity contact came with Brendan Fehr's manager, who posted as "Mr. Manager." He had seen both *Roswell* Online and Crashdown.com, and was active in informing the production office and the cast of the sites' activities. First, William Sadler took the plunge and posted on the *Roswell* Online message board as MrV. Next Brendan Fehr posted using the name Spiderman. At Christmas time, William Sadler created Real Player singing postcards for the 'Net fans in order to wish them a Merry Christmas. While they were created for both Crashdown.com and *Roswell* Online, the latter postcards were lost due to the hacking and the subsequent merge.

At the end of December 1999, *Roswell*'s ratings were tied with *Dawson's Creek*'s, with 1,813,000 million households watching the show. The actors now had to adjust to their newfound popularity. Jason Behr made the NY Post's TV's *Five Freshest Faces*, was a *Star of* 2000 for J-14 Magazine, and was nominated for Best Actor in the TV Guide Awards, while Shiri Appleby received a nomination for Best Actress. Brendan Fehr was named one of 2000's *Sizzling Sixteen* from *E!Online*. Brendan Fehr, Jason Behr, and Katherine Heigl even graced the cover of LIFE Magazine. A WB poll revealed Maria's (Majandra Delfino) popularity, which prompted the writers to give her more storylines. Not only were the actors garnering attention, but talk of bringing on a "fourth alien" was brewing.

The first organized effort of the *Roswell* fans involved Jason Behr's official Web site. The Webmaster of the site attempted to take down copyrighted photos from the different Jason Behr fan sites, causing quite a stir. The fans all rallied together through Crashdown.com and "Fan Forum" with the other Webmasters stating their case. To calm the waters, Jason posted an appreciation to all his fans, as well as to the Webmasters of the other fan sites. While the issue was dealt with, another good thing came out of the event — *Roswell* fans uniting together with purpose!

Then, the troubles began. First, David Nutter announced that he was leaving the show. He claimed he wanted to pursue other projects, and ended up directing the pilot for the FOX series *Dark Angel*, created by James Cameron. David, who had directed five of the *Roswell* episodes, was also an executive producer of the show. It did not seem to be an issue, however, as Jonathan Frakes and Jason Katims were still heavily involved. There was every bit of confidence that the show would continue to flourish. "I think that *Roswell* is going to make it. It seems to have the teenage girl demographic, which is what The WB has circled as their goal. So I have very high hopes that we will be back next year," said Jonathan. "I think that *Roswell* is going to be one of those second-year phenomenons, where it will catch on." Certainly the creators of *Buffy the Vampire Slayer* and *The X-Files* understood that concept. Neither show received large scale attention during their first season.

It was January when Kevin Kelly Brown first approached Crashdown.com. His timing wasn't great, however, seeing as the site had been plagued by several imposters claiming to be Jason Behr or one of the other cast members. Kevin Kelly Brown, new to the Web system, kept trying despite mounting frustration to get through, while Darien was unconvinced that it was actually the *Roswell* producer. A week later, a long-time member of the "Fan Forum" community who also worked as a senior staff member on Crashdown.com used her connections at UltimateTV in the hopes of verifying Kevin's e-mail address. Sure enough, the address was correct. While the incident led to some embarrassment on Crashdown.com's part, it didn't hinder the long-term friendship from growing among the Web site, Kevin Kelly Brown, and the other *Roswell* producers.

The fans continued to bond over the show, and on February 12, the first ever *Roswell* fan gathering (organized by Vigie) occurred in Seattle, Washington. That party was followed by the Los Angeles *Roswell*ian Gathering on February 26. Two fans of the show, Kim (London2LA), and Lena (Fehrocious), were working at Paramount Studios at the time. As a consequence, they were able to organize a tour of the set for the fans that participated in the event. Seventy fans from all over the U.S. came to participate, along with two Canadian women who made the spontaneous decision to fly out for the weekend. The fans were split up into various tour groups, and given the opportunity to see Liz's famous balcony, the Evans' bedrooms, the Crashdown Café, as well as to get a sneak peek at Michael's new apartment. Brendan Fehr and Majandra Delfino took time out before heading out for dinner in order to attend the party and sign autographs. The evening ended at the Paramount Studios Commissary where the fans were treated to an advance screening of "Sexual Healing." While the event affected many fans, a bond was formed among Kim, Lena, another fan Kristi, (Kdberg), and one of the Canadian visitors, Fionna (black widow). Their enthusiasm for the show, and organizational abilities would come in very handy in the near future.

Sure enough, soon after Fionna had returned home, the rumor that *Roswell* was on the chopping block began to circulate. While the cast and crew would not officially know until May, there were concerns. "We're hopeful, but you never know for sure," said Jason Katims. "The WB has been real support-ive of the show, beginning first of all with buying the show when it was originally developed for FOX, then giving it a really strong launch and really being behind it . . . We're just going to work really hard and make the final episodes of the season great and make it impossible for them to not pick it up."

In March, *Roswell* was "the top-ranked show in the U.S. among girls aged nine to 16, [with] a median view age of 27." It meant that the age range of the fans spanned from nine to 30. So, with such a diverse group of viewers, why was *Roswell* struggling in the ratings? It wasn't just *Roswell*, but The WB who was suffering on a whole, thanks to the United Paramount Network (UPN). Such shows as WWF *Smackdown* and *I Dare You*, showcasing out-of-work stuntmen, were grabbing the attention of audiences across the U.S. It was enough to prompt The WB to move *Roswell* to Monday nights, following *7th Heaven*. There were hopes that the shuffling of its schedule would somehow boost the Nielsen ratings. Between the move and the decision that *Roswell* should focus more on the sci-fi angle, the hopes were that the viewership would improve. *Roswell*'s fate hung in the balance.

The fans, however, held on tight. They had seen into the soul of the show at this point, and they weren't letting go. It was time to form a plan to save their show. And a small group of women who barely knew each other helped get the ball rolling.

Tabasco to the Rescue

Fionna, Lena, Kim, Kristi, and a friend of Fionna's from home, Michelle (lily-bunny), made the decision that something should be done. There was no expectation that it would go very far. Still, they wanted to make the effort, and they came up with a plan. Because all of them had gotten to know each other through the posting boards at Crashdown.com/"Fan Forum," they joined up with the Crashdown.com team and used the site to spread the word.

Fionna's task was to create a Web site affiliation with Crashdown.com. Having just learned the html language, Fionna created the Web site how.to/save_roswell, which was launched March 6, 2000. Fionna and the crew only assumed a small group of people would log onto the site, but it started receiving over 1,000 hits a day, and all through word of mouth. The purpose of the Web site was to provide information for fans, to post campaign news and new strategies, and store resources. *Teen People* Online was so impressed they created a page on their Web site in order to publicize it. Twenty-two thousand e-mails were sent to The WB through their Web site. As of January, 2002, the how.to/save_roswell site had received over 117,000 hits.

The concept of Tabasco sauce came directly from the show. The aliens have a weird dietary quirk where they crave food that is both very spicy and sweet at the same time. Thus, they go through Tabasco sauce by the case as they lather it on chocolate cake and other foods. The original idea for the Tabasco campaign came from Mel at the *Roswell* Delphi Forum. Why not send The WB bottles of Tabasco to show them that "*Roswell* is Hot!"? The mail-in concept wasn't new to the *Roswell* Delphi Forum. Also, for fans of the show *General Hospital*, the forum arranged for a mail-in campaign of Lucky Charms when the character of Lucky was to be written off. (Interesting how Lucky's mother on *General Hospital* is played by Genie Francis, and the projected alien mother in *Roswell* was played by . . . Genie Francis!) Mel brought the idea to Crashdown.com/"Fan Forum," and everyone ran with it.

The plan was to send bottles of Tabasco sauce along with a polite, encouraging letter addressed to Jamie Kellner, (CEO of The WB), Susanne Daniels (President, Entertainment, The WB), and Jordan Levin (Executive VP, Programming, The WB). Crashdown.com posted details on what to do, including remembering to write "*Roswell* Is Hot" at the top of the letter. The campaign began on March 6, 2000, just days after the first rumors of cancellation began to circulate. In two and a half months, over 6,000 bottles, all in varying sizes, landed in The WB's mailroom. People were phoning up the Tabasco hotline's (McIlhenny & Co.) 1-800 number, ordering bottles to send. When people couldn't afford to send Tabasco, they sent postcards instead. Initially, The WB mailroom had no idea what to do with the bottles and were throwing them away. When the network realized the purpose behind the bottles, they began to keep them.

While the Tabasco plan was in effect, Kristi was responsible for another plan of attack. As she lived in L.A., she took on coordinating a full page advertisement in *Daily Variety* which would not only inform viewers of *Roswell*'s change in scheduling, but would be an illustration of the fan support for the network executives. The ad, which would be designed by Kim, would cost about $2,500. Kristi registered an official company with L.A. County called "Alien Blast" and then got to work setting up a bank account and a P.O. Box. Then, Kristi posted a request for donations on the *Roswell* "Fan Forum" board in the hopes they might get some response. What they got was completely unexpected. Money flooded in from Canada, Australia, France, England, as well as the United States. They ended up with $5,000 in under a month.

Kim got onto the design concept right away. After putting out a poll to the fans through "Fan Forum," it was determined that the ad would be in black and white. The concept was a silver handprint with the name of the show above, and WE BELIEVE below. The final ad read, "We would like to thank The WB for the hottest show on television. We are looking forward to next season. Paid for by the Fans of *ROSWELL*." Below that was *Roswell*'s new date and time, along with the address for the How To Save *Roswell* site, and Crashdown.com. Kim got her young son to put his handprint on the poster.

Kristi got in touch with the production office to let them know what the fans were doing, and the office helped with getting copyright clearance for the font, which was necessary in order to print "*Roswell* on The WB" on the poster. The ad ran on Monday, April 10, 2000. That day, not only did the *Daily Variety* sell out, but it sold the entire stock of back copies. Nothing was left!

"On that day, as a thank you from the production office for the work I had done, I was invited for a personal set visit. I hung out for the day and met all of the cast members — who in turn autographed my copy of the *Variety* ad with personal messages. I also got to watch that night's episode "Crazy" with the cast and crew on their lunch hour. It was an amazing day," Kristi said. The cast were all amazed at the efforts of the fans, along with the fact that they donated their own money to create the ad. They were extremely grateful.

There was also a plan to get all the fans to e-mail The WB at the exact same time. As a consequence of the massive amounts of e-mail sent, The WB's server crashed, prompting them to create a separate e-mail address specifically for fans. The WB Webmasters contacted Crashdown.com, asking them to post links with the new e-mail address. Over the course of the renewal campaign, The WB received over 33,000 e-mails. The fans were just getting started. "Fan Forum" had to split their *Roswell* fan board into two separate boards due to the amazing amount of posts flooding in each day. New boards were created for each of the actors. That meant 11 *Roswell* related boards in total.

The fan's efforts did not go unnoticed. Jamie Kellner was impressed by the fact that the fans had actually spent their own money while attempting to save their show. Susanne Daniels couldn't help but notice the campaign: she had to change her e-mail address three times due to the quantity of mail she was receiving. On March 11, 2000, executive producer Kevin Kelly Brown sent a letter to Crashdown.com, addressed to the fans of *Roswell*. His letter was from the heart, as he explained how The WB had suffered due to UPN, and *Roswell* had suffered while competing against *The West Wing* and *Star Trek: Voyager*. He also explained how the move to Monday nights was a benefit, seeing as it would follow The WB's number-one show, *7th Heaven*. At the same time, he admitted that the series had lost the careful balance of sci-fi and romance that

Roswell *writers Ron Moore, Breen Fraizer, Toni Graphia, Fred Golan, Gretchen J. Berg, and Aaron Harberts* (Courtesy Fionna)

it had achieved in the pilot and earlier episodes. He reassured the fans, however, that the final six episodes were strong, and back on track. He praised the fans on the originality of the campaign, and encouraged them to continue with their efforts. Since Kevin was the one to find and option the book series and bring the team together, *Roswell* was very important to him. "But it doesn't mean anything without people like you and your fellow Crashdown fans, because without you our work becomes the proverbial tree that falls in the forest, the one that nobody ever hears. We appreciate you guys more than you will ever know . . ."

At the beginning of April, The WB issued a press release stating that they were rerouting the Tabasco bottles to the media as gifts. The campaign was mentioned in a number of well-known media sources including *Daily*

Variety, *New York Daily News*, *New York Post*, *Time* Magazine, USA *Today*, *Entertainment Weekly*, *Seventeen* Online, *Toronto Star*, TV *Guide*, and SciFi.com, to name a few. The bottles were clogging up the mailroom, and the season finale scheduled for May 15 was fast approaching. On May 16, The WB would make their official announcement about the returning shows at a press conference in New York City.

The tensions were high, but the fans, cast, and crew held on to their hope. The season finale came, and left the viewers in suspense, ending with a dramatic cliffhanger. The other major cliffhanger was about to be addressed, however: did all the hard work pay off?

Yes, it did. On May 15, 2000, The WB announced *Roswell* would be renewed, guaranteeing 13 episodes for their second season. A spontaneous party broke out in Crashdown.com's chat room, where over 70 fans from all over the world celebrated the news. Liz, a "Fan Forum" site administrator, was in attendance at The WB announcement, calling the results in to Darien so that the good news could be posted immediately. While that wasn't exactly what everyone had been hoping for, it was enough. Their efforts had saved their beloved show, and it was time to officially celebrate *Roswell*'s resuscitation. And what better way to do that than with a party.

Roswell Is Hot, Hunger Is Not

Before the campaigning and before the concerns about the show's cancellation, there was a concept floating about: a giant *Roswell* L.A. Party. Mandy, the main news poster on Crashdown.com, had posted the concept and was set on organizing it. Meanwhile, the rumors began, and the first set of Tabasco bottles reached The WB. Then, Brendan Fehr's manager annoyed the fans by suggesting on the posting boards that if the fans who worked to save *Roswell* put as much effort into something worthwhile, there would be a cure for cancer by now. The charity concept wasn't new to posters Betty and Danette, who had been sending out non-perishable food items to The WB instead of Tabasco. When The WB was flooded with Tabasco bottles, the fans suggested a way to ensure they wouldn't go to waste.

The idea of raising money for World Vision's 30 Hour Famine originated with the campaign organizers; after all, Brendan Fehr was involved with the charity. The plan was simple — they would take the loads of Tabasco bottles off The wb's hands, try to get the cast to autograph them, and arrange for a small table at the *Roswell* party in August. They could sell the bottles to the fans and raise money. When Michelle posted the idea on the Roswell2 board, she received a positive response. Danette and Betty came up with the slogan "Roswell Is Hot, Hunger Is Not" (rihhin). Meanwhile, Michelle created a Web site for rihhin. Later, when Brendan's manager's comment made the *New York Times*, Darien and Michelle discussed hosting the site on the "Fan Forum" server with a link to the charity site through Crashdown.com. So, in March, the group had a charity, the rihhin team had gathered 30 volunteers, and the Crashdown.com/"Fan Forum" crew was advertising the concept as much as possible.

Michelle and Kristi got in touch with executive producer Kevin Kelly Brown hoping that he might be able to help them. Kevin was happy to help, but he told them The wb had already determined the fate of the bottles, and were sending them out to the media as promotional items. While it was disappointing, it wasn't the only plan that had been circulating.

Fionna had suggested a first season Crashdown yearbook, which could be sold at the party with the proceeds going to World Vision. The yearbook would include an episode breakdown, trivia, fan art and fiction, breakdowns of the different "shipper" groups, along with other *Roswell* "Fan Forum" fun facts. The yearbook, finished just in time for the August party, was extremely popular, and sold out. Copies were given to the entire cast and the production office.

The extra money received for the *Daily Variety* ad was donated to the rihhin fund. As planning was getting underway, a date and venue hadn't yet been chosen so Fionna, Michelle, Kristi, Kim, Vigie, and Lena took over as the main party organizers with dozens of others also volunteering their time on various committees. They declared the party would be a charity event, complete with a charity auction.

As they prepped for the party, the fans participated in a "Without Weekend." The idea was a twist on the usual weekend of fasting — instead of going without food, the participants would "fast" from their computers for 30 hours. Kevin Kelly Brown personally sponsored both Kristi and Michelle. In the end, Blue Angel raised the highest amount — $367.50.

In June, with the help of the RIHHIN group, Michelle started coordinating a Crashdown Cookbook with SilverRain and Sozment, pulling together recipes which incorporated Tabasco sauce. The recipes were all named after aspects of the show — Kyle's (Not for Wussies) Chili, Pod Squad Pasta, Czechoslovakian Chicken, and Nasedo's Shapeshifter Soufflé. They told McIlhenny & Co. what they were doing, and the Tabasco company was happy to help print out the book and ship it down to the L.A. party. They also donated miniature bottles of Tabasco to go with each book, along with a bunch of other prizes. Unfortunately, the books did not arrive in time for the August 2000 party, and were sold at the following party in 2001.

Meanwhile, Levi's had announced that *Roswell* would be affiliated with its spring marketing campaign. That meant print and television ads, with pictures online and at retail outlets showcasing the cast of *Roswell*. The campaign featured Levi's new line of casual clothing "Lot 53" (which has a similar ring to Area 51). The ads were in magazines ranging from *Rolling Stone* to *Seventeen*. The cast toured to different stores for promotional events and autograph sessions. The campaign led to an "Official" *Roswell* fan site that didn't hold a candle to Crashdown.com, and omitted the characters of Kyle, Jim, and Alex, who had all been left out of the Levi's campaign as well.

When Brendan was signing autographs at Macy's in New York, Fionna, Michelle, and other members of the team stood in line to get autographs on some of the items they planned to auction off at the party. They also wanted to let him know what they were doing for his pet charity. Just before the fans got to the front of the line, the bouncer announced that there would be only one autograph per person. Michelle had brought two items: a giant blow-up bottle of Tabasco and a show script. First, she asked Brendan to sign the script, and then explained the situation. Seeing as they chose World Vision's 30 Hour

Brendan Fehr during the Roswell/
Levi's *campaign (Photo by Christina
Radish)*

Famine due to his connection with the charity, would he mind signing the Tabasco bottle as well? The bouncer immediately said no, but Brendan told him to back off — he was more than happy to do it. In fact, snapshots were taken of Brendan with the giant bottle, and one found its way into a magazine.

Donations from fans started coming in, starting with Catalinay, who donated over 70 photos, some autographed, of various teen celebrities. The photos were later used as pre-party auction items and prizes for the individuals who could not make it to the event. On the "Fan Forum" boards, the fans discussed the idea of donating other items for the auction. Between May and August 2000, fans made their way to the various Levi's promotional signings, asking the cast members to autograph a variety of items. In all cases, the fans explained the items were for a charity event, and through these encounters the cast first heard about the party.

Kevin Kelly Brown helped out tremendously by donating old costume items, along with other prizes (like autographed scripts and posters), and he agreed to be the Master of Ceremonies for the auction. In conjunction with the official party T-shirts made and pre-sold before the party, one fan, Clint, created four polo shirts with small silver handprints. Two sisters — tjulianne and ESQ2B — spent $1200 of their own money to create fabulous thematic gift baskets — one representing Max/Liz, one of Maria/Michael, and one of Isabel/Alex. Each basket held items pertinent to the selected couple. Levi's donated 400 T-shirts, along with large posters of their *Roswell* cast ads. Mudd Jeans sent in clothing, socks, and purses. Krispy Kreme donated 45 dozen of their popular donuts, and Power Star Merchandising provided previews of their *Roswell* trading cards and *Roswell* buttons. Scholastic Inc. donated copies of their unauthorized biography *Meet The Stars of Roswell*, while Melinda Metz and 17th Street Productions sent three autographed sets of her 10-book series *Roswell High*.

One of the more unusual items was the set of Barbie *Roswell* Theater dolls donated by MariaB. Barbie *Roswell* Theater first premiered on the Roswell1 message board. MariaB took Barbie dolls with similar looks to the characters, created tableaux images, added screencaps to tell different stories, and displayed them. The concept was completely original, and ended up with an ardent fan following. *And* the dolls made over $100 for World Vision's 30 Hour Famine.

The date had been set for August 5, 2000. The next plan was to secure a venue. The first thought was to have the party in the old bank building which acts as the UFO Center on the show. The problem was, it was located in Covina, an hour outside of Los Angeles, and if it was held there, the odds were the cast wouldn't make an appearance. Also, there were no toilets, and absolutely no air circulation. So, that venue was out.

The group managed to secure a venue at Paramount Studios, but Magic Johnson's charitable foundation had precedence, so the *Roswell* party was bumped from the venue. In the end, the group settled with the Key Club on Sunset Boulevard. While the club wasn't the ideal setting (it was dark, there was only a small area downstairs for auction prizes, etc.), it was their only choice.

The ticket price was set at $65 per person. At the door, the guests would receive a goodie bag filled with a party T-shirt and other small gifts, including one raffle ticket. Also, for every non-perishable food item brought, the guest would receive an extra raffle ticket. Camryn and Shaz took responsibility for organizing the food donation. First, they obtained boxes and decorations donated from the store chain Sam's. Later, Kristi and Camryn made their way to a children's day-care center in Covina for the afternoon so the kids could decorate them. At the end of the evening, the food items would be stored in the decorated boxes. The two tons of food would then be taken on a flatbed truck to Covina Emergency Aid, which helps with disaster relief; the fans would support starving children at home as well as on a global scale.

The fans were excited and ready for the party. The night before the event, 400 fans mobbed the Covina set and stayed until 4 a.m. Kevin Kelly Brown sent out a panicked e-mail to Crashdown.com, asking them to post a request to fans not to go to Covina because the filming was behind that night. The cast and crew had begun production on season two, and were working on the episode "Ask Not." What was the attraction? Jason Behr was filming the opening sequence, running up and down the Covina streets, shirtless.

The cast was in town, the party was in one day, and there was no indication that they would attend, even though they had been invited. No one expected that they would actually come.

They were in for a surprise.

The First Annual Crashdown.com/"Fan Forum" Summer Party

The group was frantically completing the final stages of the party. Over 450 people from all over the U.S., Canada, and even Singapore were expected. The guests had all been told that the cast would not be there; after all, the party crew didn't want to get their hopes up. Then, the morning of the party, Kim received a phone call from Nick Wechsler, asking if he could bring along a guest. Then the production office phoned to get details on the party security. After that, it was pretty apparent that the cast would be making an appearance. Knowing it was a charity event, the *Roswell* cast and crew wanted to thank the fans for all of their support. The organizers kept it to themselves, however, planning on surprising the guests.

The place looked great, decorated with giant inflatable Tabasco bottles, and photos of the cast everywhere. Kevin Kelly Brown was all set to be the auctioneer, while Kristi and Fionna were the designated Vanna Whites for the evening. The guests were enthusiastic, and ready to have fun! Kevin really got into his role, hyping up all the items, and working the audience. The fans were extremely generous as well — a signed copy of "Heatwave" went for $800

U.S. Autographed posters and scripts were auctioned off, along with Isabel's silk pajamas and Sheriff Valenti's gray Stetson cowboy hat.

When the hat came up for bids, suddenly Bill Sadler appeared onstage, and put it on. As Kevin dealt with the bidders, Bill hammed it up, clad in jeans and red shoes. MistyMue ended up winning the coveted item, and Bill hopped off the stage, put it on her head, and gave her a kiss. Not only was it an amazing moment for MistyMue, but the audience now knew that some, if not all, of the cast was in the club. The most popular item of the night, were the scrubs Jason Behr wore in the episode "The White Room." The party-goers went mad. Kevin riled them up with comments that the scrubs had touched Jason's naked flesh — and had never been washed! That was it for the bidders. Hands flew into the air, but one remained there, unwavering. The amount grew from $1,000 to $2,000 . . . and then to $3,000. The number of competing bidders grew smaller, but the price continued moving up. Still, one arm stood straight up. That arm belonged to the winner — Mad4Max got to take home Jason's scrubs for $4,000 U.S.

Down in the VIP room, the cast were curious as to what the commotion upstairs was all about. When Kenn, Kristi, and Fionna told Jason that his scrubs had just brought in $4,000 for charity, he was stunned. He joked about taking off his underwear to see how much money that would raise. Someone else in the room suggested $8,000! Jokes aside, Jason then offered to meet the winner. So, the party crew asked Mad4Max to follow them downstairs. She was concerned at first that something was wrong, and then she saw Jason. Shocked, she quickly recovered herself, and Jason offered to buy her a drink as a thank-you. A lap-top had been set up in the VIP room so that the cast could post a message on the "Fan Forum" Roswell2 message board for the fans that could not make it. Mad4Max quite happily typed out Jason's message. Colin, Emilie, Katherine, Jim Ortlieb (Nasedo), and Nick also got on the computer to post messages. Back in their homes, so many fans attempted to access the site that night that they overwhelmed the servers.

In the small area downstairs, the tables had been set up with some merchandise and prize items, and the VIP room was next door. The cast had not yet made an official appearance, and the fans were curious. People kept trying to peek into the VIP room to see just who had shown up. Finally, the cast decided to venture into the party. Brendan followed Majandra in, keeping close to the petite actress's side. Bill Sadler mingled with the crowd, and Jason Katims, Katherine Heigl, Colin Hanks, and Nick Wechsler went out to meet the fans. Shiri Appleby went out with her bodyguard. Concerned about being mobbed, Jason played it safe, asking if it would be okay if he could make a quick stage appearance to say hello and thanks.

Fionna remembers a fabulous story of one fan of Shiri's. "One fan wanted to meet Shiri at the first party, but couldn't because this 'guy' wouldn't leave her alone all night. Anyway, in frustration, he finally approached the guy and told him to back off so someone else could spend time with Shiri, and the guy smiled and left. Turns out later on, the fan saw the 'guy' on stage . . . it was Jason Katims!"

Michelle also had a lovely memory of the party. Three months pregnant and running around like crazy all night, Michelle was exhausted. While Jason Behr's manager had been very thoughtful to her, offering to have bodyguards help her through the crowds, it didn't mean Michelle could slow down. With all the work to do, one of the things she had missed out on was meeting the cast. When she got to the VIP room, Kim took her over to Nick Wechsler and introduced them. The two of them started chatting, and Nick asked if Michelle had met everyone. She told him, "No," and at that point, Nick took her hand and proceeded to lead her through the crowds. He personally introduced her to every cast member. She still hadn't met Majandra or Brendan when the cast was called off to take an official photo with Yvonne from World Vision. Nick told her to wait exactly where she was, that he would be right back. He left, took the photo, then returned to her, took her hand, and they continued on. Michelle appreciated his warm nature and the fact that he took a personal interest in her life.

Yvonne Bennett, a young representative from World Vision's 30 Hour Famine, drove down from the Washington area to be at the event. Initially, it seemed as though the donations had to be cash-only, which wasn't ideal.

Yvonne managed to arrange it so that credit cards could be used, and she spent the whole night writing out every slip by hand. Later on, she wanted to present Michelle and the RIHHIN group with a plaque, but Michelle didn't want to get up onstage — she had been running around all night. Finally, Nick Wechsler and Bill Sadler insisted Michelle get up there. Yvonne was so overwhelmed by the money raised she grew teary.

Soon, the cast got together onstage to say a few words to the audience. Poor Colin missed the call, however, and was outside having a smoke. The microphone was passed to each actor in turn. Overwhelmed, Nick was speechless. Katherine was polite and thankful, as were Shiri and Emilie. Brendan and Majandra were more comical. Brendan jokingly cried out "You guys suck!" which was met with cheers. Majandra teased the crowd by saying that she would sing, then jumped straight to the "thank you very much" without uttering a note. Jason commented on Brendan's words, then ended on a serious note by thanking the fans for their support. As the cast made their way off stage, Colin appeared. Alone on stage, Colin took the microphone and addressed the audience. He came across as a natural, comfortable and fun.

When the cast left the stage, the first chords of Dido's "Here With Me" filled the air. Soon, the entire crowd was singing along, with many of the fans tearing up. It was a highly emotional moment for both the guests and the organizers. The party had been a success! The goal the RIHHIN crew had set for themselves was $10,000. In fact, the total amount raised for World Vision's 30 Hour Famine was over $28,000 U.S. The party was covered by KTLA news in Los Angeles and on SciFiwire.com. It was also mentioned in *Teen Magazine's* August 2000 issue.

That next day, there was a special event arranged — the first ever Valentine's Dinner at the Gaylord of India celebrating Sheriff and Kyle Valenti. Both Bill Sadler and Nick Wechsler came to meet 40 of their personal fans. Bill brought his guitar and serenaded the group with silly songs. The room was only booked until 10, but Bill quickly changed that. Paying out of his own pocket, he arranged to keep the room for another hour. Then, the time came for the Rosquilters to make their presentation.

The Rosquilters were a group of fans whose love of the show and characters prompted them to create a special gift for the cast. Asking the fans to send in personally designed squares for whichever actor they chose, the Rosquilters then joined them all together to create personalized quilts for each cast member. They presented their special gifts to Nick and Bill, who accepted all the quilts on behalf of the cast. Nick was given the hand-scripted scroll to read out to the room, and was so overwhelmed he fought back tears. Bill was also presented with his own personal Hollywood "star," while Nick received a statuette even though he was "just happy to be nominated!" ("Blind Date").

The cast was more than thrilled with the quilts and all of the other wonderful gifts and support they received from their fans. Everyone finally settled down to enjoy a second season of *Roswell*, the Tabasco days a happy memory from the past. Or so everyone thought.

Tabasco to the Rescue — Again!

The party had been a success, but there was a bit of backlash that had to be addressed. Some people were under the impression that the organizers had more time with the cast in the VIP room (which wasn't true, because they were running around most of the night) and that the cast wasn't announced until later in the evening. Also, there were a few issues with the chosen charity, because it was a Christian charity. As a consequence, some fans felt unable to donate. The interesting thing was, the charitable element was organized by a Wiccan! The original party organizers and campaign leaders were burnt out from all of their efforts, and more charity campaigning was on the rise. So, a new team formed, while the first team continued to participate on an advisory level. Mary (Thicket), Scott (Scott73), Pam (provence), and Jen (Kaye), with the help of the Crashdown.com/"Fan Forum" crew (and hundreds more — including members of the site: theddd.com) became known as the new Campaign Crew.

The WB stated that if *Roswell* was to return for a second season, they needed to explore the sci-fi angle more. This wasn't an issue for Jonathan Frakes, who thought ["The show] evolved, in all honesty, into a show much more about the mythology of the aliens than about the angst about teen romance. It's really become, in a lot of ways, about Max, who is, as [creator] Jason Katims likes to refer to him, not unlike Michael Corleone — he tried to get out, but he's always brought back. He is the leader, he is the number-one alien." Ron Moore, whose previous experiences included writing for the various *Star Trek* series, was brought on as the new *Roswell* writer/producer. The fans were concerned that the relationship element to the show would become defunct, but Ron Moore reassured the fans that it would not be sacrificed. On October 23, The WB picked up four more episodes of *Roswell*, giving it a total of 17 episodes. Then, on November 6, an announcement in the *Daily Variety* stated that The WB had extended *Roswell's* run to 21 episodes. The future looked bright once more!

At this point, the infamous Tabasco campaign had inspired other campaigns. Tapes were sent in to The WB in order to save the show *Felicity*. When Joey and Pacey got together on *Dawson's Creek*, daisies were sent in protesting the union, and when the show *Popular* was on the brink of cancellation, the fans sent in tampons, hoping to change its fate. Even the *Roswell* fans followed their own trend by sending in strawberry applesauce (which broke in the mail and turned out to be quite messy) as a way of telling the producers they wanted Liz and Max back together. The strawberries came from the opening scene of "Sexual Healing," while the applesauce represented Shiri's last name: Appleby. The WB producers contacted "Fan Forum," asking them to advise fans *not* to send any more applesauce due to the mess. When "Fan Forum" posted the request, however, the fans only mailed in more.

Meanwhile, Crashdown.com/"Fan Forum" was growing. On December 15, Crashdown.com's official birthday, it received its five millionth hit. The fans remained active, and a group of Appleby's fans took out a quarter-page ad in the February 23, 2001 edition of the *Daily Variety* to show their appreciation of her work on *Roswell*. Preparations for the second annual *Roswell*ian Gathering in Los Angeles had already begun, with Kim and Lena once more taking the helm.

Before the Christmas episode aired, a small group of fans in Chicago decided to take matters into their own hands, and promote *Roswell* offline. They stood in front of the Chicago Tribune Tower and handed out packets of hot chocolate to passers-by. On the packets were labels asking people to watch *Roswell*. They also handed out flyers and bags of candy, getting people in to the Christmas spirit. In the end, they passed out over 200 flyers, and the four fans who made the effort had a great time.

The Christmas *Roswell* episode, "A Roswell Christmas Carol," included a scene where Max heals a group of children in the hospital's pediatric oncology ward. After it aired, the Campaign Crew not only promoted online Christmas cards, but along with the fans, they began supporting the Pediatric Cancer Foundation. Fans sent in toys and donations, helping in whatever way they could just before the holidays. The Campaign Crew hooked up with the PCF charity, and raised money to send a young cancer patient to the set of *Roswell* at Paramount Studios in Los Angeles. The selected child would fly there with his or her family for two days, and also get the opportunity to visit Disneyland. The actual trip would cost several thousand dollars, and any money raised beyond that would go to cancer research.

In January, there was a plea once more to send in letters to The WB executives — not because the show had been threatened, but to show the executives that the fans were still out there and still loved the show. Not only that, but February sweeps would soon be approaching, and the *Roswell* ratings needed to be high. The Campaign Crew worked hard to encourage fans to promote the show anywhere they could. For every dollar a fan donated to PCF, Save*Roswell*.com (the new Web site) would mail a postcard to that individual so they could send it to a friend to help campaign for the show. The Campaign Crew also encouraged the fans to thank *Roswell*'s sponsors, letting them know just how much they loved the show.

Lena and Kim organized the Second Annual *Roswell*ian Gathering, held on February 24th at Q's Billiards in Los Angeles, with Kevin Kelly Brown, Jason Katims, and other members of the production team in attendance. While Jamie Kellner, CEO of The WB was unable to attend, he wrote a personal message thanking fans for their support. There was another interesting attendee at the party, however. Working as a bartender that night was *Survivor: Africa* contestant, Silas Gaither. The party happened before Silas went off on his adventure, however, so when *Roswell* fans took photos with him, it wasn't his fame they found attractive! A photo of Silas with a fan was posted on the Crashdown.com Web site, and later, when *Survivor: Africa* was airing, someone saw it and assumed the fan was actually Silas's girlfriend. Suddenly, the photo found its way to a variety of *Survivor: Africa* Web sites, with the caption of Silas with his "girlfriend." The night of the party, Silas's co-workers acted as security for the second annual "Fan Forum" party, held in August 2001. That party started a relationship between Silas and the "Fan Forum."

The following day, the Rosquilters had a dinner in Los Angeles, and Nick Wechsler and Kevin Kelly Brown came as guests. There, they were presented with scrapbooks and quilted pillows for the cast — all personalized — and quilted wall-hangings for the executive producers. While not all of the cast members were attending events, they still kept active with the fans. Bill Sadler and Brendan continued to post on their boards while Shiri ventured out onto "Fan Forum," posting as killercat. Meanwhile, the fans had reached a global scale at this point — North Americans, South Americans, Australians, Europeans, and Asians of all ages were bonding over their favorite show: *Roswell.*

There were some other issues brewing, however. Some of the fans weren't happy with the way the show was moving, especially when it came to Max and Liz's relationship. There is speculation that, due to the success of the campaigns, certain fans thought they should have more say in the upcoming plotlines. A lot of people were upset over the fact that the character Max was with Tess and not Liz, sparking debates over fan boards everywhere. "Fan Forum's" firm policy against the bashing of other posters led to the formation of a couple other boards, but this did not affect the popularity of "Fan Forum."

And then . . . the all-too-familiar rumors started to circulate. *Roswell* was in danger of not being picked up for a third season. The fans got to work preparing to save *Roswell* from extinction once again. An online season three petition was created by Kim and Lena, with the goal being 10,000 signatures;

it ended up garnering 30,000. Kristi pulled together addresses of various UPN contacts and some of *Roswell*'s sponsors. Fionna wrote a covering letter on behalf of all *Roswell* Internet fans and the petition was mailed out. In appreciation for all the efforts made by fans, the Campaign Crew and theddd.net (definitive dreamers dictionary — celebrating Max and Liz) created a giveaway campaign, acknowledging individuals who had made outstanding efforts by giving away prizes such as a color ink jet printer, and *Roswell* trading cards and scripts. At the same time, other countries were also working hard to save the show in their neck of the woods. Fans from Australia, New Zealand, the United Kingdom, and Singapore had begun campaigning in order to get the *second* season of *Roswell* aired in their respective countries!

In April, the Campaign crew sent out a desperate plea to the fans to make one last-ditch effort by sending in kind letters to The WB about how much they love *Roswell*. The clock was ticking, and it didn't look like The WB was going to keep *Roswell* on its roster this time. Still, the fans kept going. What was it about *Roswell* that was too hard to give up? Daniela Pulice, a librarian from New York, says that "the character interaction is evocative of many old-time Hollywood classics. Is Liz's sacrificial love for Max any less poignant than Rick's classic farewell to Ilsa in *Casablanca*? The depth of emotion while surrounded by suspenseful intrigue is what keeps us all coming back for more." It also has huge international appeal. In Brazil, Mariana Carrilho stated, "There are many reasons why *Roswell* needs to be saved. But, personally, I'd like to have *Roswell* renewed first because it made me see and believe that love can win any barrier, of time, genre, species, and any obstacle. But, the most important reason is that it made me have hope that, someday, we will find people that can heal wounds. Maybe not the way Max Evans does, but maybe with the words he uses, with the way he treats the ones he loves, and even with the kindness we can feel from him. If the world had a little bit of this 'alien' temper, we wouldn't have so much sadness."

Many shows took time to get off the ground, including the original series *Star Trek*, as well as *Star Trek: The Next Generation*. *Roswell* had proved that they had an extensive fan base, and yet, it wasn't enough. At the end of April,

Buffy the Vampire Slayer was picked up from The wb by the United Paramount Network (upn) with the hopes that upn could broaden its female audience. Still with no news, it left the *Roswell* cast and crew feeling less optimistic than before. It also was never in *Roswell's* favor that it was produced by 20th Century Fox and was not a wb original show. *Roswell* continued to be "on the bubble."

upn was considering picking up the show, but didn't believe that the fan base was as large as they had originally heard. So, AlleyKat created a new campaign idea. The plan involved returning to the original Tabasco campaign, but instead of targeting The wb, the target would now be the executives of upn. A new slogan was created by Emily_A: *Spice Up Your Line-up! Add Roswell to* upn*!* Fionna posted a challenge to the fans on the Roswell2 board. For the first campaign, 6,000 bottles of Tabasco piled up in The wb's mailroom over 12 weeks. Now, the question was, could the fans reverse that, and get 12,000 bottles to the upn mailroom in six weeks? Sure enough, the fans came through. And not just fans from the United States. The countries who participated either by sending in Tabasco, or in other ways, were: Argentina, Australia, Austria, Brazil, Canada, Denmark, Finland, France, Germany, Holland, Mexico, New Zealand, Panama, the Philippines, Singapore, Slovenia, South Africa, Sweden, Switzerland, and the U.K.

The final countdown had begun with no news from either The wb or upn. The season finale of *Roswell* was approaching, and the producers were trying not to rule out any possibilities. There were undeniable issues to look at, however. "The fact that [*Buffy*] went to upn could negatively affect the way The wb looks at *Roswell*. It was hard to predict what was going to happen to *Roswell* before the *Buffy* move, it's even harder to predict now. I'll just have to wait and see," Jason Katims said.

May brought with it two potential upsets. The first involved "Fan Forum," and Crashdown.com on May 3. The site had become so popular that it was serving approximately 1,200 gigabytes of information a month, which caused the server bills to escalate. At the same time, as the dot-com industry suffered, the banner ads which brought in revenue started to disappear. Like they did with the show, hundreds of "Fan Forum" posters rushed in to save the day, donating money to keep the site up and running. Then, May 15 arrived and the bomb dropped. The WB made the official announcement that *Roswell* would not be picked up for a third season.

Two days later, UPN came to the rescue by announcing that they had picked up *Roswell* for their new line-up. Once again, Liz, the "Fan Forum" administrator, was at the forefront, quickly calling up Kenn at Crashdown.com to deliver the news. It was scheduled to follow *Buffy* on Tuesday nights, going up against the popular show *Gilmore Girls*, and new WB show, *Smallville*. Only time would tell as to how the shows would fare against each other. On May 21, the season two finale of *Roswell* hit the airwaves, leaving fans hungering for more. A season two finale party was held in New York, with Kevin Kelly Brown in attendance. At the same time, parties were also held in Arizona and L.A. The fans wanted to do something to thank UPN for renewing *Roswell*, and the initial thought was another page in the *Daily Variety*. Instead, keeping with tradition, Kenn and Leif came up with a unique idea that the Campaign Crew embraced immediately. Fans could send donations to the Pediatric Children's Foundation in the name of UPN and *Roswell*. The Thank-UPN campaign was scheduled to end on June 1, after which the PCF would send a letter to UPN president Dean Valentine informing him of what the fans had done, and the money they had raised in the name of UPN.

The producers were pleased about the situation. "We're in a good place. *Buffy's* a tremendous lead-in for us, that's for certain. We're in the perfect slot in the schedule at the moment," said Ron Moore. Apparently, Jason Katims felt so confident that a third season would come about that he didn't write episodes that would wrap up the series.

In June, Melinda Metz, the author of the *Roswell High* books, and Laura Burns, the editor who created the characters, were brought onto the staff writing team. It was an exciting step for both of them. "When Jason [Katims] offered us staff jobs, we were . . . thrilled!" said Burns. "It's weird because, in one way, we have a lot of history with *Roswell*. But in another way, we're just big fans of the show. The books are very different, and it's been years since we worked on them. So working on the show is like working in an alternate universe." Metz was looking forward to learning "all the production part. The kind of considerations you have to think about when your script is actually going to be made . . ."

The *Roswell* fans ended up raising $16,400 for the PCF through the Thank-UPN campaign. The spirits were high, and August was approaching. There was a party to plan!

The Second Annual Crashdown.com/"Fan Forum" Summer Party

July was a hectic time for many of the crew. To begin with, on July 11, "Fan Forum" was attacked by a hacker and was almost completely destroyed. Having lurked around for a few weeks, the hacker was able to change the automated back-up system. This led to chaos on July 11 as 3,000 of 25,000 member accounts were destroyed. The site administrators rushed to fix it. "Fan Forum" pulled through, however, and now grows by about 300 members a day. Also in July, Fionna was furiously trying to finish the Season Two Yearbook in time for the party on August 18. Many people had ordered copies in advance, and were expecting to pick them up at the event.

The cast had finished filming and were on a press tour for UPN. There were some issues, however, surrounding some of the cast members. There were rumors of the possibility that 20th Century Fox was threatening legal action against Brendan Fehr for not showing up to promote *Roswell* at the Television Critics Association Press Tour, taking place in Pasadena, California. Jason Behr was also absent. Both men, however, had reasons for missing the event. Brendan was filming public service announcements (regarding sexual abuse prevention) for the Ontario government. Jason was working on another project. Rumors had also been circulating that not all the actors were pleased about the show's renewal. "I think it's already been expressed that not everyone was particularly excited about going back for a third season," said Jim Sheasgreen, Brendan Fehr's manager.

Meanwhile, the preparations for the party continued. That year's Party

Producer Kevin Kelly Brown with Shiri Appleby (Photo by Gregory Schwartz, courtesy Crashdown.com)

Colin Hanks signing posters at the party (Photo by Gregory Schwartz, courtesy Crashdown.com)

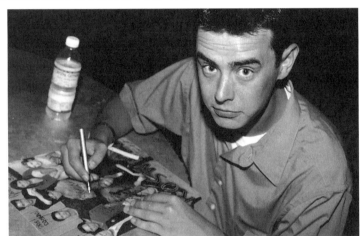

Jason Behr, holding the infamous scrubs, with his manager and Jason Katims (Photo by Gregory Schwartz, courtesy Crashdown.com)

Emilie de Ravin hugs Majandra Delfino at the party (Photo by Gregory Schwartz, courtesy Crashdown.com)

The cast of Roswell with a representative from the charity organization (Photo by Gregory Schwartz, courtesy Crashdown.com)

Brendan Fehr and Majandra Delfino mingle with the fans (Courtesy Fionna)

Executive Committee consisted of Angela, Vigie, Kristi, Fionna, Melanie, Nephele, Cameron, Cindy, and Kenn. The staff of "Fan Forum" and Crashdown.com had a more active role in organizing this party, since all the promotional and charity campaigns were done through Crashdown.com/ "Fan Forum." It was only right to make sure the event was a success for the PCF.

The group tried to incorporate all the suggestions they had received after the first party. Also, due to complaints from fans of other shows, Leif informed the *Roswell* party crew that if they were going to use the "Fan Forum" boards to advertize the party, they needed to open up the invitation to fans from other television boards, such as *Dawson's Creek* or *Felicity*. Of course, it would be too difficult to incorporate more than one show theme at the party, so the message was sent out in a general capacity. While a few fans of other shows did attend, 95% of the guests were there because of *Roswell*.

The event was held at the Sheraton Universal Hotel mirrored ballroom in Los Angeles, and hosted by "Fan Forum." The ballroom offered more space than the Key Club and had a stage. A full buffet was arranged, with the plan to donate any leftovers to a local homeless shelter, and there were plenty of tables and chairs to accommodate the guests. A DJ was hired, along with some live music from a singer named Magdalen Hsu-Li. It looked to be a much saner, more organized version of the first party.

A few days before the party, Fionna sent off the prototype of the yearbook to Kristi in L.A. so that copies could be made before she got there. When she arrived, however, all 600 bound copies had been badly printed. The sheets had been photocopied on an angle with the binding obscuring the copy on most of the pages. After much debate with the copy store until the wee hours of the morning, they agreed to redo all 600 of the yearbooks on the night before the party, and they were finished 15 minutes before the party began. Like the first book, it was extremely well-received. A few members of the *Roswell*/UPN staff attended the party, saw the yearbook, and requested copies for their entire marketing department. The yearbook was then used as their "bible" as they came up with ideas for how to market the show. There was also a discussion with UPN about Crashdown.com becoming the official *Roswell* site. While

Fionna and Kristi hold up one of the Roswell *quilts (Photo by Gregory Schwartz, courtesy Crashdown.com)*

Majandra and Brendan answer questions from the audience (Photo by Gregory Schwartz, courtesy Crashdown.com)

Kevin Kelly Brown and Bill Sadler auction off a pair of Sheriff Valenti's jeans (Photo by Gregory Schwartz, courtesy Crashdown.com)

there were complications with that concept, UPN and Crashdown.com still formed a strong relationship.

Over 500 guests attended, excited to meet up with their Internet friends. Brendan Fehr, Majandra Delfino, Bill Sadler, Kevin Kelly Brown, and some of the *Roswell* writers also attended the Second Annual gathering. The fans took the opportunity to talk with the writers: some were more confrontational about storyline choices, while others were in awe, asking questions about their careers. Magdalen performed for the crowds, at one point making a comment that *Felicity* was actually her favorite show, which did not bode well with the *Roswell* fans! Majandra and Brendan were in the back room, and came out when they heard her performing. The appearance of the stars caused a bit of chaos with the crowds. Magdalen's set finished early as a consequence, and Majandra approached the drummer, Dan Fanning, to talk about working together in the future. Then, at Kevin Kelly Brown's insistence, Majandra and Brendan took the stage while security got the crowds under control. Later in the evening, Brendan ended up showcasing his musical "talents" on the drums, with Majandra and her musical producer offering him tips. They also held an impromptu Q&A session for the fans as well as taking the time to post a message on the "Fan Forum" boards for the absentee fans. The "Fan Forum" crowd also had the privilege of hearing the Q&A session live on the Internet, thanks to former "Fan Forum" administrator Mark McLeod.

Once again, there was a live auction in conjunction with the silent one. Kevin Kelly Brown reprised his role as auctioneer, with Fionna and Kristi helping display the auction items. Brendan Fehr donated many of his personal items to the event, including several T-shirts, a few pairs of jeans, and his beloved pair of Doc Marten boots, all of which he autographed. A complete set of season one and two scripts was also auctioned off, along with autographed photos, posters, and numerous second season costumes donated from wardrobe. Bill came onstage with an autographed poster reading "Valenti And Son." Karen (Rosburtie), one of the Rosquilters, brought quilts to auction off. In May, Majandra had auctioned her gift quilt on eBay, then donated the $1,375 to the PCF. Fans also donated to the PCF on behalf of UPN rather than

Brendan Fehr lets loose on the drums at the second annual Crashdown/ "Fan Forum" party (Photo by Christina Radish)

send thank-you notes. At the end of the evening, over $14,000 U.S. had been raised for PCF, which was, on its own, a reason to celebrate.

"What happens now, Max?"

The Canadian TV *Times* poll listed *Roswell* as the number one drama series in August 2001. The future looked bright once more. Jason Behr's fans followed in the footsteps of Shiri Appleby's, putting an ad in the *Daily Variety* to thank him for his work on the show, and wishing him best of luck in the third season. Everyone was gearing up for the premiere episode, curious to see what changes the move to UPN brought. The change everyone noticed immediately was Heigl's hair: pulling a *Felicity*, she had chopped off the blonde locks for a short, stylish hairdo. She had also dyed it brown. It was minor compared to the changes her character was about to make in season three.

UPN was promoting the show through billboards, promotional events, and contests. The producers had more freedom to return to the writing style of the first season. "What [UPN] wants from the show is what I wanted to do with it," said Jason Katims. "We've added a little more humor. And we've simplified it in terms of mythology and sci-fi. I think the last season was confusing to people, even if they were watching the show regularly. So, the move has been exciting. It has given us new life."

The horrible events of September 11, 2001, rocked the world. Knowing some of their own had been personally affected by the terrorist attacks on the World Trade Center, the Rosquilters quickly organized a new quilt theme: Healing Hands. They put a request to all the fans to send in pieces of material with a silver handprint on it, along with their name. Once the pieces were collected, the quilters put them together, not only creating quilts for the few fans who had been directly affected, but also sending a quilt to the New York Police Department, the New York Fire Department, and finally, one to the Pentagon, as a gesture of support. The Pentagon staff were so touched that fans of a television show would go to such an effort, they hung up the quilt in their official museum. A fan quickly noted: "Now there is a real *Roswell* cover-up in the Pentagon."

Roswell still seemed to be doing well, despite the tragic events. In the September issue of *Entertainment Weekly, Roswell* won out as favorite show in their Fall TV poll. UPN soon picked up more episodes, bringing the count up to 20 episodes for the year. Still, *Smallville* opened with amazing ratings, turning out to be more competition than they had expected. Ex-*Roswell* producer David Nutter had directed the *Smallville* pilot episode and comparisons between the two shows were immediate. Both series feature dark-haired sensitive heroes with extraordinary powers. They also feature long, dark-haired, intelligent heroines, and each has a spunky blond. It was still early, however: "[W]e were prepared to let them have a big premiere and a solid follow-up rating or two," said Ron Moore, "But after the bloom is off the rose, and they have to do it every week, then it's going to be a fair fight, and we'll just see what happens."

While *Roswell* continued to "re-invent" itself, so did the Crashdown.com/ "Fan Forum" Campaign Crew. In October 2001, they began recruiting volunteers to help out with different committees. Those committees included a Grassroots Team (dealing with e-mail reminders, flyer posting), the UPN Appreciation Committee, the Sponsor Support Group (helping fans contact sponsors), the Affiliate Advocates (amassing contact info), and the Media Club (media exposure/publicity). Of course, it didn't take long for the *Roswell* fans to sign up. Christmas brought a new charitable campaign with it — Toys for Tots. The Toys for Tots charity was chosen by the *Roswell* production group because it is run by military personnel. As a consequence of troops heading for Afghanistan, it had a shortage of help. Postcards were also created to send to Dean Valentine, the CEO of UPN, thanking him again for *Roswell*. Dean Valentine later donated $500 to the Crashdown.com Toys for Tots campaign.

Meanwhile the fight between the small Kansas town and the small New Mexican town continued. It wasn't looking too good for the aliens (wait, they're *all* aliens!), with *Smallville* pulling in four times as many viewers as *Roswell* by the end of October. Soon, *Roswell* was on the fence once more, getting lower ratings than the UPN executives, or even the producers, had expected. At the beginning of 2002, UPN made the decision to shelve *Roswell* for seven weeks, starting in March, and air two of their new sitcoms in the timeslot. There was also the very real possibility that the number of *Roswell* episodes would be cut down from 20 to 18. In *Roswell*'s case, the expression "three time's a charm" just wasn't true.

Another online petition was created, suggesting the exchange of the Tabasco bottles for Snapple caps in reference to the third season episode "Michael, the Guys, and the Great Snapple Caper." Instead, the campaign involved the arrival of new UPN president, Dawn Tarnofsy-Ostroff.

As she would be taking over the position close to Valentine's Day, the latest campaign was a mass-heart-mailing to UPN. The slogan was "Follow Your Heart . . . Let *Roswell* Capture It." With the fans of Sheriff and Kyle Valenti calling themselves the Valentines, the campaign had a nice double meaning. Once again, the fans wanted UPN to know that they were out there, regardless of what the Nielsen ratings suggested.

The question was, did the cast want to stay? Jason Behr, Majandra Delfino and Brendan Fehr had all stated publicly that it wasn't necessarily their first choice. Even though Jason was grateful for the opportunities *Roswell* had given him, his life was changing. "When we first started this, it wasn't a job — it was fun," Behr said. "It was showing up today, working with friends and telling a good story. I felt really positive about everything. I told myself the moment it becomes a job, when it becomes work, it's not worth it anymore for me. There are days [now] when I walk on that set, and I laugh so hard and have such a great time. But there are days when it is work. It can be hard." Like Brendan Fehr, he's working on making a career for himself in movies. Brendan's view on the show is more blunt. "I'd never do TV again," he says. "I'd do guest-stars; I'd do recurring — three or four or maybe six-episode arc deal. . . . this would be my last stint in TV and after this I would either do movies or go poor."

There were other rumors circulating that some of the cast members didn't get along at the start. While that may have changed over three seasons, it was still an issue. Teenmag.com stated, "[S]everal of the stars feel like they should be doing more big-screen work, and were actually hoping that the show would be cancelled at the end of last season, so they would be free to go on to these movie careers . . . So, when UPN picked up the show for this season, those stars weren't at all looking forward to returning, which, as some fans and critics of the show have been noticing, has been showing in their performances this season, which, according to those fans and critics, have seemed half-hearted. Given all this, the stars who actually *do* want to be on the show . . . are rather resentful of the fact that their co-stars have such bad attitudes, and this often causes clashes among the cast." The teen aliens may be growing up, looking to branch out, but one thing is for certain. Their moving performances, along with the strong, compelling scripts, have touched the lives of people all over the world.

Jason Katims is interviewed during the filming of the final episode, "Graduation Day" (Photo by Christina Radish)

While the audience members had been receiving hints for weeks regarding *Roswell's* impending fate, it didn't stop fans from continuing their quest to save their show. The "Passion Through Compassion" campaign was well underway at this point. The plan arose after *Roswell* writer/producer Garrett Lerner sent out a plea to the fans. His 20-month-old son, Zeke, suffers from a debilitating disorder known as Spinal Muscular Atrophy. Knowing the history of the *Roswell* fans and their charitable events, Garrett appealed to their generous natures in the hope to raise money for the FSMA charity. Sure enough, the Campaign Crew decided to incorporate this charity with their latest attempt to reach out to UPN. As well as sending donations to Families of Spinal Muscular Atrophy, the plan involved sending cards to the CEO and President of CBS Television, and the chairman of Fox Television Entertainment Group. The cards state simply that: "I am a *Roswell* fan. I could have sent Tabasco but instead I'm sending $ . . . to Families of Spinal Muscular Atrophy to show my compassion as a *Roswell* fan." Both McIlhenney and Co. (Tabasco) and Cadbury Schweppes PLC (Snapple) provided large, corporate donations as well, bringing the total donations over $20,000 U.S. While the fans efforts may not have saved *Roswell*, they certainly had a hand in helping to save lives.

The official cancellation announcement came on April 10, 2002. Jason Katims brought the series finale story line back to the roots of the show: Max and Liz's relationship. Even though the fate of the television series has been sealed, the fans refuse to give up. This time the campaigns have taken a different spin on things; the fans are asking for a *Roswell* feature film. In a Crashdown.com interview with Jason Katims, he revealed: "I also worked on *My So-Called Life* and that was a show that also inspired this big passionate fan base, but at the same time the Internet was very new, and not as pervasive as it is now — and the television audience was not as sophisticated as it is now, and this Crashdown audience is such a sophisticated audience . . . I think there's just something special about *Roswell*'s audience in their passion."

While we may have to accept *Roswell*'s departure, we will always hold it dear in our hearts.

Chapter 4

Roswell on the Internet

"The point is that we don't know anything about these Czechoslovakians. Are they good Czechoslovakians? Bad Czechoslovakians? We don't know."

WEB SITES AND SHIPPER TERMINOLOGY
THE ROSWELL SHIPPER ALPHABET

Internet posting boards are quite the phenomenon. Everyone has a preference of character relationship combinations, be it either platonic or romantic. Some people prefer to discuss storylines, or general themes. The discussions on "shipper" groups are completely diverse, and quite unique. Here is a list of some of the different "shipper" groups that have graced the posting boards of "Fan Forum" and other posting boards, courtesy of the Crashdown Yearbook.

Abductees – Brody fans

African American Roswell Lovers
   (AARL)

Alleycats – Ava fans

Applesaucers – Shiri Appleby fans

Aussie Roswell Embassy

Awakened Dreamers – Liz/Zan fans

Balcony Sirens – Liz/Lonnie fans

Band Candy – Maria/Alex/Michael fans

Band Geeks – Maria/Liz/Alex fans

BBQ M&M's – Maria/Michael/Kyle fans

Behrians – Jason Behr fans

Bicker Brigade/Cool Kids — Maria/Kyle
(platonic relationship) fans

Big Pimpin' — Liz/Maria/Nasedo (as
Max) fans

Blond Ambition — Maria/Tess/Isabel
fans

Blond Attitudes — Maria/Isabel fans

Brats — Nick Wechsler/Kyle fans

Breakfast Club — Liz/Michael/Maria fans

B-Team — Kyle/Alex fans

Canadian Roswellian Embassy

Candy Clan — Michael/Maria fans

Catfighters — Liz/Tess fans

Cliffhangers — Michael/Isabel fans

Continuity Hole and/or Discrepancy
(CHAD)

Conventioneers — Max/Milton fans

Copy Catfighters — Liz/Tess/Ava fans

Copy Cats — Liz/Ava fans

Corn Fed Ladies — Betty/Hal fans
(Summer of '47)

Cruel Desires — Liz/Nicholas fans

Delinquents — Sean fans

Desert Dwellers/Three Musketeers —
Maria/Michael/Isabel fans

Donors — Alex fans

Double Dippers — Liz/Max/Zan fans

Dreamers — Max/Liz fans (also TNT
Dreamers, and Reject Dreamers)

DreamPole Nuts — Liz/Max/Michael
fans

Dupes Appreciation Thread (DAT)

Dutch Embassy

Fantastics — Liz/Nasedo fans

Fehrians — Brendan Fehr fans

Fifth Wheelers — Alex/Tess fans

Filipino Embassy

Friendshippers — Roswell teen friendship
fans

Fryers — Sean/Liz fans

German Embassy

Ground Zeroers — Max/Maria fans

Groupies — Alex/Maria fans

Guides — Liz/Topolsky fans

Hankies — Colin Hanks fans

Healers — Max fans

Hot Wheels — Maria/Alex/Tess fans

Hussies — Tess fans

Hustlers — Rath/Tess fans

In Crowd/Cremegirls — Kyle/Isabel fans

Interns — Liz/Congresswoman Whitaker
fans

Italian Roswell Obsessed (IRO)

Jewish Roswell Addicts (JRA)

Journal Keepers — fans of Liz's journal
entries

Juliets — Lonnie fans

Jumpers — Liz/Rath fans

Killer B's — Maria/Kyle/Alex fans

Knockouts — Michael/Alex fans

Lifesavers — Tess/Maria fans

Lizizards — Liz/Isabel fans

Lolitas — Liz/Sheriff Valenti fans

Lollies — Michael fans

Loners — fans who don't associate with any one group

Loyalists — Liz/Kyle fans

Mark of the Behr (MOB) — Jason Behr/Max fans

Marmalades — Liz/Maria/Max fans

Mental Vibrators — Michael/Tess fans

Mindwarpers — Tess/Isabel fans

Mohawks — Rath fans

New Zealand Embassy

Nickologist Project — the study of Nick Wechsler

Older Roswell Believers (ORB)

Out of Towners — Michael/Max/Isabel fans

Outsider Garden — Max/Isabel fans

Over Thirty and Obsessed (OTO)

Panty Brigade — Max/Kyle fans

Past Indiscretions — Isabel/Nicholas fans

Peanut M&M's — Max/Michael fans

Pepperjackers — Maria/Brody fans

Pixie Chicks — Majandra Delfino fans

Plasmatics — Max/Alex fans

Polar Cliffs — Liz/Isabel/Michael fans

Polarists — Michael/Liz fans

Pole Cats — Liz/Tess/Michael fans

Positive Optimistic Die-Hards (POD)

Rebel Alliance — Max/Tess fans

Rebounders/Lamptrimmers — Tess/Kyle fans

Rebounding Loyalist Catfighters — Liz/Kyle/Tess fans

Riot Grrls — Liz/Maria/Tess fans

Roswell Addicted College Students (RACS)

Roswell Beauty Divas — fans of the fashions

Roswell Bureau of Investigation/Liz Mythologists (RBI)

Scandinavian Embassy

Science Fiction of Episode

Second Generation — Maria/Kyle (romantic relationship) fans

Shades — Nicholas/Miko Hughes fans

Shared Gomez — Liz/Isabel/Max fans

Singapore Roswellian Embassy

Sirens — Sheriff Valenti/Isabel fans

Snake Charmers — Courtney fans

Snap Dragons — Liz/Isabel/Maria fans

Snickers — Max/Michael/Maria fans

Soul Mates — Michael/Rath fans

South African Roswellian Embassy

Spanish Speaking Roswell Lovers

Spurs — Michael/Kyle (romantic relationship) fans

Stargazers — Isabel/Alex fans

Star Sightings — Maria/Isabel/Alex fans

Streetwalkers — Maria/Rath fans

Studs — Michael/Kyle (platonic relationship) fans

Sugar Daddies — Liz/River Dog fans

Teenage Roswellians United Eternally (TRUE)

Teflon Babes — Maria fans

Trespassers — Liz/Eddie fans

Truckstopperz — Zan fans

True Bluers — Liz/Alex fans

Twisted Desire — Maria/Agent
   Pierce/Sheriff Valenti fans

Twisted Destiny — Liz/Tess/Max fans

UK Crew

United French Organization (UFO)

Untuckables — Sheriff Valenti/Amy

DeLuca fans

Valentines — Sheriff Valenti/Kyle fans

Waitresses — Liz/Maria fans

Warped Lizizards — Liz/Isabel/Tess fans

Whirlwind Romantics — Isabel/Jesse
   fans

Wild Ones — Katherine Heigl/Isabel fans

WipeOuts — Liz/Kyle/Maria fans

ROSWELL WEB SITES
So many wonderful sites . . . so little time . . .

Unfortunately in the last short while a lot of *Roswell* sites have closed down. Still, there are a whole range of different *Roswell* fan Web sites on the Internet, so don't despair! Here is a short list of sites that have interesting and inform-ative elements for you to enjoy. An easy way to explore the Internet world of *Roswell* is to click on links that may be provided by some of the pages, so you can experience a whole range of sites dedicated to this fantastic show. The list here is limited to my own personal favorites, and I've tried to be diverse in my choices. Don't be discouraged if the list doesn't provide what you are looking for . . . just take off from one of the site links and enjoy the adventure!

GENERAL ROSWELL SITES
Crashdown
www.crashdown.com

While Crashdown isn't the official Web site, it might as well be. Since it first appeared Crashdown has been one of the most popular *Roswell* Web sites, and rightly so. Full of detailed up-to-date news and information, it also has great episode transcripts and reviews, fantastic photos, and a truly impressive "links" section that details almost every available site out there! And of course, it is linked with "Fan Forum," the popular posting board site where fans get together to discuss the show, and a whole variety of topics. Brendan Fehr, William Sadler, Majandra Delfino (Nephelite), Emilie de Ravin (Diva Duck), and Shiri Appleby have all graced the *Roswell* "Fan Forum" boards. Also on Crashdown, there is a detailed news archive, cast bios and photos, campaign information, polls, and more. It is the place to go if you want to be in the know.

Oz Crash Festival
users.bigpond.net.au/ozcrash/

An Australian based site, Oz Crash Festival is totally unique. First off, click on one of the *Roswell* logos — the Crashdown Café sign perhaps? West Roswell High? Soap Factory? Maybe you prefer to stop by KROZ Radio first. And that's only the beginning. The episode guides not only include sound bytes, but continuity comments, pop culture references, bloopers, alien elements, and production notes. More? How about taking the *Roswell* Virtual Tour and check out the floorplans for the different *Roswell* sets? Looking for more info on the alien elements of the show? Check out the UFO Center for details on alien powers and mythology. Informative and fun, the Oz Crash Festival is definitely worth a visit.

Roswell Mp3's
roswell.na.nu

One of the elements that can make or break a show is the music. If you are looking for all the fabulous tunes that compliment the show, look no further. This is, without a doubt, the best place on the Web to download *Roswell* Mp3's. Not only do you get a mini episode synopsis, but details on the circumstances linked to each song. A truly impressive site that cannot be missed!

Images of Roswell
mmmgraphics.fanforum.com/main.shtml

Not only does this site have a whole array of cast photos, it also provides great wallpaper, screensavers, fan art, icons, themes, avatars, CD and video covers, animations, and a multimedia section. Take your time on this site and enjoy browsing through all of the different images it provides. It's called Images of Roswell for a reason — and is the first place to head to if you're looking for visual stimulation.

Antarians Crashed Into Roswell
www.geocities.com/antarianscrashedintoroswell/home.html
Another fabulous "general" *Roswell* site, Antarians Crashed Into Roswell has sections like the Destiny Book and Liz's Journal. It also has some fun puzzles, good news articles, episode transcripts, and you can download the *Roswell* font.

A Night on the Town
anightonthetown.tripod.com/index4.html
Ever hear of the *Roswell* dance? You'll know what I'm talking about after visiting this site. A Night on the Town is a fun site that has animations, puzzles, and fan art and fiction, and free e-mail accounts.

SITES DEVOTED TO COUPLES

If you have a favorite relationship paring on *Roswell,* or would like to see one that doesn't exist on the show, odds are you can find a "shipper" group on the 'Net that supports your choice. Even if you can't find a Web site, there are some amazing pieces of fan fiction out there to explore! If you're not sure what to look for, the easiest thing to do is to use one of the search engines, and search for UC's (or unconventional couples), and start there! There are so many shippers out there, but again, not enough space. So below are just a few sites that have more than just shipper memberships to give you a taste of what is out there.

Roswell's Definitive Dreamer Dictionary
www.theddd.net
Love Max and Liz? Love Shiri and Jason? The artist index on this site is massive. Slide shows, animations, wallpapers, and more. The best part,

however, is the Max Evans photo alphabet — the definitive dictionary. There is a selection of pictures for each letter from ABSOLUTELY Max to ZZZZ's Max. Even if Max and Liz are not your favorite couple, it's worth checking out some of the art and poetry the dreamers have come up with.

Wicked Game
www.geocities.com/kyletess/

I completely stumbled upon this site, and was glad I did. Aside from the very cool black and white design, this site is completely dedicated to Tess and Kyle. With bios, fan fiction, pictures and stills of the couple, you can also buy Emilie/Tess and Nick/Kyle merchandise! Even if you aren't a fan of the couple, it is worth taking a look at.

Mud Pies
mudster.brinkster.net/home.html

While this site is named with M&M in mind, it offers a range of fan fiction. It's also a very clear and comprehensive site. And it looks cool, too.

Following Your Heart
www.geocities.com/followingyourheart/

With a very funky design, this Max and Liz site stood out. Check out the Crashdown Café for quotes, and the Art Class and English Lit for some cool fan art and fiction.

As for the unconventional couples, here are a few interesting sites to explore:

Girlfriends
www.geocities.com/pezgrrrlz/girlfriends.html

A site dedicated to Max and Maria.

The Panty Brigade
members.aol.com/rinisengir/tpb.html

A gay-related site dedicated to Max and Kyle.

On Fire
www.geocities.com/max_and_tess/on-fire.htm

A site dedicated to Max and Tess.

In Crowd
www.geocities.com/incrowd47/

A site dedicated to Isabel and Kyle.

SITES DEVOTED TO CAST MEMBERS
Jason Behr Unlimited
jasonbehr.fanforum.com/

Filled with up-to-date news, and some great pics, this site is one of the best ones to go to if you're a Jason Behr fan. Check out the TV & Movie section to see pics of Jason through the ages. You can also link directly to the message board and post with other fans.

Shiri Online
www.efanguide.com/~shiri/

Of the Shiri sites out there, I found this one to be the best with a whole variety of elements to choose from. Aside from being extremely informative, this site lets you see Shiri in the Bon Jovi music video "It's My Life," and contains sound bytes of Shiri from *Xena: Warrior Princess*.

Katherine Heigl Online
www.kheigl.com

Katherine's official site offers an extensive biography, current news on Katherine, a wide selection of photographs, and more. Along with an extensive print archive, the site also has film clips of past interviews that are great to watch. It definitely provides you with all you need or want to know about Katherine's life and career.

China Doll: MD
www.chinadollmd.cjb.net/

This Majandra Delfino site may be difficult to read (the print is rather small) but of the sites I saw, it had the most variety. If you're a fan of Majandra's music, you can download MP3's from both the show and her new album. It also provides a fairly extensive photo and news archive.

Brendan Fehr
www.brendan-fehr.com

What makes this site great is the fact that Brendan posts regularly on it, answering questions and sharing opinions, which gives insight into Brendan as an individual. Like the other cast sites, it is always kept up-to-date and has extensive archives with past chat transcripts and interviews. It also has an extensive photo gallery to browse though, so you can find your favorite photos of Brendan.

William Sadler's Wild on the Web
www.williamsadler.com

Even if this site had little information on it, just the opening page showing Bill by the water makes it worthwhile. Aside from providing a fabulous biography on Bill, this site is just a lot of fun. Some highlights include a Bill Board to post on, fan fiction on the sheriff and other roles Bill has played, and a shop to purchase fun Bill items. Right now the Webmasters are working on setting up a section for Bill's tunes. Have I said "Bill" enough yet?

The Nick Wechsler Fan Base
members.aol.com/BigGuyFlash/nickfan.html

With pics, fic, and more, this site is a great tribute to Nick. For all you N.I.C.K. fans out there (Notably Interested in the Character Kyle) who are searching for some general information on Nick, this is a great place to start. Check out the final section for a couple of fun Nick sites as well!

Blood Brother
colinhanks.hk.st/

Even though Colin is no longer on the show, he remains an integral part of the *Roswell* world. There's an amazing amount of video clips to sift through, and some pretty wild fan art. Visiting this site is definitely recommended for any Colin fans out there.

Emilie de Ravin Online
www.efanguide.com/~emilie/

Sure, like Colin, Emilie is no longer a regular on the show, but who could ever forget Tess? This site boasts that it has the largest Emilie gallery on the Web. With lots of information on Emilie's career, video clips, and general news items, this site is a great resource on the Australian actress we've come to know as "the fourth alien."

THE SITES ARE OUT THERE . . .

On my journeys, I stumbled upon a whole array of sites that didn't fit in any particular category, but are definitely worth a visit.

Majandra's Diary
majandra.com/cdc/diary/

Majandra writes her thoughts and views for all the world to see in this site. While she's not always up-to-date with her entries, it's still worth a peek at the previous ones.

The Jason Behr Birthday Project
behritall.tripod.com/default.html

The Jason Behr Birthday Project was created in October 2000 as a way for the fans to thank Jason for his portrayal of Max Evans. Instead of sending presents to Jason on his birthday, his fans raised money for different charities in his name.

The Nick Wechsler Research Institute
www.geocities.com/nickologists/research.html
This site is the home of the "nickologists" who are involved in "the careful and cautious study of the actor known as Nick Wechsler." While the official "Nicktionary" hasn't been posted yet, keep an eye out.

Michael Guerin — Viva la captain hairdo!
www.captainhairdo.iwarp.com
You knew it had to happen — a site dedicated specifically to Michael/Brendan's hair. There's even five theories given behind the mystery of the do. This site is hilarious.

Kyle Valenti Estrogen Brigade
www.fortunecity.com/lavender/hoskins/263/
We just can't get enough of Kyle. Want to relive some of those great lines from season one? There are sound bytes, a quotes section, and a major array of fiction all about Kyle.

Roswell — The Television Show Season One Theories Archive
www.ulink.net/plum/Roswell/
This is a fabulous site that studies the sci-fi theories on the show, based on the "Fan Forum" posting thread 'The Science Fiction of Roswell.' Go to "search the site" to get sci-fi breakdowns of each episode.

Roswell Communicators
roswellcommunicators.tripod.com/
A cute *Roswell* site with lots of links, and the daily weather report from Roswell,

New Mexico. The coolest part of this site is the True Believers archive and links.

Cherry Coke
www.liquid2k.com/cherrycoke/milkyway.htm

Got Milk? These are some fun "creations" of the cast with the famous mustache.

Hollywood On Location
seeing-stars.com/Locations/RoswellPhotos.shtml

This is an interesting site showing the shooting locations in Covina.

Roswell Virtual Season 3
www.geocities.com/roswellvs3/vs3.html

Not happy with season three? Check this site out to read the fan version.

Chapter 5

Leaving Normal....
The Roswell Quiz

So, you're a fan of the show, and you've seen every episode — more than once. Here's a little test to find out just how well you know the world of *Roswell*. There are questions on specific character lines, episodes, and more. Don't get caught in a Tess mindwarp, however — some questions aren't as easy as they look. Grab a note pad and write down your answers — score one point for each correct answer unless otherwise indicated (and an extra point for correct answers to bonus questions) and then turn to page 131 for the results!

THE WORLD ACCORDING TO KYLE

In the middle of season one, Kyle's humorous side came out to delight us all. In season two, he discovered Buddha after Max healed him, and had us rolling around in stitches. Which episodes do the Kyle Buddhist quotes come from?

1. "My strength fails. My vitality exhausted. I cannot find the bull. I only hear the locusts chirping through the night."

2. "Buddha teaches us that some of us are born with stones and some

123

of us are born with jewels, but the most fulfilled of us are those who were born with stones and turn them into jewels."

3. "Actually Buddha himself first coined the phrase 'know when to hold 'em, know when to fold 'em, know when to walk away and know when to run.'"

4. "I'm here to help. My body's merely a vessel."

5. "Buddha, forgive me, but I'm gonna kick your ass!"

6. "His mind and body are in deep conflict. When one's heart and one's mind are not in balance, one's body is the first to fail."

7. "No, no, no, no. I'm here for inner peace, not that science fiction crap."

8. "In order to trim the lamp of wisdom, we must attend to our bodily needs."

9. "Now that my mortal soul has been cleansed, on to more terrestrial concerns. It's been a dry couple of years. Kyle needs a woman. Kyle needs her badly. Kyle needs her tonight."

10. "It's Buddhism. And if you're asking about my spiritual journey, I'm touched."

BONUS QUESTION: What two magazines is "Buddhist for Beginners" sandwiched between under Kyle's bed?

SAY THAT AGAIN?

There are some classic lines from *Roswell.* In the next section, try to identify who said the line, and what episode it was in. Each question is worth two points.

1. "Nothing's ever simple with you people, is it?"

2. "It's like the porno version of *Aladdin.*"

3. "Well, I'd have to be a special kind of stupid not to have figured that out."

4. "You know, I don't think it's the kissing, but the actual volume that's the issue."

5. "Yes. It is a very small thing, and that's why a person who can't even get the cheese right does not deserve to live!"

6. "I mean, think about it. We not only *met* aliens, but they killed us. How many people can say that?"

7. "You could say I was born to fly."

8. "Someday I'll be buzzing and crackling like tinfoil in a microwave and I'd just as soon be with my own kind when it happens."

9. "Oh, so community college wants to know if I'd marry an alien?"

10. "I was at a party! And my only wish was that while I was there, I engaged in some sort of depraved activity, like drinking or sex, but I didn't. I didn't break any laws."

11. "So, what's a chick got to do to get a cake out of a guy like you?"

12. "I'm not avoiding you. We destroyed a race of people. I'm just trying to get past it. Juice?"

13. "I'm very concerned that you're starting to make sense to me."

14. "Oh, please don't let me die like Elvis."

15. "Good looking pile of dust."

16. "Why don't you just tell them about us? I mean, eventually the smell of microwave burritos is going to kill the mood."

17. "Save me. Save me. I'm a human trapped in an alien body."

18. "Okay. But I'm warning you. I'm a man on a mission. Sex or death, so don't get in my way and don't cramp my style."

19. "You mean horrible disgusting creatures from outer space who sneak into your room at night and perform excruciating experiments?"

20. "Well, you're here for a reason, or you rushed right over 'cause you sensed I might be experiencing some actual joy?"

21. "My God, yeah, here it is: she's really a shape-shifting alien also known as Nasedo."

22. "Keep watching. Make sure it doesn't hatch and release an army of enemy aliens."

23. "I'm sorry. When humans need rides, they take Jettas. And when aliens need rides, they take spaceships. Oh! Find one."

EXCUSE ME

It's tough being a teenager, but even worse when you have to cover your tracks all the time. Some call it a simple excuse, others, a downright lie. In this section, try to name the guilty party or the excuse they gave.

1. Who claims to have had a bad relationship with Congresswoman Whitaker's stepson, and what was his major problem?

2. What excuse does Jim give Dan in "To Serve and Protect" when Dan asks about Isabel and Max's visit to the station?

3. What excuse does Air Force use for locking down Roswell after Tess escapes in "Four Aliens and a Baby"?

4. When Max arrives at the hospital after Liz's Grandmother's stroke, what excuse does he give for being there?

5. Who lies to Agent Duff about Laurie Dupree's whereabouts?

6. What excuse does Tess give Max in order to stop him from killing her when she returns to Roswell in season three?

7. Who told Isabel that the facial bruises Max received from Kyle's buddies were actually from falling on the basketball court?

8. When the gang prepared to head for Vegas, what excuse did Max come up with for the school?

9. What excuse did Liz give to Mrs. Evans when Isabel disappeared from her surprise party?

10. When Mr. Evans asked Max about the jeep, what was Max's excuse for getting rid of it?

11. At Congresswoman Whitaker's family home in Copper Summit, what did Isabel say her relationship with Vanessa was like?

12. Where did Liz claim she was the night that she took off to Marathon, Texas, and who figured out the truth first?

13. When Philip Evans asks Jim Valenti about Tess' whereabouts in season 3, where does Jim say she is?
14. What's Liz's excuse for leaving Winnaman Academy?
15. When Nasedo/Hank showed up at the sheriff's office, what was his excuse for the gunshots fired in the trailer?
16. Who lied to Liz in order to get her to meet secretly at Señor Chow's, and how did this person do it?
17. Who said he needed a cheeseburger after a formal dinner in order to pull off a very sweet maneuver, and what did he do?
18. When did Liz plan on using the excuse that a friend in Florida was having a crisis?

I HAVE THE POWER!

As the aliens discover their powers, the humans also unearth their own hidden talents. Not only that, but evil forces are at work. Can you name who is responsible for each act, or what that act was? One point per correct answer.

1. Who heals a broken ankle?
2. Who has Max healed the most number of times?
3. Who were the four people Max failed to heal (not including Clayton Wheeler)?
4. Who apparently didn't sleep for a week after being dreamwalked by Isabel?
5. Which two characters use their intellectual skills to return the human population to Roswell in "Wipe Out"?
6. When Michael tries to blast Courtney, what object does he destroy?
7. What power does Max hold over Kal Langley?
8. What two episodes actually showed Alex's technological skills in action?
9. What power does Max use on Isabel and Michael in the UFO Center that he had never told them about?

10. What two alien powers does Kyle attempt to use?

11. In what episode does Liz first mention getting flashes from kissing Max?

12. What side of Michael does the "Royal Seal" appear on?

13. Who is capable of accessing memories other than Tess?

14. How many times does Larek use Brody's body as a communication device?

15. Who told Liz she had changed "physically" as a consequence of Max's healing, and what is the first change Liz experiences?

16. What does Nasedo teach Michael to do with his powers?

17. What physical symptoms does Michael show when his balance is disrupted?

18. Which alien teen has not healed someone in any way, shape, or form?

19. What episodes involve Maria using the detective skill she learned from her babysitting days?

20. Who are the two unfortunate receivers of Michael's "itchy rash"?

21. What metal did Nasedo reveal the teens would not be able to manipulate?

BONUS QUESTION: What is the ratio of people on earth who have the genetic flaw required for the Gandarium to infect their system?

WHEN WAS THAT?

Match up the event with the episode.

1. When do we hear Maria sing for the first time?

2. In what episode does Mr. Seligman talk about the Big Bang theory?

3. In "Michael, the Guys, and the Great Snapple Caper," what are the two reasons we see for Michael needing a second job to improve his financial situation?

4. Name the episode where Max first admits to remembering Tess.

5. In "Summer of '47," when do Richie and Hal get in trouble for stopping to buy Zagnuts?

6. When is "Kivar" first mentioned?

7. When does Isabel insist she and Jesse have sex on the bathroom floor?

8. What does Maria use for her audition song in Las Vegas, and what key is it in?

9. Who were the four guests scheduled to show up for "The Convention"?

10. When do we meet Zinaplox from the planet Zedagon?

11. What are the names of the four leaders at the summit in "Max in the City"?

12. What episode has Liz asking Max to move in with her?

13. In "Missing," where does Liz first tell Max that her journal might be missing?

Jason Behr and Brendan Fehr crack up on the set of Roswell *(Photo by Dale Josephson)*

14. What distracts Michael and Maria from watching the sheriff's station in "Disturbing Behavior"?

15. Name the two episodes where Max and Liz dance while Maria sings.

THE TRUTH IS OUT THERE

Answer the following questions with "true" or "false" and make sure to correct the false statements!

1. Maria's favorite flavor of ice cream is pistachio.

2. Max is the only one who has not used his alien powers to kill someone.

3. Michael reached out to Max in the pod chamber after they had hatched.

4. The highest grade point average in Tess's school file is 3.4.

5. Grant fights against the Gandarium Queen in order to save Isabel's life.

6. The first time Amy and the sheriff met was when she was arrested at the age of 18.

7. According to Future Max, Liz and Max made love for the first time after the Gomez concert.

8. Zan told Larek not to introduce him to Ava on his behalf.

9. Jesse made his own brown Christmas stocking when he was in grade two.

10. Liz's new powers cause her to melt a payphone receiver, a plate, and to set fire to a book.

BONUS QUESTION: Alex's gravestone reads: "Always Sing Your Song."

Chapter 6

Answers

THE WORLD ACCORDING TO KYLE

1. "Ask Not"
2. "Baby It's You"
3. "Viva Las Vegas"
4. "The End of the World"
5. "Wipe Out"
6. "A Roswell Christmas Carol"
7. "To Serve and Protect"
8. "The End of the World"
9. "A Tale of Two Parties"
10. "Heart of Mine"

BONUS QUESTION: *Hustler* and *Busty Biker Babes*

SAY THAT AGAIN?

1. Kyle in "Interruptus."
2. Maria in "285 South."
3. Lonnie in "Max in the City."
4. Nancy Parker in "Sexual Healing."
5. Maria in "Meet the Dupes."
6. Alex in "How the Other Half Lives."
7. Michael in "Summer of '47."
8. Kyle in "Graduation."
9. Maria in "Significant Others."
10. Alex in "Heatwave."
11. Courtney in "Surprise."
12. Isabel in "Wipe Out."
13. Sheriff Valenti in "A Roswell Christmas Carol."
14. Maria in "Wipe Out."
15. Tess in "The Harvest."
16. Jesse in "Michael, the Guys, and the Great Snapple Caper."
17. Max in "The Convention."
18. Kyle in "A Tale of Two Parties."
19. Isabel in "Monsters."
20. Kyle in "The End of the World."
21. Liz in "Four Square."

22. Max in "Four Aliens and a Baby."

23. Maria in "Summer of '47."

EXCUSE ME

1. Courtney. His problem involved drugs.

2. They were there to report a stolen bike.

3. Someone stole an Air Force truck with three tons of explosives inside.

4. He says his cousin was in a car accident.

5. The sheriff.

6. She claims she is linked to the baby; if she dies the baby dies.

7. Michael.

8. He put them on the list for the debate team's two-day meet in Santa Fe.

9. Isabel spilled something on her dress and had to change.

10. Max claims he got sick of the plastic doors, and the time it took to take the roof off and on.

11. "She was like a mother to me."

12. She said she was at Maria's, but Kyle figured it out.

13. He tells Philip that Tess was with her uncle and aunt back east.

14. Her drug-addicted roommate wanted Liz to have a three-way with her teacher.

15. Hank was drunk while cleaning his gun.

16. Topolsky did it. She sent Liz flowers from "Max" telling her to meet him there.

17. Michael. He had arranged for Maria to sing in a Las Vegas supper club.

18. She planned to tell her parents that before taking off to Sweden.

I HAVE THE POWER!

1. Michael ("Into the Woods").

2. Michael: with the gang's help in "The Balance," and alone in "Independence Day" and in "Who Died and Made You King"?

3. Alex in "Cry Your Name," Nasedo (with the gang) in "Ask Not," Samuel in "Samuel Rising," and Liz in "Ch-Ch-Changes."

4. Mrs. Evans.

5. Kyle and Maria.

6. A perfectly good television set.

7. Kal must follow any direct order Max gives him.

8. In "Blood Brothers." Alex broke into Topolsky's laptop and in "Tess, Lies, & Videotape" he set up complicated surveillance equipment.

9. His force field.

10. He tries to use the power to change television channels (including unscrambled porn) in "To Serve and Protect," and to heal Isabel in "Chant Down Babylon."

11. "Independence Day" (she had the flash in "Blind Date")

12. The upper left side of his chest.

13. Nicholas.

14. Three. In "Max in the City," "Disturbing Behavior," and "How The Other Half Lives."

15. Ava. Liz melts a plate.

16. Alter his fingerprint.

17. Fever, delirium that includes chanting, convulsions, his eyes turn white, and cocoon-like webbing forms around him.

18. Isabel (Tess healed a bruise on Max, Michael healed River Dog).

19. "Blood Brothers" and "Heart of Mine."

20. One of the jocks in "Leaving Normal," and Larry in "The Convention."

21. Depleted uranium.

BONUS QUESTION: One in 50 million people.

WHEN WAS THAT?

1. "Monsters," singing "Genie in a Bottle" by Christina Aguilera.

2. "Sexual Healing."

3. His power has been cut off, and Maria refuses to pay the restaurant check anymore.

4. "Off the Menu."

5. When they arrive at the crash site.

6. Kivar's name is first used in "The Harvest" by Nicholas.

7. "Behind the Music."

8. "I've Got The World on a String" in the key of E.

9. William Shatner, Leonard Nimoy, Jonathan Frakes, and Patrick Stewart.

10. "The Convention"

11. Larek, Kathana, Sero, and Hanar

12. "Significant Others"

13. A storage room in the UFO Center.

14. A couple having sex in Garrison's Hardware store.

15. "Viva Las Vegas" and "Ch-Ch-Changes"

THE TRUTH IS OUT THERE

1. False. It's Michael's favorite.

2. True. He strangled Meris Wheeler with his bare hands.

3. False. Isabel did.

4. True.

5. True. It's an internal struggle, mind you!

6. False. The first time they actually met, Jim almost ran over Amy and Curt Pressman with his dirt bike.

7. False. They never made it to the Gomez concert.

8. True.

9. False. He made it in kindergarten.

10. True.

BONUS QUESTION: False. It reads "May Your Song Always Be Sung."

TOTAL POINTS: 120

Chapter 7

Off the Menu.... The Roswell Chicken Jokes

The chicken jokes began on a *Roswell* "Fan Forum" thread, and spread from there. The original jokes written by the fans were compiled and presented in the "Crashdown Yearbook" after season one. I've updated the jokes to fit season two and three, and am very grateful and proud to showcase a few of the season one jokes, too. The hardcore *Roswell* fans will recognize what season each element is from.

Why did the chicken cross the road?

(in alphabetical order)

AGENT DUFF: I don't know, but I appreciate honesty so I'm gonna be straight with you. I like to catch chickens and if that means busting my butt and asking for help, I'll do it.

AGENT PIERCE: Just tell me which way the chicken went and no one will get hurt. And when I find it, I will take that chicken apart piece by piece, and make sure it stays conscious enough to feel every second of it.

AGENT TOPOLSKY: Because it learned things and saw things that no one would believe, and now its life is in danger! But if I bring the chicken the other communicator orb, if I risk my life for the chicken . . . maybe it will take me with it when its people come to get it.

ALEX WHITMAN: It's already gone. But I think we both know that I loved it, too.

AMY DELUCA: Well, on this glorious, rebellious road trip this chicken is on, it better not get tattoos, or pierce any part of its body that cannot be shown in polite company, and if it has sex of any kind I will hunt it down and kill it. Oh, and it should call if it needs bail money.

AVA: The chicken is out there in the street! It's all my fault! I should have stopped it! I'm not sure it ever loved me back, though. That chicken was always waitin' for someone else to walk into its life.

BILLY: It crossed because it was following its dream. If I hadn't met that chicken, I'd still be playing "Stairway to Heaven" in my mom's garage.

BRODY: It was probably abducted.

CONGRESSWOMAN WHITAKER: What? The chicken dumped me? On voice-mail? Don't let any chicken pull that crap on you.

DEPUTY HANSON: Uh . . . Sheriff? Chicken's crossed the road. We have kind of a situation brewin' here. I was thinking this might be what you call a P-O-U-L-T-R-Y situation.

DOUG SHELLOW: Because it was tired of being chased by a radio station DJ all night long. All it wanted was a "normal" date.

EDDIE: Because you broke the chicken's trust and now it's really pissed!

HUBBLE: I haven't had a good time since it crossed. Not that night. Not any night since. I know who it really is, what it is capable of, and I won't let it kill again.

ISABEL EVANS: It *crossed*. Without discussing it with me. Fine, I'll follow the chicken. The chicken may be my home, but there's no way I'm bowing down to it.

JENNIFER: The chicken is chasing UFOs. In the beginning I was kind of into it, but now I'm tired of adventure. It consumes every waking moment of its day!

JESSE: I used to think I knew the chicken, but it's not the chicken I married.

KAL LANGLEY: That chicken has always been selfish and ungrateful. I might have genetic encoding that makes me protect it, but I'll never stop hating it.

KIVAR: It doesn't matter. It will stop itself. It will always be mine.

KYLE VALENTI: Buddha tells us that . . . wait, does he have a quote about chickens? Look, so long as it doesn't use any creepy powers on me, it can do whatever the hell it wants.

LARRY: Look, I don't want to become a major chicken hunter. I'm a gatherer . . . of . . . information! And I gotta say that Mr. Jonathan Frakes is a god. I get goose bumps!

LAURIE DUPREE: What??? It's dead! It's dead! Don't let it touch me!

LIZ PARKER: Because it didn't want to think that Alex was killed by a chicken because that would mean IT was responsible.

LONNIE: So . . . the chicken's off to make the beast with two backs. It is in for a treat.

MARIA DELUCA: One thing's for sure — by crossing the road it's just taken a huge step in chicken/human relations.

MAX EVANS: Because it has to save its son.

MICHAEL GUERIN: Because for years it has been on a quest to figure out where it belongs and it finally found home.

MILTON ROSS: The chicken crossed! There's been a sighting! I have unmitigated proof that chickens walked this earth. I was that boy next to the chicken shadow! And I swear on my mother's grave that one day I will stand face-to-face with that chicken and say "I told you so!"

MR. EVANS: My biggest concern is that the chicken has terrible secrets, and is in trouble . . . and that I can't help it out.

MR. PARKER: All I can say is that chicken is a bad influence and it better stay away from my daughter or she's off to boarding school!

MRS. EVANS: It's crossing too young. If it rushes into this then one day it's going to wake up bitter, living at home, and alone. What's happened to our family?

Majandra and Nick share a laugh at the UPN All-Star summer party
(Photo by Christina Radish)

MRS. PARKER: It crossed the road? [sigh] Why did it have to stop being my baby?

NASEDO: All I have to say is, if I have to kill the chicken in order to protect the Royal Four, I will.

NICHOLAS: If only people could see the chicken now. Clueless, groping for its own identity. It's lost that legendary aura.

RATH: The chicken and me, we were closer than brothers, man. I mean, all my life I looked up to him and then just one day . . . bam! He crossed!

RIVER DOG: Beware the chicken. It can pull you in if you are not careful.

SEAN: Hey, I'm on parole, I'm not saying anything. Unless the chicken's cute, and then I'll consider breaking the law for it.

SHERIFF VALENTI: I don't care where it's from or what it is, that chicken saved my son, and I'll be there for it.

TESS HARDING: Because it was the chicken's *destiny*. And, well . . . because 40 years ago a deal was made with the chicken's former enemies to return home carrying the child of a king. But you could never understand, could you?!

ZAN: That chicken may cross the road, but it ain't goin' nowhere. *I'm* the man.

Chapter 8

Roswell Episode Guide

Warning . . . the following guide contains some spoilers for each of the episodes (namely, plot details are discussed). If you are someone who likes to be surprised, I would skip any episodes that you have not yet seen. The guide offers some explanations of references used in the show. The opinions expressed in these entries are mine and are completely debatable. The guide is written in a review format, not as a plot summary, and you will see that a lot of details have been left out. So if I haven't mentioned your favorite moment, it's not because I didn't find it important; I had to leave it out because of limited space.

There are some other terms to explain. In reference to Liz's famous "flashes," the **FLASH** section points out a small but very cool moment that stood out in each episode. **IRKS** are elements of the show that I got annoyed with, and in many cases include continuity errors. **DOUBLE TAKE** looks at bloopers from each episode (I'm sure I missed a few, but I did look). **ALIENISMS** catalog the alien powers used on the show, as well as other alien references such as The Gandarium. **SODA MOMENT** explains a pop culture reference used by one of the characters. Sometimes I've added one or two **COOL FACTS** that relates either to something said on the show or something that happened in production. Finally, I've listed the **MUSIC** from each episode. For this segment, I have to give a tremendous thank-you to Fionna for her work on the Crashdown Yearbook, Wisters26 for the list, and the Roswell MP3 General

Discussion Board for the information regarding season three. I could not have done this without their outstanding effort. (Notice how the titles of the songs used each episode actually fit the theme of the show.)

SEASON ONE (OCTOBER 1999 — MAY 2000)

STARRING: Jason Behr as Max Evans
Shiri Appleby as Liz Parker
Brendan Fehr as Michael Guerin
Katherine Heigl as Isabel Evans
Majandra Delfino as Maria DeLuca
William Sadler as Sheriff Jim Valenti
Nick Wechsler as Kyle Valenti
Colin Hanks as Alex Whitman
Emilie de Ravin as Tess Harding (season two)
Adam Rodriguez as Jesse Ramirez (season three)

1.1 Pilot

ORIGINAL AIR DATE: October 6, 1999
WRITTEN BY: Jason Katims
DIRECTED BY: David Nutter

GUEST CAST: John Doe (Geoff Parker), Michael Horse (Deputy Blackwood), Wendle Josepher (Jennifer), Kevin Weisman (Larry), Richard Schiff (Agent Stevens), Volanda Lloyd Delgado (Ms. Hardy), Vance Valencia (Mayor Sandler), Joe Camareno (Paramedic), Daniel Hansen (young Max), Channing Carson (young Liz), Zoë Nutter (young Isabel), Jonathan Frakes (uncredited — Master of Ceremonies)

When Liz Parker is shot at her father's diner, Max Evans miraculously heals her, prompting him to reveal a surprising secret to her.

Not only do we gain a fabulous sense of the characters while incorporating the major theme of teen alienation, but a sense of the world of *Roswell*, a brief history of the 1947 incident, and a strong conflict that continues throughout the season. This episode is truly outstanding.

Based on the *Roswell High* book series by Melinda Metz, the show's concept tends to veer away from the original series. The pilot episode takes certain plot elements from the first book, however, including the opening scene. With *Romeo and Juliet* references, both stories explore the idea of romance blooming from a tense, life-threatening situation. Max risks exposure in order to save the woman he loves. Liz, in turn, risks her life to protect him, and so it goes. While the book series is suspenseful, it is obviously written for young teens, and does tend to dwell on the more romantic elements. Some of the characters are more two-dimensional as well, with Sheriff Valenti as the unsympathetic villain and Kyle Valenti as a meathead jock.

Jason Katims's pilot may touch on the world of *Dawson's Creek*, where emotional dramas take precedence, but on *Roswell* we are constantly reminded that there is a larger pressure out there to deal with: namely, the enemies out to capture the alien teens. Lives are on the line, not just relationships. Like on *Buffy the Vampire Slayer*, the *Roswell* teens are special, and while they crave normalcy, they will never truly capture that normal life. That is what makes them compelling.

"I'm Liz Parker and five days ago I died." The pilot episode opens with Liz writing in her diary, flashing back to the life-changing events from less than a week before. While the reflective flashback framework is too often used and abandoned (remember Felicity and her tapes to Sally?), in the case of the pilot episode, it works. Then, BOOM, we're at the kitschy UFO-themed Crashdown Café, where Liz and her best friend are serving up lunch to a packed restaurant filled with high school students, alien chasers, and burly men who are better suited to a roadside bar. We have a brief moment with Liz's wacky friend Maria, catch a soulful glance from Max, and then a fight breaks out between our burly friends. We hear a shot, and Liz is on the floor, bleeding. Max rushes to her aid even though his moody friend Michael tries to stop him. Placing his left hand on her chest, Max gets to work. He has only moments before the ambulance arrives. A grimace, a long moment filled with flashes of Liz's childhood . . . and he's done. Suddenly, he breaks a ketchup bottle and pours it on her. Max quickly instructs a dazed Liz to tell them she was never shot, then just as quickly Max rushes out. The audience is left in as much of a stupor as Liz. *What just happened?*

While the audience may not know the details, one thing is for certain: Shiri Appleby and Jason Behr have *amazing* chemistry. Shiri does a wonderful job as Liz, portraying a strong and scientifically minded young woman who has opened her eyes for the first time. She is continually struggling with growing up and the confusion that comes with discovering new things about herself. Behr has easily moved away from his rebel roles for The WB, and is completely convincing as a shy, cautious young man who longs to stop hiding. Jason's intense looks and tortured soul routine make Max vulnerable and instantly appealing to a female audience.

Brendan Fehr may closely resemble David Duchovny, but what makes him stand out as

Michael Guerin is his strong rage and James Dean rebelliousness. It's a perfect contrast to Max's quiet nature. A defensive teenager whose skin is thick from years of neglect, Brendan does a great job of slowly opening up as the season progresses. Right from the beginning, Brendan starts to show the cracks in Michael's stone wall, exposing a hurt boy desperate for a father figure and longing to belong. And then there's Majandra Delfino. As Maria, she describes herself as the "wacky best friend" to Liz's straight character. An incense-sniffing, slightly neurotic yet fiercely loyal girl, she is a nice parallel to Michael's intensity as the season progresses. Nick Wechsler is introduced as Kyle, the sheriff's son, and Liz's sort-of boyfriend. Nick really starts to shine later in the season when his humor is utilized. Katherine Heigl is very well cast for the role of Isabel Evans, the glamorous, aloof teenager who uses her powers for recreational purposes, and on some level, to spite her younger brother Max. Like Michael, she slowly chips away at her aloof exterior through the season. Like many teenage beauty queens, Isabel really just wants to belong. When Isabel is the one to reach out to Liz's plan, it is done with a balance of arrogance and humility. William Sadler joins the cast as the token veteran actor. William plays Sheriff Valenti as a force to be reckoned with. A single father dealing with his own father issues, in many ways Jim Valenti undergoes the greatest journey of all the cast members. William Sadler's range is as admirable as his resumé.

Yes, the theme of "teen alienation" becomes a bit of a tag-line for the show, but it is certainly a serious topic in the pilot episode. No one wants to be seen as "different," especially when it escalates to the level of "freak." Max, Michael, and Isabel are seen as a threat, when in reality they are just teens. It appears their fears are justified when we see the Crash celebration. A group of eager partygoers count down as a replica of a flying saucer slowly slides towards the dirt. The crowd cheers as the saucer crashes and the four alien bodies burn on the ground. Isabel, Max, and Michael are afraid for their *lives*, not their social status. Like the human teens of Roswell, all they want is to be normal, and to belong. The alien teens also want to know about their "home." Figuratively speaking, home is longing to belong in your own skin. That's something every teenager — and human being — searches for.

With strong dramatic undertones, an excellent cast, and a compelling storyline, the pilot is a strong start to a fabulous series.

FLASH: Max, Isabel, and Michael's intense, reflective expressions as they watch the four small alien bodies burn on the sand. Suddenly, the cheerful mood seems hideously morbid.

IRKS: In the first episode, we don't really get a clear picture of Kyle's relationship with Liz. At the beginning, in the band room, they act as though they've only just started dating (and yet they apparently have been seeing each other over the summer), and then before the Crash

Festival, Liz is kissing him rather intimately in the hopes of coaxing him into joining her. If there is one major flaw in the pilot, it is that Liz and Kyle's relationship is never really defined, and feels rather vague and unbelievable. While that could sum up most high school relationships, in this case, it's hard to suspend the belief that Liz and Kyle ever had a mutual attraction. It doesn't help that Shiri's on-screen chemistry with Jason makes Liz's scenes with Kyle seem as passionate as a warm glass of milk. It is also a bit difficult to believe that there would be no questions about two naked six-year-olds (Max and Isabel) holding hands while walking along a desert road. The Evanses found them, but they asked no questions? Wouldn't they have taken the children in for check-ups with a doctor? And wouldn't the doctor have taken blood tests? There are many consistency problems with the "discovery" of Isabel and Max throughout the season, including the location. A general nitpick for all three seasons: if you watch, the sets are constantly changing.

DOUBLE TAKE: Max heals Liz with his left hand. The first time she notices the silver hand-print, it is the left hand. When she shows it to Max, and when Kyle notices it, it appears as though made by the right hand.

ALIENISMS: Aside from the burning alien reference at the Crash Festival (based on myths surrounding aliens of the Roswell Incident), we discover that the teens had hatched from incubation pods that had been hidden by the aliens of the 1947 crash. A body was found in 1959 with a silver handprint on its chest. Max heals Liz, and in the process, has visions about her childhood memories. He later helps her to see visions of his past, and manipulates the molecular structure on a clay statue. Isabel heats her food with her hand and can play a CD by holding it up to her ear. And they all put copious amounts of Tabasco sauce on their food.

SODA MOMENT: Liz's opening line in the book (in reference to the burgers she is about to serve) is exactly the same as her opening line in the diner: "One Sigourney Weaver and one Will Smith." This particular line has a nice irony for later on in the pilot, when Max and Liz attend the annual Crash Festival. Liz arrives dressed in Sigourney Weaver's *Alien Resurrection* costume, while Max comes as one of the *Men in Black* (co-starring Will Smith). It's a nice little twist that Max has costumed himself as one of the men *"protecting the earth from the scum of the universe."* The aliens in Barry Sonnenfeld's film tend to disguise themselves as humans, hiding from the top-secret agents (*Men in Black*) who police alien activity on earth. In *Roswell*, Max works to keep his alien identity a secret from the law. So, who better to dress as than an ally to the government! Then, there's Liz dressed as the character Ripley in *Alien Resurrection* (appropriately, a FOX picture). In the fourth film of the *Alien* series, Ripley has been resurrected by cross-breeding her DNA with that of an alien. A hybrid — just like Max. Throughout the film, Ripley struggles to determine which part of her is more prominent: the alien or the human. Since Liz has just been healed by an alien, and later undergoes changes on a physical level, her costume is very appropriate. The two costumes not only help define the characters of Max and Liz, but parallel their journeys as well. And of course, while not "pop" culture per se, we do have the many *Romeo and Juliet* allusions: Max calling up to Liz as she lounges on her balcony, for example.

COOL FACTS: Festivals resembling the Crash Festival actually do exist. In fact, it's a tradition in Roswell, New Mexico. For the 2000 New Year's party, a high-power laser carried over 10,000 electronic messages into space in the hopes that there would be a response from beyond. An interesting casting note involves John Doe, playing Liz's father Geoffrey Parker. John Doe headed up the influential 1970s/'80s punk band "X."

MUSIC: In the pilot, we hear "Save Tonight" by Eagle Eye Cherry in the Crashdown just before Liz is shot. Sarah McLachlan's "Fear" is played when Max is healing Liz, and when Liz is witnessing Max's memories. "I Think I'm Paranoid" by Garbage comes on during the scene in the girls' washroom where Maria challenges Liz about the Crashdown shooting. Hole's "Boys on the Radio" is what Isabel is listening to while using her powers in the jeep. When Liz leaves Kyle's place on her way to the Crash Festival, Filter's "Hey Man, Nice Shot" is in the background. Finally, at the festival when Max and Liz discuss their future, "Crash Into Me" by The Dave Matthews Band rings through the air . . . a most fitting musical ending. Julius Robinson is responsible for determining the songs used on *Roswell*, while the original music is composed by W.G. Snuffy Walden and Joseph Stanley Williams.

1.2 The Morning After

ORIGINAL AIR DATE: October 13, 1999
WRITTEN BY: Jason Katims
DIRECTED BY: David Nutter

GUEST CAST: Julie Benz (Kathleen Topolsky), Mary Ellen Trainor (Diane Evans), Michael O'Neill (Philip Evans), Richard Schiff (Agent Stevens), Robert F. Lyons (Hank Whitmore), Jason Peck (Deputy Hanson), Michael Horse (Deputy Blackwood), Reggie Hayes (Agent Hart), Christopher Holloway (Paul Aronson), Ebonie Smith (Genevieve), Marc Brandon

Daniel (Boy in Class)

Just when it seems as though things have settled down, a new threat comes to town — Kathleen Topolsky, a substitute teacher who is asking a lot of questions about Michael. Meanwhile, Michael is determined to find out what the sheriff knows about the mysterious corpse from 1959.

While the first episode focuses on Max and Liz, this episode showcases Michael. Opening with the diary-entry framework, this one takes a more humorous approach. Liz moons over Max, unable to sleep, and wonders if he is as emotionally tortured as she is . . . and then we cut to Max snoring. The humor is shut off just as quickly, however, when Max prepares to strike someone breaking into his room. When Michael identifies himself, Max immediately rolls out a sleeping bag by his bed. It's a subtle yet defining moment, showing us the sort of relationship the two men have. It is obvious that both Isabel and Max take responsibility for Michael, as though watching out for a rebellious younger brother. Isabel's comment — "Michael's AWOL" — reinforces the idea that he can't be left alone without supervision.

"The Morning After" gives us some subtle Michael moments, allowing him to break away from his "alone against the world" routine. When Liz shows up at the shabby trailer Michael shares with his foster father, Hank, Michael apologizes for Hank's behavior. While it's hinted at (and later shown) that Hank is an abusive jerk, here he comes across as more of a pathetic wimp. Later, Michael simply states to Liz, "It's where I live. Thanks." The tone isn't a self-pitying or angry one . . . it's just his reality. The episode really shows Michael's alienation from Max and Isabel. He is the only one who receives psychic flashes from the key. He is the only one of the three who has no control over his powers. He has nothing to lose by leaving town, while Max and Isabel have attachments. It's heartbreaking at the end when he silently watches the Evans family from a distance as they play basketball together. It's no wonder that he doesn't mind risking everything to find out about their past — Michael wants to belong.

The FBI enter into this episode, adding a new dynamic to the scene. Now the sheriff isn't the bigwig anymore, and is being investigated as much as the teenagers are. This is the first instance of Valenti breaking the law by hiding something from the FBI. The enemy has enemies, which is a nice twist. We are also introduced to the somewhat clueless Deputy Hanson. He's a replica of the endearing yet dopey Deputy Andy Brennan from David Lynch's show *Twin Peaks* (Jason Katims is a fan of the show).

Julie Benz is a good choice as the teacher-who-obviously-isn't-a-teacher (a triangle is 180 degrees, not 360. . . we all know that!). She comes across as kind and dedicated, yet there's something a little suspicious about her eager behavior. We're also introduced to Max and Isabel's parents. The Evanses are the caring suburban family who act like they are straight out of *7th Heaven*. While they are only briefly introduced in this episode, Mrs. Evans has a larger role later on in the season.

Jason Katims adds some humorous elements to this episode that don't get explored in the pilot. Having Maria and Liz use the word "Czechoslovakians" to replace the word "aliens" is very funny, especially since Maria gives it different intonations every time she uses it. "The Morning After" also starts to touch on Nick Wechsler's humorous side. Kyle approaches Liz in the hallway, mentioning how he's had a heart-to-heart with his fellow jocks on the importance of promptness in a relationship. Michael gets the opportunity to lighten his mood as he cheerfully attempts to sell chocolates for the Westlake orphanage in the sheriff's office. Even the sheriff has his moment as he goads Agent Stevens — "Agent Stevens. You don't write, you don't call . . ."

Liz's reflective voice-over on the nature of secrets sums up the episode quite well. After all, this is a show about hiding and uncovering secrets . . . and there are many more to come.

FLASH: Alex trying to impress a group of girls by twisting his double-jointed arms together, then looping them over his head.

IRKS: It's rather convenient that the eraser room, best known as make-out central, has a vent that looks straight into Kathleen Topolsky's makeshift office. Secondly, there is no way that the sound of pulling up blinds matches the sound of two teenage boys landing in a dumpster. And the whole Kyle/Liz relationship thing is way out of whack here. Liz claims they just had a summer fling, then Kyle calls her his "girl." While it's obvious that we have some miscommunication happening here, if Kyle really believes Liz is his girl, why doesn't he react with more anger when he confronts Max and Liz in the jeep — even if Liz isn't doing what he suspects she is. Liz's feelings for Kyle don't seem to really exist, which makes it difficult for Kyle to react to her. Maybe she just likes his snazzy red Mustang convertible.

DOUBLE TAKE: Somehow Kathleen Topolsky knows Liz's full name even though she never gets past Michael Guerin's name during roll-call. Max's jeep has a mind of its own — first it has a windshield (at trailer park), then it doesn't (outside Crashdown), then it does (driving with Isabel to find Michael), then it doesn't (inspecting the key).

ALIENISMS: Michael may be unable to control his powers, but he does manage to blow out the police station's security system and break open the protective metal bars. The photo from 1959 is of a corpse with a silver handprint — the same mark Max left on Liz — which means there may be another like them out there. Max can fuse metal together. When holding the key, Michael has psychedelic flashes of a geodesic dome.

SODA MOMENT: Maria makes a comment about the aliens being able to "wiggle their noses and poof [them] to oblivion." This is a reference to the television series *Bewitched* (1964–1972). (In the third season, *Roswell* does a spoof of the show in the episode "I Married an Alien.") Elizabeth Montgomery plays Samantha, a witch who falls in love and married a mortal. She vows to her husband that she will give up witchcraft and take on the role of suburban housewife. However, that is not always an option, and the antics ensue as her powers and troublesome family members bring about entertaining conflicts in the Stephens household.

COOL FACTS: Julie Benz is known for playing Darla on *Buffy the Vampire Slayer*. Darla is the vampire who turns Angel over to the dark side centuries earlier. She comes to Sunnydale to try and bring him to the dark side once more, but he slays her. Then, she is resurrected, brought into human form, but is dying. She redeems herself in Angel's eyes, regretting her past. Interesting that Kathleen Topolsky will eventually do the same thing — hunt the teens, work to bring them down, and then later regret her actions and try to do right by them.

MUSIC: This is actually the first time we hear the theme song to *Roswell*: "Here With Me" performed by British singer Dido. "My Favorite Game" by the Cardigans plays at the Crashdown when Liz and Maria brush off Alex's question about the Czechoslovakians. The Smashing Pumpkins's song "Blank Page" comes on while Max and Liz are in the eraser room. "Ladyshave" by Gus Gus is the background music when Liz and Maria explain their strange behavior to Alex. When Max and Liz discuss having lunch outside the Crashdown, "I Never Thought That You Would Come" by Loni Rose is playing. Finally, Dido's "Honestly OK" comes on as Liz ends the episode with her journal entry.

1.3 Monsters

ORIGINAL AIR DATE: October 20, 1999
WRITTEN BY: Jason Katims
DIRECTED BY: David Nutter; David Semel

GUEST CAST: Julie Benz (Kathleen Topolsky), Steve Hytner (Milton Ross, UFO Center curator), Amy Lyndon (Mother at Crashdown), Daryl Sabara (Corey), Zack Aaron (Heavy Metal Student), Maria Bembenek (Crashdown waitress), Donna May (UFO Museum tourist), Adam Weisman (UFO Center), Christos (Mechanic)

Maria struggles not to be intimidated by Isabel and expose the alien secret to Sheriff Valenti, while Future Week progresses at West Roswell High and the students contemplate possible careers.

The diary opening has been abandoned for this episode. Instead, the episode starts on a desert highway with Maria. Actually, it is the first official episode incorporating Majandra Delfino's vocal talents. (Mind you, she's singing along with Christina Aguilera, but still!) Maria notices Isabel at the side of the road, the jeep hooked to a tow truck. This becomes the framework for this episode as we also end with Maria picking up Isabel by the side of the road.

"Monsters" gives us more insight into the characters of Maria and Isabel. We begin by seeing Isabel's constitution of steel and how fear turns Maria into Jell-O. Yet, by the end, Isabel's vulnerabilities have been exposed and Maria proves to be stronger than anyone thought. As the only two blond leads on the show, it isn't only their personalities that contradict each other. Isabel is sophisticated, with long hair and a classy wardrobe. Maria's short *Star Trek* haircut and casual, hippy clothing is in total contrast. Yet, as both women will discover, people aren't always what they seem.

It is completely understandable that Maria would look at Isabel, Max, and Michael as monsters. They're *very* different, after all, and as history dictates it is common to fear what we don't understand. Before the films *Close Encounters of the Third Kind* and *E.T.*, aliens were depicted as monsters out to take over the planet. Look at *Invasion of the Body Snatchers* (1956) or *Day of the Triffids* (1962) to name just a couple. Even on a more recent note, the *Alien* series (starting in 1982) and the recent *Independence Day* (1996) portrayed aliens as evil creatures. Either that, or they were goofy, similar to the vein of the 1965 television show *My Favorite Martian*.

If Maria didn't know Isabel is an alien, she would probably still find her threatening. After all, Isabel comes off as aloof and glamorous: the antithesis of Maria. Maria is clutzy (tripping outside at lunch and trying to cover her embarrassment) and insecure. She isn't attached to any of the aliens like Liz is, and wants very much to feel safe again. What is interesting, however, is her dream in the Crashdown that Isabel invades. While she sees Isabel and Max as rather comical yet creepy green aliens, she puts Michael at a separate table, dressed in a tux. When Isabel questions her choice, Michael turns into an even creepier, fly-like creature that starts to strangle her. Perhaps this is foreshadowing, considering later on, in the third season, Maria feels her relationship with Michael is suffocating. Maria's not wearing blinders, however. She does see the human element in Isabel when Isabel hugs Mrs. Evans good-bye. It is at that point when she realizes Isabel is not a threat. The sheriff reaches out to Maria, sharing the fact that they both are from broken homes, and showing why Maria, like Michael, might envy Isabel. In fact, the sheriff's words later work against him.

Shiri and Majandra at the UPN summer press tour in 2001
(Photo by Christina Radish)

Isabel comes off as cold, snobbish, and almost arrogant at the start of the episode. And yet, in "Monsters," we not only witness her fear of Valenti and all he represents, but we see her longing for the love Max has, and how her fear of exposure won't allow her to let down her guard. With Max, she discusses their real parents and their adoptive family. The issue of finding their "real" parents is one most adopted children face. Max and Isabel *have* parents who love them, and yet they are curious about their heritage. In many ways, teenagers look to their parents as they start to define their own personalities. Isabel tells Topolsky she wants to be a supermodel, but her test comes back saying she is a caregiver, showing that Isabel works hard to guard herself *because* she is sensitive and vulnerable. While we see less of a transition in Isabel than we do in Maria, we still have the opportunity to get under a few layers.

While "Monsters" isn't as suspenseful as the first two episodes, it's a nice introductory episode for Maria and Isabel.

FLASH: Kyle Valenti's expression when he discovers he's best suited for law enforcement — "This is a joke, right?"

IRKS: Twice in this episode Isabel finds herself at the mercy of her vehicle's shortcomings, and yet she is able to fix Maria's car's air conditioning and improve the sound system. That being the case, why is she unable to fix her own car?

DOUBLE TAKE: Maria goes to see Sheriff Valenti wearing a gray school-girlish type outfit (which really doesn't seem to fit her character at all). She then picks up Isabel by the side of the road. When they return to West Roswell High, Maria is wearing an entirely different outfit — a dark sport jacket over a white blouse, and dark pants. When did she change?

ALIENISMS: Isabel can manipulate both air conditioning and stereo systems (how she does it is still uncertain). She can also invade other people's dreams by touching their photographs.

SODA MOMENT: Maria makes a comment that Isabel is "Queen Amidala." She is referring to the character from *Star Wars: Episode One: The Phantom Menace*, who seems emotionless and cold at the start, but eventually the audience learns that it is only a "mask" kept up for safety reasons. Maria's comparison is very accurate.

COOL FACTS: While Max is in the UFO Center, he scans over photographs of both Glenn Dennis (mortician in Roswell in 1947) and Walter G. Haut (the lieutenant ordered to write a press release in 1947 stating the debris was from an alien saucer). Walter Haut and Glenn

Dennis are co-founders of the present-day UFO Museum and Research Center in Roswell, New Mexico, which was incorporated on September 27, 1991, and was soon recognized as a non-profit organization.

MUSIC: The episode begins with Maria singing along with Christina Aguilera's hit "Genie in a Bottle." When Isabel manipulates the Jetta's sound system, the song playing is "Head" by Tin Star. After Max's interview with Topolsky, "The Background" by Third Eye Blind is playing. "Drip" by Other Star People is on when Isabel orders fries from Maria at the Crashdown Café. When Sheriff Valenti orders the Heavenly Hash special from Maria, "My Ritual" by Folk Implosion is in the background. Finally, Semisonic's "Made to Last" comes on at the end of the episode when Maria and Isabel return to West Roswell High.

1.4 Leaving Normal

ORIGINAL AIR DATE: October 27, 1999
WRITTEN BY: Jason Katims
DIRECTED BY: Chris Long

GUEST CAST: Jo Anderson (Nancy Parker), John Doe (Geoff Parker), Carroll Baker (Grandma Claudia), David Smigelski (Tommy), Troy Robinson (Paulie), Marisa Ramirez (Isabel's friend #1), Sarah Laine (Isabel's friend #2), Eve Sigall (Agnes), Paul Hayes (Orthodontist #1), Kent Kasper (Orthodontist #2), Floyd Vanbuskirk (Angry Customer), Michael Hernandes (José), Octavia L. Spenser (Nurse), Harry Johnson (Doctor), Charles Martinez (Janitor)

Liz's beloved grandmother is rushed to the hospital after having suffered a stroke, while Max is beaten up by Kyle's friends and told to stay away from Liz.

"Leaving Normal" deals with a universal issue: losing a loved one. Liz's Grandma Claudia, a trendy, vibrant woman who is full of life, suddenly has a stroke. When she appears to be getting better, she has a relapse. The moral of this episode is pretty clear: embrace life to the fullest and follow your heart. While that is a totally acceptable theme to work with, the writers really hammer it home by having Grandma Claudia make Liz promise to follow her heart "wherever it takes you. Trust it." Then, we follow with Liz's voice-over on the tough part about trusting your heart and how once you leave normal you can never go back. The episode is setting up a relationship between Max and Liz, which is expected, but it doesn't need as much justification as it gives.

It's interesting that the title "Leaving Normal" is opposite to what Max attempts to do —

which is return to life as it once was. After being beaten up by Kyle's buddies, Max does not heal himself, but instead keeps his bruises and refuses to retaliate. He tries to stay away from Liz, as instructed, and gets angry at Michael for pulling pranks on the jocks that hurt him. In some ways, Max is "chasing" normal, only he never quite gets back to it. Meanwhile, Liz pulls away from Kyle, and follows her heart by phoning Max at the hospital, then later by coming to his house to ask for help. Since Liz is highly analytical, loves science because it's factual, and believes that "you can be in control of everything," her choice of intuition over intelligence is definitely leaving normal.

When Max knocks down a bathroom stall wall with his fist, Michael responds with "Gandhi feeling frustrated?" While in this case, it's a sarcastic reference considering Gandhi's staunch belief in non-violence, at the same time it's quite appropriate. Max's whole attitude towards his beating was to keep the peace and stay away from any sort of retaliation. Gandhi was known for his peaceful protests, fasting instead of fighting. Max is suffering by denying himself love. Later, when Max arrives at the hospital to try to help Liz communicate with her grandmother, we delve into the question of faith even further. Hindus believe the soul is distinct from the physical senses and the mind, and that the soul transmigrates from the dead into another birth. Grandma Claudia's body and soul separate for that brief moment, and it seems, in a way, that she has been reborn in Liz. Yes, some would say that these parallels are leaning towards the realm of far-fetched, but they are still interesting to ponder.

The other alien teen characters get to "leave normal" for a bit in this episode. It's nice to see Michael having some fun and acting like a teenager for a change. His retaliatory pranks are fairly harmless, allowing him to break away from that dark cloud that looms over him. Isabel also gets to explore her goofy nature when she agrees to help out at the Crashdown as a waitress.

Maria shows her depth in this episode as she goes out of her way to be there for Liz. From taking control of the diner to simply stroking her hair and listening, Maria's friendship is really touching. We also get to see more depth in Kyle. Not only does he stay by Liz's side while she is in hospital, but he chastises his friends for beating up on Max. We receive a glimpse of Kyle's relationship with his father. Showing viewers the softer side of Sheriff Valenti is a nice touch as the two men attempt to talk about Kyle's relationship issues.

"Leaving Normal" takes us away from the sci-fi suspense world for a short time, and examines relationships with others, and with ourselves. Oh, yeah, and it's about following your heart!

FLASH: Isabel "lowering herself" to help Maria out at the Crashdown.

IRKS: Well, the diary framework has returned once more, though it's still not clear as to why she always has to write her *own name* in the diary. Doesn't she *know* that she's Liz Parker? Because *we* do. I know this is a broken record, but once again the Kyle/Liz relationship leaves me completely boggled. Liz tells her grandmother that Kyle is somebody that she has a "good time" with. Not her boyfriend, just a good time guy. Kyle tells Max that he really likes Liz, but never mentions being her boyfriend. Then, later at the hospital, Liz tells Kyle that she doesn't think they should be together anymore, and Kyle asks if she's breaking up with him. When did they become a couple? It's very complicated.

ALIENISMS: Interesting how Michael has now suddenly learned to control his powers. He touches one jock, making him intensely itchy. He manages to change the answers on someone's exam paper, and melts the metal hinge of Kyle's locker. Isabel cooks a hamburger with her hand, and heats coffee. It's not really clear *exactly* what Max does, but somehow he connects with Grandma Claudia's spirit, allowing her to leave her body and communicate with Liz.

SODA MOMENT: In response to Isabel's sarcastic comment as she watches him re-stuff the alien autopsy doll, Max replies, "Gotta feed the monkey." It's a slang term referring to feeding an addiction, habit, or craving. In this case, Max's monkey involves working at the UFO Center in order to gain more information on their past.

COOL FACTS: The 1992 film, *Leaving Normal*, directed by Edward Zwick, touches on the theme of running away, only to realize that peace comes when you stop searching and learn to love what is already there. Edward Zwick also directed an episode of *My So-Called Life*, created by Jason Katims.

MUSIC: Mandy Moore's "Candy" is playing in the Crashdown when Max enters at the beginning. "Then The Morning Comes" by Smashmouth plays when Michael touches the jock in the hallway, and gives him the itch. Geoff Parker sings along with "The Weight" by Nazareth just prior to Grandma Claudia's arrival. When Agnes goes on her smoke break, "Mistaken" by Save Ferris plays on in the Crashdown. Sugar Ray's "Someday" plays while Isabel works as a waitress. Finally, Sarah McLachlan's "I Love You" is in the background while Liz and Max embrace outside the Crashdown.

1.5 Missing

ORIGINAL AIR DATE: November 3, 1999
WRITTEN BY: Jon Harmon Feldman
DIRECTED BY: David Semel

GUEST CAST: Julie Benz (Kathleen Topolsky), Jo Anderson (Nancy Parker), Steve Hytner (Milton Ross), Robert Clendenin (Mr. Cowan), Robert Neary (Agent Moss), Richard Anthony Crenna (Agent Baxter)

When Liz's journal goes missing, everyone becomes a suspect.

"Missing" takes us back to what *Roswell* is all about — a show that balances human relationships with great suspense. The episode involves three different searches, and explores how friends can appear to be enemies, and enemies can enter our lives disguised as friends. It is an interesting episode because all three storylines end up coming together at the end.

The framework device becomes a main plot line for this episode. "Missing" may open with Liz's voice-over, but it leads to her furiously searching her drawer for her journal. In its own way, the journal does begin the show. The reason Liz is devastated when her journal goes missing is because it not only contains all of her personal secrets, but those of Max, Isabel, and Michael. Once again, the alien teens' lives are on the line. With Maria's help, Liz begins to narrow the possible suspects. Could it be Alex? After all, he's been dying to know their secret. Or Liz's mother? Teenagers are often quick to jump to the conclusion that their parents are snooping through their personal things. Or maybe Kyle? Kyle has abandoned all sympathy when it comes to Liz, and keeps dropping hints that he knows something. He's acting like a classic rejected boyfriend, yet when the stakes are high, it's easy to misinterpret someone's words.

Then, there is story number two: Michael's obsession with the image from his "vision" from "The Morning After." The vision has lain dormant for awhile (which explains why he hasn't done anything over two episodes), but returns to him one night while sleeping. He wakes up and begins the process of recreating it. As Liz searches for the journal, Michael searches his mind trying to conceptualize his vision. It's a great moment when Michael saunters into his art class and informs his teacher that he "kinda just really want[s] to draw." Offering no apologies for his absences, he takes an easel and begins a series of drawings of the same image. His obsession with creating the ideal picture of the geodesic dome is a nice allusion to the Stephen Spielberg film *Close Encounters of the Third Kind* (1977). In the film, Richard Dreyfuss plays Roy Neary, one of many who witness three UFOs soaring through the night. As a consequence, he becomes obsessed with recreating an unknown image that haunts him. Like Michael, Roy doesn't know what it is he is trying to recreate, only that he must keep going.

The third, and much smaller subplot involves Max's search to find out more about their alien past. His boss at the UFO Center gives him a book called *Among Us* by James Atherton. Steve Hytner is fabulous as the wacky UFO Center curator Milton Ross, a "true believer." Highly paranoid and very suspicious, Milton Ross feeds Max with lots of information because he believes Max to be a believer like himself. He's a great element of comic relief, especially since his lifetime goal is to come face to face with an alien so he can stand on his mother's grave and say "I told you so!" Like most fanatics, they are so caught up in their heads they fail to see what is in front of them.

The three threads come together nicely in this episode through a touching scene and a suspenseful cliffhanger. The scene where Michael pays a visit to Liz at the Crashdown truly showcases Brendan Fehr's skills as an actor. In a touching moment, Michael says to Liz, "Thank you for giving me one more reason to envy Max Evans." Although his next line may be flippant and amusing, one thing is for certain: Michael does have a soft side. Ending on a high-note, "Missing" is a well written, compelling episode.

FLASH: When Mr. Cowan suggests that Michael abandon his geodesic dome drawing and put his talents to work sketching the statue of a nude female bust, Michael takes a long look, then draws a stick figure. "Stick with the dome," is his teacher's response.

IRKS: Nancy Parker's incriminating comment is a little too "convenient" for this episode.

ALIENISMS: Max's boss at the UFO Center mentions theories about the 1947 crash. Michael sharpens a pencil and erases paint with his hand. Max causes the food vending machine to vibrate, and has a "flash" after holding a CD that Kyle touched. Isabel speed-reads the book "Among Us."

SODA MOMENT: Topolsky calls her agency and "Control" answers. On the television series *Get Smart* (1965–1970), Maxwell Smart (Don Adams) calls into "Control" to get his assignments.

COOL FACTS: The 1982 film *Missing*, starring Jack Lemmon, is about a man searching for his son in Latin America. His character is unable and unwilling to accept the idea that the American representatives there might not be telling him the truth. Like the alien teens on *Roswell*, he's dealing with enemies who are disguised as friends.

MUSIC: When Maria questions Alex about Liz's journal, "Pick a Part That's New" by the Stereophonics is playing. Filter's "Take a Picture" plays while Michael sketches the geodesic dome in the Crashdown. "Novocane" by Beck is what Michael is listening to while he paints in the art room. When Michael goes to the Crashdown to see Liz, "Torn" by Creed is in the background. Finally, "Colorblind" by the Counting Crows plays when Isabel discovers the photograph in the book.

1.6 285 South — Part One

ORIGINAL AIR DATE: November 10, 1999
WRITTEN BY: William Sind, Thania St. John
DIRECTED BY: Arvin Brown

GUEST CAST: Julie Benz (Kathleen Topolsky), Michael Horse (Deputy Blackwood), Daniel Hagan (Steve Sommers), Steve Hytner (Milton Ross), Richard Anthony Crenna (Agent Baxter), Michael Garvey (Highway Patrolman), Frankie Ray (Biker), Marilyn Sue Perry (Secretary)

On a search for Atherton's dome, Michael kidnaps Maria and her car, driving them down 285 South to Marathon, Texas — with Liz, Max, Isabel, Kyle, Sheriff Valenti, and government agents in pursuit.

"285 South," and the second part, "River Dog," are considered by many to be two of the best episodes of *Roswell*. Fast-paced, this episode explores relationship dynamics and how they change during the race to the dome.

It opens with Michael getting caught after breaking into the UFO Center. The next scene takes us into West Roswell High, where Liz, Isabel, Maria, Max, and Kyle receive instructions about their history oral report. Their teacher, Mr. Sommers, hands them all a sheet of questions. Some are minor ("What's your favorite flavor of ice cream?") and some are more personal ("What are you afraid of?"). The assignment is to pose the questions to their partner in order to learn something new about them. He pairs up Liz with Isabel, Max with Kyle, and Maria with Michael. When Maria tries to reject her new partner due to his absence from class, Mr. Sommers's response is "Well, then it'll be like true field work, tracking down your subject." A nice touch, considering what happens next.

The majority of this episode is divided into three parts: Michael and Maria's journey; Liz, Max, and Isabel in the jeep; and Kyle, the sheriff, and Topolsky together. One of the strengths of this episode is the explosive dynamic between Maria and Michael, whom we haven't seen together before. Their journey is the catalyst in the episode as Maria and Michael undergo their own relationship shift. When Maria runs into Michael, desperate to get her assignment done with him, he agrees to help her . . . only if she gives him a ride to the gas station. The first great line is when Maria argues that Michael's favorite television show couldn't possibly be *The View*. "Keeps me in touch with my feminine side," he tosses back. Their dialogue is like a well played tennis match, with one-liners thrown back and forth at such a pace that you almost wish there were instant replays. It helps that, like Shiri and Jason, Majandra and Brendan have great chemistry. Interesting that like their characters Maria and Michael, the two actors did not get along at first, and then ended up in a serious relationship. Who says life doesn't imitate art?

Once again, Michael's layers are brilliantly displayed. From his humiliation about his dysfunctional powers to his sensitive moments with Maria, Michael continues to show us cracks in the wall. He's met his match in Maria, however. Her spunky personality, along with her loyalty and strength, all come into play. These two discover that while they seem very different at first, in actuality they have a lot of similarities. There's a lovely moment at the motel where both Maria and Michael realize they share the same dream: that there is something better for them outside of Roswell, New Mexico. These two certainly achieve the aim of the history assignment by discovering that "people aren't what they appear to be."

The second journey involves Isabel, Max, and Liz. Isabel deals with the idea that she might be losing her brother to Liz. For years, Isabel has been the main woman in both Max and Michael's lives. Now she worries that she might not hold the same place in their hearts. In a poignant scene, as Liz attempts to bring over a peace offering (coffee) to Isabel, it spills on both of them. Isabel uses her powers to clean herself up, but makes no effort to do the same for Liz. What makes this episode powerful isn't so much what is said, but what is not said in all of the scenarios.

Max and Michael's testosterone levels continue to be on the rise. Michael is obviously tired of relying on Max to come to his rescue, just as Max is frustrated by always having to take the responsible route. And yet, the two men obviously care a great deal for one another. The nice shift comes when Max stops trying to be safe and lets Michael's excitement envelop him. When Michael's key is unable to open the door, he defers to Max, whose powers can solve the problem. At this point, the power struggle ceases and the men come to a new understanding in their relationship. Like two young bucks fighting over a doe, these two rarely give it a rest.

A fabulous episode, "285 South" leaves us desperate for more!

FLASH: While there were *many*, the scene when Isabel opens the motel room door and Maria falls on top of Michael was great. She jumps up, bumbling that the situation is not what it seems, then Michael casually replies with: "Come on, honey, we don't have to lie."

IRKS: First of all, Kyle doesn't hear Liz mention the words "285 South" in the Crashdown, nor is it mentioned when he confronts Max, Isabel, and Liz outside by the jeep. When Kyle calls Liz's cell phone, the only indication that Liz is on the highway is the sound of a truck in the background. How on earth did Kyle know to take 285 South? Also, Max, Isabel, and Liz take off on the long trek to Marathon in the afternoon and Kyle leaves at night, yet he shows up at Maria and Michael's motel room right after the other three do. And the government agents are desperately obvious. Weren't they trained to track people? Finally, how did Topolsky know where the teens were going when her agent was foiled halfway there?

ALIENISMS: Isabel makes coffee stains disappear, opens a chain lock, and lights an old lantern with her hand. Max causes two tires to go flat, seals up a rip in the jeep's fabric roof, and unlocks the front door of the geodesic dome. Michael sets Maria's car engine on fire, tosses Kyle across the room with superhuman force, and gets another flash from the key.

SODA MOMENT: "Come on. Wiggle your nose, blink your eyes, do the Samantha-Jeannie alien thing. Come on." When Maria's car breaks down, she makes reference to the television shows *Bewitched* and *I Dream of Jeannie* (1965–1970). *I Dream of Jeannie*, starring Barbara Eden, starts when astronaut Captain Tony Nelson discovers a magic lamp on a desert island, and rubs it . . . only to end up with Jeannie, a magic genie who is so thrilled to be free, she swears to serve her "master" however she can. She makes things happen by blinking her eyes.

COOL FACTS: James Joyce's acclaimed novel *Ulysses* is considered a modern-day interpretation of Homer's *Odyssey*. It was first written in installments, then later published in Paris in 1922. While the critics appreciated Joyce's wit and genius, there were issues regarding his "outhouse" humor. The novel was considered pornographic and was banned in the U.K. and the U.S. It didn't stop Joyce's literary status from rising, however, and over a decade later, Random House won a court case which led to the first American publication of *Ulysses*. Two years later, the book was made available in Britain.

MUSIC: The episode begins with "The Dreamer" by Euphoria, as Michael breaks into the UFO Center. "Delerium," also by Euphoria, plays during history class when the assignment is given out. Stroke 9's "Little Black Backpack" is heard at the Crashdown while Max, Kyle, Liz, and Isabel attempt to do their assignment. "On Any Given Day" by Laura Webb plays in the jeep when Max and Liz discuss the terms of their relationship. Finally, "Safe" by Grassy Knoll is on at the end of the episode while the team goes through Atherton's abandoned home.

1.7 River Dog — Part Two

ORIGINAL AIR DATE: November 17, 1999
WRITTEN BY: Cheryl Cain
DIRECTED BY: Jonathan Frakes

GUEST CAST: Ned Romero (River Dog), Tod Thawley (Eddie), Toochis Morin (Native American Woman), Steve Hytner (Milton Ross), Julie Benz (Kathleen Topolsky), Michael Horse (Deputy Blackwood), Mary Ellen Trainor (Diane Evans), Richard Schiff (Agent Stevens), Richard Anthony Crenna (Agent Baxter)

The necklace found by Isabel at Atherton's is connected to the local Native reservation. Liz and Max meet with River Dog, who provides them with more clues to their past.

"River Dog" continues to explore changing relationships. Working together as a team, Max, Liz, Isabel, Michael, and Maria manage to escape from Atherton's dome before being caught by Topolsky. While they don't notice it's Topolsky who is following them, Sheriff Valenti certainly does. Back in Roswell, Isabel has a revelation to share with Max. The symbol on the chipped necklace she discovered was something they drew in the sand together as children. They leave all the other information from Atherton's bunker in Max's room as they head off for school. Now, it's totally unrealistic of them to simply leave the information at home, especially since it could provide them with answers to their past; after all, they know that they were followed. Of course, they don't think of this, and the house is robbed. Firstly, the scene allows the sheriff to grill them once more on their odd behavior. Secondly, it's the perfect time for Deputy Blackwood to identify Isabel's new necklace as something he had seen years previous at the Mesaliko Reservation outside of Roswell. While that is another nice clue, people are still following them, and Max states that everyone must lay low.

Max and Liz continue to get closer, both physically and emotionally. The sexual tension between them is so thick, you could cut it. When he pulls her to him in his bedroom, resting his forehead against hers, you just want to scream at the screen, "Kiss her, dammit!" The nice dynamic shift here is when Liz tells Max clearly that she is going to the reservation for them, and is not interested in his permission. It's nice to see Liz taking charge and Max stepping back from the head honcho role.

"River Dog" takes Michael and Maria's new relationship dynamics to the next level. No longer afraid of Michael, Maria carefully flirts with him, testing the waters of their new relationship. Michael has started to view her in a new light as well, but refuses to let go of his gruff exterior. Later, at the Crashdown, Michael continues to be insensitive while Maria responds with disgust. What is realistic about these characters is that they *act* like teenagers, pretending not to like each other when in fact, they really do. While Michael still tends to push the envelope to the extreme, he makes up for it by doing something spontaneous and lovely. In fact, it becomes his trademark. Their humorous courtship is a nice contrast to the intense longing of Max and Liz.

Kathleen Topolsky really isn't cutting it as an undercover agent. Considering her boss is ready to pull her from the case if she doesn't shape up, it's a little ridiculous that she pursues Michael in a high-speed car chase around the small town. Besides, what exactly would she do if she caught them? She is supposed to be *undercover*. It doesn't help her image when we find out that the sheriff has been able to follow Topolsky without her knowledge. So, when she attempts to form an alliance with him, you have to wonder *why* he'd want to agree to it.

"River Dog" introduces a new Native American element to the series. Until this point, Deputy Blackwood has been the only Native character. Now we have River Dog, Eddie, and their community. While Mesaliko is a fictional term, in reality there is a Mescalero Apache Indian Reservation located right next to the White Sands Missile Range, just outside of Roswell. Located on the reservation are the Three Rivers Petroglyphs. Over 15,000 Mongollon Indian petroglyphs (designs that are cut or scratched out of rock) are at the site, dating between 900 and 1400 AD.

"285 South" begins as a quest for clues, and at the end of "River Dog," there is the suggestion that the gang can no longer turn back.

FLASH: Michael kissing Maria "to calm [her] down."

IRKS: The incompetence of the FBI is a little ridiculous. They are federal investigators, not the Keystone Cops. Also, while they know something happened with Liz and Max Evans at the Crashdown due to the blood on the waitress uniform, there has never been any indication that Isabel or Michael should be watched. Milton, the head of the UFO Center, acts more suspicious as a grown man than the teenagers do. Also, the timing is a bit off at the beginning of the episode. When they leave Atherton's, the sun is already out and bright. Then, there is the over three-hour drive back (as stated in "285 South"). So, how is it that Max and Isabel are back in their rooms before breakfast?

DOUBLE TAKE: At the beginning of the episode, in Atherton's secret bunker, Liz spies something and points it out to Maria. A rat runs down an anonymous arm (blue shirt, bottom left of screen). Liz immediately notices the rat disappear through the tunnel, but makes no reference to a body. Obviously, there wasn't supposed to be an arm in the shot!

ALIENISMS: Max creates light with his hands in order to find Liz in the cave. Whether or not he makes the pendant glow is debatable. We finally discover the reason for the Tabasco sauce — the aliens like things to be very sweet and very spicy at the same time.

SODA MOMENT: The two films playing at the Roswell movie theater are *Secret Agent* (1936) and *The Lady Vanishes* (1938) by Alfred Hitchcock. While the plots aren't pertinent to the show, the titles are. A "secret agent" (Topolsky) watches as Max enters the movie theater with Liz, and Michael and Isabel take off as decoys. When "the lady vanishes" they are safe to head out to the reservation.

COOL FACTS: The Mescalero Apache tribe was formally the Nde tribe. Rounded up in 1863, they were forced to live under appalling conditions along the upper Pecos River at the Bosque Redondo reservation, and the American government forced the name Mescalero Apache on them. When the Nde rebelled two years later and escaped into the night, the U.S. Army hunted them down, and killed them. Then, in 1873, the Mescalero Apache Indian Reservation was established by President Ulysses S. Grant, and the remaining Nde (approximately 400) were moved there. The survivors of the Lipan and Chiracahua Apache bands were also taken there. While they are a very private people, their reservation is a popular tourist site. (Also, Mary Ellen Trainor had a role on Jason Katims' short-lived series *Relativity*.)

MUSIC: As Max, Isabel, and Liz ride home in the jeep, we hear Euphoria's "Delerium." When Maria and Michael drive back from Texas, "Blown Away" by Bachelor Girl is playing. Later, when Eddie shows up at the Crashdown, "Quicksand" by Finger Eleven is in the background. "Get You In The Morning" by Crash Test Dummies plays while Isabel, Michael, and Maria wait for the others to return. When Topolsky and the Sheriff have a drink at the bar, Bramhall's "Snakecharmer" is playing.

1.8 Blood Brothers

ORIGINAL AIR DATE: November 24, 1999
STORY BY: Barry Pullman, Breen Frazier
TELEPLAY BY: Barry Pullman
DIRECTED BY: David Nutter

GUEST CAST: Julie Benz (Kathleen Topolsky), Mary Ellen Trainor (Diane Evans), Johnathan

Nicholas (Doctor), Hilary Shepard-Turner (Nurse Susan), Victor Campos (Principal Bruckner), Eric Jungmann (Lester), Joe Camareno (#1 Paramedic), Paul Palmer (#2 Paramedic), Kevin Calishner (Bob the Jock), Zack Aaron (Heavy Metal Student)

When Max ends up in hospital after a car accident, the gang is dependent on Alex's blood to help them out.

"Blood Brothers" finally brings Alex, who has been absent for a while now, back into the fray. When we last saw him ("Missing"), he was not only angry at Liz and Maria for keeping secrets, but for being accused of taking Liz's journal. This episode gives us more insight into Alex, as well as dealing with issues of loyalty and trust. Alex is torn between his loyalty to Liz and his conscience. Liz, in turn, is torn between her promise of secrecy to Max and her friendship and loyalty to Alex. Ultimately they both need to make a choice.

Max takes Liz out for a drive when their fourth period class is cancelled, and of course disaster strikes. Unconscious, Max is rushed to the hospital and the gang is faced with a new dilemma — Max's blood tests. They need the blood of a human male to keep the secret. Liz knows just who she needs to turn to.

Alex is one of those comedic characters just on the verge of cool, but not quite making it. Like Xander was with Buffy in the early days, Alex is completely mesmerized by Isabel, but completely hopeless when it comes to talking with her. His loyalty to Liz is admirable, however, as the risk he takes for Liz is huge. Colin Hanks does a great job, showing his hurt and disbelief when Liz, his best friend, lies to him point blank. Liz's first explanation should have been that it wasn't her secret to tell (she doesn't use that until next episode). Instead, she gives him nothing. Cue Topolsky, who slithers in with her "you can tell me anything" approach. It's hard to know whether or not to betray a friendship to an adult. Topolsky puts the "safety" card on the table, which is even more incentive for a hurt, confused teenager to confess. Interesting how Alex never questions how his *guidance counselor* knows what happened at the hospital. All in all, Alex's character is nicely fleshed out, and is a great complement to the cast.

Liz is less sympathetic in this episode. If Liz and Alex had been so close for so long, why does she not work harder to persuade Max to let Alex in on the secret? It's also a little unfair that Max doesn't think harder on the topic, considering the sacrifice Alex makes for him. The only response Max can give Alex is, "I'm trying to protect you." Max isn't trying to protect Alex. He's trying to protect himself and the others. Liz does redeem herself for a moment when she relives her friendship with Alex at the Crashdown. While Alex's dilemma is very intense, Liz's is not, simply because we know she's already chosen Max.

While Alex has some really strong moments in "Blood Brothers," the plot has some really weak ones.

Colin Hanks, looking very dapper (Photo by Albert L. Ortega)

FLASH: Maria, Michael, and Isabel are about to tail the agent, and Maria puts on Terminator-style sunglasses.

IRKS: What exactly do the FBI agents need a blood sample for anyway? DNA? They could have gotten that from hair left behind on Max's pillow. Topolsky slips Alex a drug that makes his nose bleed, which seems a little far-fetched. And where was Sheriff Valenti? When the Evans's house is broken into in "River Dog," he has cops crawling all over the scene. A car accident is definitely something he would be aware of. And finally, where did they get a vial with an identical Max Evans sticker on it for Alex's blood?

DOUBLE TAKE: Alex is carrying his books in one hand. His nose starts bleeding, and suddenly, both hands are free to deal with the blood. We cut to a long shot, and it seems Alex is still carrying his books.

ALIENISMS: Michael unlocks the door to the motel room with his powers. The aliens apparently don't get sick.

SODA MOMENT: When the crew first see Max after he's woken up, Michael says: "Heard you saved Mister Ed." He's referring to the television show, *Mister Ed* (1961), where the title character was a talking horse.

COOL FACTS: While in the hospital, the doctor suggests that Max have a head MRI scan. The Magnetic Resonance Imaging scan (MRI) uses extremely powerful magnets and radio waves in order to create clear, detailed pictures of different tissues. Using the MRI scan, doctors are capable of making a diagnosis much earlier than from using standard diagnostic techniques.

MUSIC: While Max and Liz drive down the highway at the beginning, "Learn to Fly" by the Foo Fighters is playing on the radio. Following that is the song Liz makes reference to in her voice over: "You Make Me Feel" by Jeremy Toback. "Alien" by Pennywise plays while Alex and Kyle talk over lunch. Citizen King's "The Long Walk Home" is on at the Crashdown while they all discuss what happened in the motel room. When Alex gives Liz one more opportunity to tell the truth at the end, "If You Want Me To" by Ginny Owens is playing.

1.9 Heat Wave

ORIGINAL AIR DATE: December 1, 1999
WRITTEN BY: Jason Katims
DIRECTED BY: Patrick Norris

GUEST CAST: John Doe (Geoff Parker), Diane Farr (Amy DeLuca), Jason Peck (Deputy Hanson), Meghan Gallagher (Vicky Delaney), Trevor Lissauer (Octavio), Eamon Behrens (Metal Head), Fred Estrada (Jailed Kid), Jodi Taffel (Secretary), Dan Martin (Principal), Yolanda Lloyd Delgado (Ms. Hardy), Save Ferris (as themselves)

A heatwave hits Roswell, causing the townsfolk to boil over with passion. Later, a fire at the old soap factory causes Sheriff Valenti to break up the party.

"Heat Wave" addresses a major teenage issue — sexuality. The teens soon discover that while making out is good, it's not everything. Maria and Michael set the pace in the opening scene of the episode, which feels more like a steamy romance novel. It's all very sexy and stylized and far from the usual awkward groping that happens for many in high school.

One thing that really stands out in this episode is the difference between Liz and Maria, and Max and Michael. Michael feels something, and acts accordingly, while Max thinks and plans, which is why the two constantly clash. It's the exact same situation for Maria and Liz. Liz analyzes everyone's behavior, including Maria's, while Maria follows her emotional impulses. When Michael and Maria are forced to think about their actions, conflict arises. The biggest problem this couple has is communication, which ends up dogging them throughout the season.

On the other hand, Liz and Max think things through rather than act on their impulses. They haven't even kissed, and already they seem to have analyzed their future relationship to death. It's rather curious that Liz would be left alone in a dark biology lab encouraging two slugs to mate, but it does seem like a strangely appropriate venue for Max to show up so they can (sigh) discuss their relationship once more. Only this time, Liz confronts Max about their lack of lovin'. Max relays his major concern, while Liz, in turn, reminds him that it is her choice. This is actually the conversation that Michael and Maria should have had. We are teased through the entire episode until, finally, we have another *Romeo and Juliet* balcony scene, and are left satisfied. Phew!

This episode first introduces the idea of Alex and Isabel as a potential couple. Using the same dreamwalking technique she uses on Maria in "Monsters," Isabel takes a peek into Alex's world. What she discovers, however, is not what she expects. The vulnerability Isabel shows as she watches Alex dance with her dream image is beautiful. Alex's desire to see who Isabel "really is" touches her, considering Isabel admits that she keeps her distance because she is afraid of emotional rejection. Alex's awkward response to Isabel's invitation to the dance is a lovely contrast from his confident persona in the dream. All in all, Katherine and Colin gave touching performances, showing that there is much more to Alex and Isabel below the surface, and in their own way, they both just want to be noticed and appreciated for their inner selves.

Diane Farr is introduced in this episode as Maria's mother, Amy. Amy is a wonderful addition to the cast, and is just as wacky as Maria. Brought on as a love interest for Jim Valenti, the two adults share a fabulous chemistry, flirting just like teenagers.

All in all, this episode is more of a device to move the romantic relationships to the next level. Once more we are reminded that regardless of their differences, they are all still *teenagers*.

FLASH: The balcony scene!

IRKS: Since the sheriff knows that Topolsky is an agent, wouldn't he just phone the FBI to find out why she has suddenly disappeared? (Not that he seems too concerned with her disappearance.) I find it hard to believe that Kyle's new girlfriend would not only be eager to invite Liz, his ex, to a party, but that she actually *thought* about it beforehand. When Alex takes on Valenti at the prison, it's nice to see his strength, but it's a little hard to believe that his words alone get both himself and Liz released *without* their parents having to pick them up.

DOUBLE TAKE: At the beginning of the episode, as Liz walks down the school hallways, her hair is down. Moments later, when she runs into Kyle and Vicky, her hair is up.

ALIENISMS: Isabel dreamwalks, and changes the color of Liz's nail polish with her hand.

SODA MOMENT: Maria tells Michael that she is not "some Pollyanna." *Pollyanna* (1960) is the story of a young girl who comes to live with her intimidating aunt in a town filled with bitterness. Her unfaltering optimism puts a spell on the town, changing everyone for the better.

COOL FACTS: Diane Farr was the former co-host of MTV's *Loveline*, and the author of *The Girl Code*. Most recently, she can be seen on the ABC show, *The Job*, opposite Dennis Leary.

MUSIC: When Michael and Maria start going at it in the Crashdown, "Put Your Lights On" by Santana is playing. "Got You (Where I Want You)" is on when Liz walks through the lust-ridden school hallways. Save Ferris (in a cameo) performs "Let Me In" during Alex's dream while he dances with Isabel. "Situation ('99 Remix)" by Yaz is on at the start of the soap factory party. Warren G's "I Want It All" comes on when Max and Liz try to exit the factory. Finally, "We Haven't Turned Around" by Gomez is the song Max and Liz first kiss to on the balcony!

1.10 The Balance

ORIGINAL AIR DATE: December 15, 1999
WRITTEN BY: Thania St. John
DIRECTED BY: John Behring

GUEST CAST: Ned Romero (River Dog), Tod Thawley (Eddie), Steve Hytner (Milton Ross), Daniel Hansen (young Max), Zoë Nutter (young Isabel), Nicholas Stratton (young Michael).

Michael's experience in a Native sweat ritual gives him a strange illness that threatens his life.

Jumping off from the joys and heartbreaks that came at the end of "Heat Wave," "The Balance" almost acts as a balance of the extreme events that occurred in the previous episodes. This episode explores spiritual powers on a variety of levels, along with giving us more insight into the history of the Pod Squad.

"The Balance" begins at the Crashdown, with a cross-cut scene showing Liz and Maria's viewpoint in contrast to Michael and Max's. Liz and Max are still a-glow from their kiss, while Michael and Maria are griping about each other. As usual, Majandra and Brendan deliver their lines with great sarcasm, while Shiri and Jason continue to gaze at one another with puppy-dog eyes. Liz and Max are idealistic, and Maria and Michael are realistic. In the teenage world, both options are viable. *Roswell* continually shows how much of a roller coaster ride teen relationships can be, especially when future plans and perceptions of relationships are still idealized.

This episode looks at the mystery of the alien powers, the spiritual practices of Native Americans, and even touches (with humor) on voodoo. It explores the validity of both human and extraterrestrial powers. While Michael takes off to find River Dog and is thrown off-balance by the sweat ritual, it is River Dog helps restore the balance. River Dog helps to heal Nasedo, which shows how human support can make a difference. The circle created to heal Michael involves two humans and two aliens. A balance of both powers helps to bring Michael back, not one or the other.

The Apache tribe believes that the supernatural power that envelops the world offers its services to their people through visions. The sweat lodge ritual helps to unify the body, heart, soul, and mind. The steam helps the body release impurities, the heart is cleansed through prayer, the soul through spiritual communication, and the mind through full unification of the four human elements. Michael's strange reaction to the sweat (cleansing the body) first causes him to mumble the native chant (cleansing the heart), then puts him into a comatose state, where he has visions (cleansing the soul). Michael then reconnects with a past moment that has overlapped onto a present one. He takes Max's hand, both as a child and as an adult, bringing him back in balance (cleansing the mind).

Max and Liz, caught up in their "normal" romantic date, find themselves thrown into this drastic "abnormal" situation. Max recognizes he has left one extreme (being alien), to delve into another (being human). Liz represents a normal human world, while Isabel and Michael represent his heritage. Max's conflict is symbolized in the "trance" scene when each character approaches Michael. Max moves towards him, but gets distracted by Liz's image. He needs to restore his own balance on an emotional level.

Maria introduces a form of magic in "The Balance." She stabs away at a silver alien toy representing a voodoo doll of Michael. While it is only meant as an amusing reference, it's interesting to note how afterwards, Michael does experience sickness. The voodoo religion originated in Africa, and was brought over to Haiti through the slave ships. Recorded uses of voodoo dolls originate in New Orleans in the early 1900s, where hexes were cast on an individual to bring them either good or bad luck. When pins were stuck into the doll, the spell was reinforced. Based on Maria's mood towards Michael at the beginning of the episode, it's pretty clear that she wasn't wishing him well. Maria goes through her own spiritual growth by coming through for Michael without hesitation. Like Liz before her, Maria works to find the balance with Isabel while they both care for Michael.

"The Balance" delves further into the alien heritage questions and allows for more character growth and maturity. All in all, it's a strong episode.

FLASH: Michael's "visions" while unconscious. John Bartlett's cinematography is creative and visually compelling.

IRKS: When did Alex change his mind and decide to believe Liz about the alien teens? Also, when Michael heads into the sweat lodge with Eddie, how does River Dog know that he is associated with Max and Liz? Sixth sense? Later, Eddie tells Max that River Dog "tested" him but he didn't pass. What is the test — that he would instantly react negatively to the ritual and get sick? Even so, it would mean that he knows Michael is affiliated with Max, and unless he is psychic (which is never implied), he wouldn't know. Also, why does the reservation look as though it only consists of trailers?

ALIENISMS: Isabel messes with the molecular structure of ketchup, turning it into mustard. As a consequence of his imbalance, a cocoon-like web forms around Michael's comatose body. River Dog brings Nasedo's healing stones to restore the balance in the alien bodies. The stones fit into different hieroglyphs on the wall, glow, and reveal a map — like stars in the sky.

SODA MOMENT: After speaking of how Michael's ways are hurtful, Maria says she's like "Teflon." Namely, that whatever he does to her doesn't stick, but slides right off without leaving any pain behind.

COOL FACTS: Alex takes Isabel to the UFO Center to show her a display that he feels has some connection to the hieroglyphs that Max recreates. The display involves Machu Picchu, in Peru. The ancient Inca civilization that inhabited the mountain town vanished over 400 years ago. Its oddly shaped, colored stones were thought to be record keepers. There are people who believe that Machu Picchu was also the home of the original Inca tribes. An advanced society, the Inca religion involved both male and female deities, worshipped a Sun God, and was in harmony with the natural world. Where the last Incas disappeared to remains a mystery.

MUSIC: When Liz opens the episode with her voice-over, "Troubled Times" by Fountains of Wayne is in the background. Cirque du Soleil's "Incantation" is the Native American chant during the sweat ritual. "Everyday" by Angie Stone plays while Isabel explains her heritage to Alex at the Crashdown. While Liz and Max shoot pool on their date, Third Eye Blind's "Deep Inside Of You" plays. Later, when Liz bonds with Maria over ice cream, "Everyone Can Fly" by Gigolo Aunts is in the background. "Absence of Fear" by Jewel, plays on Liz's balcony at the end, when Max comes to talk.

1.11 The Toy House

ORIGINAL AIR DATE: January 19, 2000
WRITTEN BY: Jon Harmon Feldman and Jason Katims
DIRECTED BY: Michael Fields

GUEST CAST: Mary Ellen Trainor (Diane Evans), Gil Colon (Firefighter), Zoë Nutter (young Isabel), Daniel Hansen (young Max)

Max uses his powers to put out a nasty kitchen fire and save his mother, who begins asking questions about her son . . .

What's so wonderful about "The Toy House" is the subtle emotional moments. The entire cast shines in this episode as they deal with mending broken or wounded relationships.

When Max puts out the roaring grease fire with his hand, he triggers his mother's memory, causing her to look back on a childhood incident when Max had healed a wounded bird, sending it soaring into the sky. The lovely dynamic between mother and son is genuine, and Mary Ellen Trainor and Jason Behr should be applauded. When Diane starts asking questions, Max closes off from her. While they have an unearthly secret to hide, being secretive is a very pertinent situation for teenagers. As he grows older, it's common for a teenage boy to back off from his mother's affections and keep his life to himself. After all, puberty isn't exactly something a guy wants to get into with Mom. So, in this case, while Max's reasons for guarding his privacy from his mother are more extreme, the situation is still easy to relate to. The fact that Diane does not judge her son or become fearful of him is also a nice touch. Instead, she wants to reach out the way parents often try to do with their children. When she shows Max the video, it's heartbreaking to watch his expression. He knows she knows, and that he has to say something. Giving his mother the toy house is his way of recognizing her love, but it also suggests that he is growing up.

The other element in this is Isabel, who, in contrast to Max, wants to reach out to her mother and let her in on their secret. Katherine's performance is amazing in this episode. We really get to see her as a teenage girl struggling to connect with a female mentor. Her desire is such that she openly challenges Max's authority in the matter. Her scene with Max in the desert is both heartwrenching and poignant. It really makes the audience ask the question: could you risk revealing your true self if it possibly means losing someone you love?

Liz regains her confident nature in "The Toy House," as she takes it upon herself to make things right with Kyle. Kyle is growing into a more understanding human being, and his comment about learning emotional maturity from Sally Jessy Raphael is priceless. Michael makes his own attempts to fix his relationship with Maria, in his own backward way, of course. Brendan really manages to capture the teenage spirit through Michael's frustrated and confused reactions to Maria's anger. He is the classic guy who just doesn't "get" women. When Maria finally tells him the problem, he comes back at her with accusations, not gratitude. She claims his problem might very well be that he's not a "normal" human being. The irony is, Michael is acting in a totally normal teenage way. Maria and Michael continue to bring humor to the show, but in this episode, we really see a tenderness from them both.

While "The Toy House" really examines trust and the fear that comes with letting down your guard and exposing your true nature, there is another message. Sometimes there is no magic out there that can fix a problem. When it comes to healing, the best medicine is time and a little effort.

FLASH: Michael's incensed reaction when Maria tells him her woodworking project receives a failing grade.

IRKS: Max has no hesitation about trusting Liz, and yet he can't seem to at least consider telling his mother the truth. It seems a bit odd seeing as he's known his mother more intimately than he's known Liz. While his fear of her reaction is understandable, she gives him no reason to think that she would hurt him. Also, the adoption concept becomes a bit confusing. In the pilot episode, we find out that Max and Isabel were found at the side of the road by Mr. and Mrs. Evans. That is reiterated in "The Balance." In this episode, Isabel mentions the day that the Evanses walked into the orphanage to adopt them. I presume that means they found the kids, took them to the orphanage, and later adopted them. How long were they there for? Also, Max mentions how Isabel is immediately comfortable with their new home, but Max would cry himself to sleep at night, wanting to go "home." In "The Balance," Max tells Liz that Isabel would cry herself to sleep at night because they had been separated from Michael. "The Toy House" doesn't give that impression.

DOUBLE TAKE: The Crashdown Café door seems to change the way it swings. One episode it swings in, and other it swings out. Also, when Isabel and Max hug each other at the end, she leans in with her right arm over his shoulder. When the camera zooms in, his left arm is now over hers.

ALIENISMS: Max puts out a fire with his powers. We discover Max healed a pigeon as a child. Isabel changes her lipstick color with her hand.

SODA MOMENT: Michael refers to Maria and Liz as "Frick and Frack." Frick and Frack were the stage names of the famous Swiss comedy ice skaters Hans Mauch and Werner Groebli. Involved with the Ice Follies, which began in 1936, they became extremely well known.

COOL FACTS: Before *Roswell*, Nick Wechsler had no ability to play basketball whatsoever. He had to learn, fast.

MUSIC: While Max and Diane chat in the kitchen before the fire, "Shambala" by Three Dog Night is in the background. "Amy Hit The Atmosphere" by the Counting Crows plays twice:

once when Max is moping in his room, and at the end when Max and Isabel are out at the desert arrojo. Jessica Simpson's "Woman In Me" plays while Liz explains to Maria that she's "just fine" about the breakup. Third Eye Blind's "Never Let You Go" is on during the basketball game. When Isabel changes her lipstick, "Get Up" by Amel Larrieux plays in the background. "Rodeo Clowns" by G. Love and Special Sauce is playing when Kyle comes to the Crashdown. Finally, When Max sees Liz talking to Kyle, we hear "For the Movies" by Buckcherry.

1.12 Into the Woods

ORIGINAL AIR DATE: January 26, 2000
WRITTEN BY: Thania St. John
DIRECTED BY: Nick Marck

GUEST CAST: John Doe (Geoff Parker), Garrett M. Brown (Philip Evans), Ned Romero (River Dog), Robert F. Lyons (Hank Whitmore), Steve Hytner (Milton Ross), Ted Rooney (Mr. Whitman), John Cullum (James Valenti Sr.), Jason Peck (Deputy Hanson), Tom McCleister (Coach), Tony Papenfuss (Rocky Calhoun), John Michael Vaughn (Deputy Stone), Stan Sellers (Receptionist)

A UFO sighting in Frazier Woods inspires Max and Isabel to join in on the West Roswell High Fathers' Camping Weekend.

The previous episode explores mother/child relationships, so why not follow it with an episode about father/child relationships? "Into the Woods" also returns us to the sci-fi world once more as the alien teens covertly search for clues about their past.

The opening of the episode alludes to the original sighting. A couple makes out in the back of a pickup truck in the woods, when suddenly they are interrupted by a bright flash. We cut to the Crashdown where Geoff Parker comments on how Liz has been so busy, he hasn't had time to talk with her. Well, they'll have the perfect opportunity at the Fathers' Camping Weekend, which Liz obviously feels she has outgrown.

Jeff is having difficulties watching his daughter become a woman, and misses being included in her life. Liz, however, is like many teenage girls — going away for a bonding weekend with Dad isn't the top priority. Like teenage boys with their mothers, sharing everything while going through puberty is awkward — for both father and daughter, in this case. The distance between them and their stilted conversation is enough to make him suspect Liz of taking drugs. Instead of asking about it right away, he takes the alternative approach —

snooping. Fathers are known to struggle with the idea that their little girl is growing up and away from them and John Doe does a wonderful job conveying this.

While Liz wants distance from her dad, Kyle wants his father's attention. Right from the beginning, we get a clear picture on how preoccupied Jim gets with his police work and how Kyle feels like an afterthought. Kyle keeps attempting to communicate with his father, but the sheriff just isn't listening. Jim's focus is so intense that Kyle secretly follows him just to understand what takes priority over their relationship. Jim's behavior has begun to mirror that of his own father, and Kyle calls him on it. Their broken communication represents families where the parents are so caught up in their jobs they end up alienating their kids. Kyle's words do hit home, however, prompting the sheriff to face what he has been avoiding — his past and his father. In Jim's case, there is a lot of truth to the statement "like father, like son."

Michael may act tough, but he obviously yearns for a father of his own. When River Dog comes to him to tell him of the sighting, Michael is convinced that he is the one they have been searching for, that River Dog is their "father." River Dog's astute observations lead him to respond to the question that Michael is indirectly asking. Michael keeps any disappointment to himself, which only makes you want to hug him more. Growing up with only one parent can be tough, but when that one parent is cruel, it's brutal. Still, as much as Michael wants to leave, he holds on to the only home he has known.

"Into the Woods" has some poignant moments while unraveling more of the alien mystery.

FLASH: Maria strutting down the high school hallway in her aqua bra and red sweater.

IRKS: When Isabel and Max arrive at the cave and see the symbol, they aren't remotely surprised to see River Dog and Michael, even though they weren't expecting them.

DOUBLE TAKE: When Maria and Liz discuss Max in the Crashdown, just after Alex has left, Michael and Max are at the booth with Isabel. When she turns to look at him, she turns straight to the cash at the front, where he and Michael are now standing. How would she know they had moved?

ALIENISMS: The UFO sighting apparently is like a flash of hot, white light, like "an X-ray." Michael heals River Dog's broken ankle, having another flash of the large hieroglyphs in the desert. Max changes his cards while playing poker in order to lose to Liz's father.

SODA MOMENTS: When Maria first sees Liz in the back room of the Crashdown, she tells her "Today is the first day of the rest of o ur lives." While slightly altered, the quote is attributed to Charles A. Dederich, who was famous for founding Synanon in the 1950s, a Californian self-help community for alcoholics and drug users. A recovered addict himself, Dederich received much praise for his tough-love leadership, and the members all lived together in a commune. He created the Synanon "Game" where members were free to speak their mind with no restrictions. The group eventually morphed into more of a religious cult in the mid-'70s, and Dederich was involved with a scandal where an L.A. lawyer who had fought against Synanon was bitten by a four-foot rattlesnake hiding in his mailbox. In 1980, Dederich and two others pleaded no contest, and as a part of the bargain, gave up his control of Synanon. The group disbanded in 1991 due to financial issues, and Dederich died in 1997.

COOL FACTS: The Stephen Sondheim musical *Into The Woods* is about a baker and his wife who are left childless due to a witch's curse. The baker heads off on a journey into the woods, interacting with the characters of different fairy tales (Cinderella, Jack and the Beanstalk, Rapunzel, Little Red Riding Hood) as he attempts to break the spell. Also, this is the episode that prompted the name "Stargazers" for the Alex/Isabel fans.

MUSIC: Edwin's "Theories" is playing at the beginning as the couple make out in the pickup truck. It continues as Maria and Liz discuss the camping trip at the Crashdown. We hear Billy White Trio's "Diamond" as Maria sports her aqua bra. "Stranded" by Plumb plays when Liz's father walks in on her half-dressed. Matthew Sweet's song "Faith In You" is on at the Crashdown when Michael tells the others he believes River Dog is their father. When Maria tells Liz that Max has been staring at her, "Everything You Want" by Vertical Horizon is playing. Van Morrison's "Sometimes I Feel Like A Motherless Child" plays when the sheriff goes to visit his father.

1.13 The Convention

ORIGINAL AIR DATE: February 2, 2000
WRITTEN BY: Emily Whitesell
DIRECTED BY: Tucker Gates

GUEST CAST: Jonathan Frakes (as himself), Tom Bower (Everett Hubble), John Cullum (James Valenti, Sr.), Kevin Weisman (Larry), Wendle Josepher (Jennifer), Diane Farr (Amy

DeLuca), Deron Michael McBee (Ray, the wrestler), Paul Tigue (Zinaplox), Andy Morrow (Boy at Info Booth)

The annual UFO *convention brings a variety of alien fanatics to town, including the legendary alien hunter Everett Hubble, who is out for revenge.*

"The Convention" really covers the whole spectrum, from romantic moments to intense ones. At times, it has the feeling of an old Western, where the embittered cowboy comes back into town to finish up old business. It seems Max, Michael, and Isabel aren't the only ones looking for answers about their past. The sheriff has his own mystery to solve.

The introduction of Everett Hubble is a great way to bring the sheriff and the teens together. It's also a nice way to continue with Jim's storyline from "Into the Woods." Like Captain Ahab chasing *Moby Dick*, Hubble has spent the majority of his life tracking the fourth alien, determined to bring him down at any cost. Hubble's past is pockmarked, however, with his obsession leading to the downfall of the ex-sheriff — Jim's father. Right from the beginning, the animosity Jim Valenti feels towards Hubble is apparent. The problem is, Hubble has one thing that Jim wants: answers. Tom Bower's subtle shifts in character, from being cold and mysterious to devious and manipulative, to vulnerable and tired, are excellent. He is a great match for Bill Sadler, who also displays various emotional levels as his character works to uncover the truth behind that fateful night in 1972. It's the young cowboy carefully eyeing the old, trying to figure out his game.

Jim's journey is compelling as well, allowing him to truly connect with his father from whom he was estranged for years. Dealing with a senile parent is a difficult situation, especially when you need answers. Jim keeps his frustration in check, showing his father tenderness in small ways. It's as though his eyes are opening for the first time, and he's finally seeing the light. Adults who try their whole lives to be different from their parents often find themselves discovering they aren't that different at all. In Jim's case, he needs to relive his father's obsession in order to understand why James Sr. abandoned him so many years before. John Cullum does a good job portraying the old, weak sheriff who moves from conscious thought to irrelevant rambling.

Having the final showdown at Peppers, the old store where Hubble's wife was murdered, is a nice touch. Cutting from old black and white shots of the scene in 1972 to the present day not only gives a clear picture of the past, but reinforces Hubble's haunted personality. While Max and Michael are there, the scene is really about Jim and Hubble, both out for vindication. A fabulous scene, we finally see Jim in a new light, stepping away from his father's path and finding his own. His final words to Max and Michael are from a new man, one who will not sacrifice his life or family for an obsession.

Max distracts himself with more work for the ever-amusing alien fanatic, Milton. This involves catering to Jonathan Frakes, and trying to convince Hubble to sit on the panel. It's very obvious that Jonathan Frakes has a blast portraying himself as a complete egomaniac. Max's interaction with Hubble, however, has a completely different tone. Hubble baits Max with promises of providing answers to his "alien" questions, and we get to see Max as a frightened teenager. When he lays into Jim, he tosses aside any logic, hitting home with his comments about Kyle. Considering all the pressure Max has been under — much of it self-induced — it's great to finally see him break and allow Michael to be the calm, rational one.

In the tradition of an old Western, "The Convention" provides us with a villain, a showdown after sunset, and a hero who prevails. Look out, Roswell, there's a new sheriff in town.

FLASH: The masked wrestler who comes to Amy's rescue.

IRKS: Where's Kyle in all of this? Last we see of him, he fights with his father out in Frazier Woods. Now, Jim is spending all of his time bonding with his father, but hasn't (to our knowledge) mended any bridges with his son. There could have been some really interesting scenes with Kyle while Jim works on the whole mystery of the Silo shooting. I'd also love to know what happens with the FBI. Topolsky may have disappeared, but I would've thought the sighting in the previous episode would really pique their interest.

DOUBLE TAKE: Larry states the Crashdown shooting took place on September 17. In the pilot, Liz opens by saying it's September 23, and how five days earlier, she died. Five days earlier would be September 18, not 17.

ALIENISMS: Michael causes a rash to form on Larry, making him extremely itchy (as seen in "Leaving Normal"). Max makes the gun slide across the sand. We discover "Nasedo" has killed more than once.

SODA MOMENT: While in the Café, Jennifer is reading *Men Are From Mars, Women Are From Venus*. The book by Dr. John Gray, published in 1992 by HarperCollins, explores how men and women are inherently different, using an interplanetary allegory.

COOL FACTS: The "Hubble" name is important in the space industry. The Hubble Space Telescope has been revolutionary in the efforts to further understand space. Orbiting 370 miles above the earth, it uses powerful optics and state-of-the-art instruments, bringing us incredible views of the stars. Designed in the '70s, it first launched in 1990. Its modular design allows astronauts to service and upgrade its technology in space. It also uses solar panels to convert sunlight into electricity, and is controlled through radio antennas.

MUSIC: "Waiting for the Aliens" by the Toys plays at the beginning with Max in the alien costume. Pennywise's "Alien" is on when Jennifer and Larry enter the diner. "Planet Claire" by the B-52s plays at the UFO Center when Max asks for more responsibility. When Liz approaches Max at the info booth, we hear "Calling All Occupants of Interplanetary Craft" by Klaatu. "Miserable" by Lit plays while Jennifer confides in Liz. Owsley's "Coming Up Roses" is on when the women gripe about men in the Crashdown. Finally, we hear Sheryl Crow's "My Favorite Mistake" when Larry tells Jennifer he's ready to marry her.

1.14 Blind Date

ORIGINAL AIR DATE: February 9, 2000
WRITTEN BY: Thania St. John
DIRECTED BY: Keith Samples

GUEST CAST: Matt Walden (as himself), James O'Shea (Doug Shellow), Michael Yurchak (KROZ DJ), Jonathan David Bouck (Markos), Derrex Brandy (Chris), Ben Busch (Nicky), Patricia Skeriotis (Female Talent Judge), Joshua Hutchinson (Male Talent Judge)

Liz wins the local radio station's Blind Date contest, causing Kyle and Max to get drunk and bond. Meanwhile, Michael and Isabel send Nasedo a sign.

"What's so great about normal?" Max asks Liz. Good question. "Blind Date" is the cream of the crop as far as *Roswell* episodes go. While it is certainly in the top five "romantic" episodes, it's also one of the funniest. "Blind Date" isn't all sugar, however; the reality of teenage drinking does come into play. Still, the romantic moments make up for the lack of Max/Liz time since he put the kibosh on their relationship in "The Balance."

Kyle seizes the opportunity to bond with Max. First he approaches him at school, then later shows up at his house with some of his buddies. Drunk and about to drive once more, he lures Max to join them by making him the designated driver. This episode may use drinking as a way to elicit humor, but in many ways, it's sad that Max is only able to express his true feelings when he is drunk. That seems to be an unfortunate reality for a lot of teenagers and adults. So, while it is wonderful to see Max acting silly and "teenage" for a change, it's too bad that it is only as a result of alcohol.

Jason and Nick manage to play off each other very well, creating a lot of really amusing moments as they go on their drunken journey. Kyle, especially, has some brilliant lines. His reaction to Max's decision that they win Liz back is great: "Well, how do we split her up, exactly? Every other week? Mondays, Wednesdays, Fridays, alternate Saturdays?" Instead of competing with him, however, Kyle plays bodyguard. This episode really takes advantage of Nick's talent for comedy. While Kyle is a funny drunk, Max almost regresses into a child. There's an innocence to his love, like a boy with a crush, and he abandons his fear of exposure and his responsible nature. Instead, he wants to escape with Liz, run away and embrace anonymity. Like many young people, Max shoulders a lot of heavy responsibility that he never asked for. It's no wonder he longs to take off.

Liz seems to be pushed and pulled in every direction in "Blind Date." Her life is taken out of her hands and immediately run by a contest. Considering she really didn't want to be in this situation at all, her passivity seems a bit uncharacteristic. Not only that, but she follows instructions without arguing. However, she does a great job trying to look after Max when she discovers he's drunk. While she's obviously moved by the romance of it all, she does keep a realistic perspective, recognizing that the alcohol is a factor. James O'Shea's performance as Doug is fine, but there are some issues. First of all, he is a college student — making him much older than Liz. Secondly, like Liz, Doug is hoping to just have a normal date, but that seems to be a silly remark considering the whole situation is set up through a radio contest. It's obvious that his character is only there to act as a catalyst for Max and Kyle, and to show Liz that maybe "normal" isn't what she wants after all.

Alex and Maria bond in this episode as Maria replaces the lead singer in Alex's garage band "The Whits." This episode allows both Majandra and Colin to show off their musical talents. (The other band members certainly don't look like high school students, which they are supposed to be.) Majandra does a great version of the Phil Collins song "In the Air Tonight." Michael and Isabel continue the sci-fi storyline as Michael decides to take matters into his own hands. As with Maria and Alex, it's good to explore the dynamic between Michael and Isabel without Max. Michael's intelligent and in-depth analysis of the hieroglyphs is a great touch. After all, he's never at school and is often painted as a character who tends not to think things through.

"Blind Date" takes us on the roller coaster ride of teenage romance, and leaves us wanting more. It's clear in its statement that reality always returns, and while the reality we have is not always the one we want, we still can make the best of it. "Blind Date" is arguably in the top three best episodes of season one.

FLASH: Kyle wrestling Doug onto the bed, only to have the DJ and his crew walk in on them. And, of course, the famous Max line: "You're my dream girl, Liz."

Brendan, Shiri, and Majandra helping to build a home for Habitat for Humanity (Photo by Christina Radish)

IRKS: The fact that Michael and Max are *always* arguing is getting to be a bit repetitive. Thus far, I think the only thing they have agreed upon involves not telling Diane Evans the truth about who they are. Kyle doesn't seem to find it strange that Max manages to get so drunk so quickly off one sip of alcohol. Also, Liz's parents are absent for the entire episode, which is a bit odd considering a radio station camps out in their restaurant, and their daughter is going on a date with a college guy they don't know. And wine with dinner? That's not only unlikely, but illegal, considering Liz is a sophomore in *high school*. And finally, does no one *live* in Roswell? The streets are always empty at night, which is convenient. I guarantee the whole town is *not* at the Blind Date concert.

DOUBLE TAKE: At the concert, Maria takes the microphone out of the stand. Moments later, it's back in the stand again.

ALIENISMS: Michael recognizes the constellation from his vision as the zodiac sign of Aries. By placing a map of Roswell under the constellation in April, when Aries is directly overhead, the symbols from the map all indicate locations in Roswell. Isabel removes the burn marks from the grass. Max gets drunk from one sip of alcohol, disappears for the first time, then manages to get up on an awning. He paints a heart on Liz's wall with his hand and later makes it glow, superimposes his face onto a photograph, makes a street lamp reflect like a disco ball, causes parking meters to spark like mini-fireworks, and almost turns Doug into a blond. (He had a busy night!) A mystery man sets the symbol aflame once more.

SODA MOMENT: Kyle calls Liz a "man-eater." He's referring to the 1980s hit "Maneater" by Hall and Oates. The song is about a woman in a relationship for the money, not for love.

COOL FACTS: While "K" is the first letter of the radio stations in Roswell, there is no station KROZ.

MUSIC: "Anything, Anything (I'll Give You)" by Dramarama plays in the Crashdown just before the contest winner is announced. At school, while Liz and Maria talk about the blind date, "Is Anybody Home?" by Our Lady Peace is playing. Joe 90's "Truth" is on at the Crashdown when Michael talks of Nasedo. "Adam's Song" by Blink-182 plays in Isabel's room just before Michael arrives. As Liz gets ready for her date, "24/7" by Kevon Edmonds plays. "Stand By My Woman" by Lenny Kravitz plays when Max and Kyle see Doug and Liz in the restaurant. At the end, Majandra Delfino sings the Phil Collins song "In the Air Tonight."

1.15 Independence Day

ORIGINAL AIR DATE: February 16, 2000
WRITTEN BY: Toni Graphia
DIRECTED BY: Paul Shapiro

GUEST CAST: Diane Farr (Amy DeLuca), Garrett M. Brown (Philip Evans), Mary Ellen Trainor (Diane Evans), Robert F. Lyons (Hank Whitmore), Robert Katims (Judge Robert Lewis)

Max and Isabel finally discover Michael's foster father is abusing him.

"Independence Day" deals with the very human issue of child abuse. This episode also looks at different aspects of responsibility, which also ties in with Michael's situation. It allows us to further understand Michael's guarded nature and his buried hurt.

Unable to heal his black eye, Michael's secret comes out, first to Max, and finally to the rest of the group. This is probably Brendan's best episode to date, as he really captures the essence of an abused teenager. He covers his embarrassment with a gruff tone, instructing Max to keep his secret because he doesn't want pity. Concerned, Max tells Isabel, which only makes Michael feel worse. While they try to come up with solutions for him, none of them are feasible. Finally, he agrees to stay at their house for a couple of days.

Two of the most powerful scenes in this episode involve Michael's interaction with the Evans family. He's obviously kept his distance from their parents, but not enough that they have a problem with him staying over. His inability to fit in with their family habits at dinner makes him stand out and seem ignorant of table manners. Later, when playing Monopoly, Michael's vulnerability comes through when he is unable to pay when he lands on Mr. Evans' square. Michael first attempts to brush it off as a game, but Mr. Evans is a man who plays by the rules. Having grown up with Hank's abuse, Michael masks his embarrassment with a defensive tone and takes off. After one more final blow-out with Hank, Michael finds himself homeless. His hurt is very real, and he is unable to share it with either Max or Isabel, who both tend to treat him like a child.

What is interesting here is the way the different characters react to Michael's situation. Isabel immediately starts to mother him, while simultaneously accusing him of being a child. When she threatens to kill Hank, it only makes things worse. She wants to take responsibility *for* him, which of course, won't help the situation. Max, on the other hand, tries to prevent Isabel from smothering Michael, even though he was the one to tell her about the situation in the first place. He steps back, wanting to help Michael but unsure of how to do it. He recognizes that a lot of Michael's behavior is due to his rough childhood experiences, and that it cannot be fixed in one night. Instead of trying to stop Michael from leaving, he allows Michael to make his own decision. In the past Max has always taken responsibility for Michael; it's a nice change to see him treat Michael like an adult.

Maria really shows her maturity in "Independence Day." When she looks out her window and sees Michael out in the rain, she brings him in and lets him cry without needing any explanation. It's a perfect instance of someone being responsible to Michael, rather than trying to take responsibility *for* him.

Michael finally comes of age, recognizing that it is time for him to take responsibility for his own life. He has two choices: he can run away or he can step forward and ask for help. He learns that reaching out to others doesn't always lead to rejection and hurt. In essence, while he seems to be alone, he is never alone. So many abused children struggle with feelings of guilt and isolation, as seen in "Independence Day." However, with love, support, and time, it is possible to heal.

FLASH: Maria and Liz catching Amy and Jim Valenti making out.

IRKS: It's hard to believe that Hank Whitmore would ever be allowed to be a foster parent, unless somewhere along the line he changed drastically. It also seems rather fast to have Michael declared as an emancipated minor when Mr. Evans claims it's a complicated process. Also, it's a little upsetting that Michael decides to take off without saying goodbye to Maria, or thank you for that matter (didn't he learn anything in "The Toy House"?).

DOUBLE TAKE: When Michael is throwing stones by the train tracks, something falls out of his pocket which does not get retrieved.

ALIENISMS: Liz tells Maria she had visions when she kissed Max in the previous episode. Max heals Michael's bruise. In a fit of anger, Michael causes a chair to move across the trailer and smash, and wind to break through the windows and push Hank's gun to the wall.

SODA MOMENT: Maria is really following in her "hippy" mother's footsteps, and getting into the whole "herbal remedy" experience. First, it was sniffing cedar oil to calm her nerves. This time she's using drops of "Grief Relief" in order to clear her mind of Michael. According to spiritherbs.com, "Grief Relief" allows the user to experience emotions, and quit over-intellectualizing everything. The contents include organic Nasturtium flowers, wildcrafted blackberry leaves, wildcrafted Queen Anne's Lace flower essence, and organic Burdock root.

COOL FACTS: Robert Katims (the judge) is creator Jason Katims's father.

MUSIC: Euphoria's "Delirium" is playing when Liz tells Maria what kissing Max is like. "Hand" by Jars of Clay plays in the Crashdown when Amy arrives with the pies. When Maria and Amy discuss men in Maria's bedroom, "Detour" by Bis is on. "Run" by Collective Soul plays while Michael is standing in the rain. Radford's "Closer to Myself" is on at the Crashdown when Isabel tells Maria about Michael. Finally, "40 Miles From the Sun" by Bush plays as Michael tries to hitchhike out of town.

1.16 Sexual Healing

ORIGINAL AIR DATE: March 1, 2000
WRITTEN BY: Jan Oxenberg
DIRECTED BY: David Semel

GUEST CAST: Jo Anderson (Nancy Parker), Mary Ellen Trainor (Diane Evans), Dan Martin (Principal), Michael Chieffo (Mr. Seligman), John Doe (Geoff Parker), Garrett M. Brown (Philip Evans), Rosie Taravella (Gym Teacher), Fernando Negrette (Nasedo).

When both Max and Liz start having visions when they kiss, they decide to take their relationship to the next level.

And we thought "Heat Wave" was a hot episode! "Sexual Healing" is really a vehicle for Max and Liz to make out for an hour. There are a few extra plot elements that advance the story, otherwise this episode was essentially about steamy passion and making up for lost time.

We've returned to Liz's voice-over framework. In a provocative opening (to rival Michael and Maria's in "Heat Wave"), Max and Liz toss aside the whole "just friends" thing and start making out in the back room of the Crashdown. Strawberries fall to the ground in slow motion. Liz moans with pleasure, literally seeing visions of stars. We've just begun the "Sexual Healing" journey.

The premise is that Liz's visions follow the journey Max's ancestors must have taken. First they begin in outer space. Then, she witnesses the crash. Then, the army is crawling around the area. But instead of providing answers, the experience prompts a lot of questions. What will the final vision be? Why, all of a sudden, is Liz having such precise, vivid flashes of Max's past? In "Pilot," Max helps Liz see visions of himself as a child, but now she's seeing them without his help. It's not just the passionate kisses that evoke images, but his touch on her skin. And why does Liz's hickey glow, when Maria's hickey from "Heat Wave" is perfectly normal? Also, what inspires Max to suddenly succumb to his passions, after fighting them for so long? Everything is happening very fast, which, in some ways, is the point. Liz has thrown logic to one side in order to lose herself in her physical pleasure. From that standpoint, it's believable. Liz, however, is practically having orgasms when Max touches her hand. She's certainly being vocal about the situation — it's like watching an Herbal Essence commercial. Liz's sexual awakening seems to coincide with her rebelliousness. This could have had a smoother transition, but every Liz and Max fan out there has been waiting for this to happen, so why argue the point? This episode is worth watching even if it's just to hear Max's confession to Liz in the girl's locker room.

Michael's intense fascination with Max and Liz's visions is great. He's so intrigued that he and Maria try to give it a go themselves. It's interesting how at the beginning of the season, Michael and Maria are the hot and steamy couple, while Liz and Max have more subtle, romantic moments. Now, things are trading off, allowing Maria and Michael to slowly open up to one another. In a lot of ways, Michael and Maria's relationship mirrors that of many teens. It begins in passion, and slowly grows to a more serious, emotional level. Intrigued by Liz's visions, Isabel gets into the action as well, although the results of her "experiment" are inconclusive.

It seems that Max and Liz are out to face the world together, totally enraptured with each other. That concept works, because even the most responsible teenagers can let relationships consume them. The world becomes about them, not everyone else. "Sexual Healing" really illustrates that theme, and gives us some other interesting illustrations as well.

FLASH: Michael and Isabel setting the mood in Michael's apartment for Liz's arrival.

IRKS: The FBI has completely disappeared. I'm surprised that Max isn't concerned with what he might have said to Kyle the night he got drunk. After all, he doesn't remember what he said to Liz. Wouldn't he be worried that he exposed his secret to Kyle? How many teachers leave their students *alone* for detention? And haven't the school staff realized that the janitor's closet and eraser room might be better off locked? Finally, how is it that Michael, an unemployed high school student with no money to his name, can afford an apartment? There's no explanation for it whatsoever.

DOUBLE TAKE: Isabel is unpacking a brown bag in Michael's kitchen. Suddenly it disappears and she starts polishing a glass.

ALIENISMS: Liz and Max both see visions of each other's past when they kiss. Max makes

Liz's skin glow when he touches it. Michael sees visions of Maria as a child. Isabel snaps her fingers, causing a bunch of candles to spontaneously glow with light. Max and Liz discover an oval-shaped metal object with the Whirlwind symbol from Isabel's necklace on it.

SODA MOMENT: Michael makes reference to the singer Chaka Khan. She is known for her '70s hit "I'm Every Woman" and has performed session work with Quincy Jones, Prince, and David Bowie. W.G. Snuffy Walden, an original composer for *Roswell*, once toured with Chaka Khan.

MUSIC: When Max and Liz make out at the Crashdown, and the strawberries fall, "Sex and Candy" by Marcy Playground is on. Tara MacLean's "If I Fall" plays when Liz tells Maria of her first vision. We hear "Youth" by Addict at Michael's apartment when Maria comes to apologize. Finally, Sarah McLachlan's "Fumbling Towards Ecstasy" plays at the end as Liz and Max walk towards the Crashdown.

1.17 Crazy

ORIGINAL AIR DATE: April 10, 2000
WRITTEN BY: Thania St. John
DIRECTED BY: James Whitmore Jr.

GUEST CAST: Julie Benz (Kathleen Topolsky), Kevin Cooney (Dr. Margolin), Yelyna De Leon (Senor Chow Hostess), Hugh Benjamin (Flower Delivery Guy)

A crazed Topolsky returns to Roswell to warn Max Evans and the other kids about the FBI *alien hunter Pierce. And there's a new girl in town . . .*

"Just act like normal kids" seems to be the theme of "Crazy." Topolsky wants them to act that way, Max feels it is good advice — even the sheriff seems to be on the bandwagon for this one. Normal kids should ignore the advice of a crazy woman who had previously been tracking them, trying to prove they were not of this Earth. Trust is also a major theme in this episode. Do you trust the enemy you know, or the enemy you don't?

Max and Liz continue to be completely absorbed with each other, so much so that Liz just starts making out with Max in the Café, unconcerned that she's supposed to be working. Later, Topolsky bangs on the jeep window at Buckley Point, tells them they are in danger, and runs off. Neither Max nor Liz seem particularly shocked by her presence, which is really out-of-character taking into account the fact that a) Topolsky is an FBI agent who was investigating them, and b) she disappeared seven episodes ago. The question remains, is Topolsky telling the truth, or is this another trap? Still unsure, they decide to follow her advice and just act like "normal teenage kids."

Julie Benz does a good job as the terrified agent, leaving the audience to wonder if she's really crazy, or if, in her traumatized state, she is telling the truth and wants to protect the teens. While her paranoia is believable, her description of Pierce, the vicious FBI agent, doesn't really paint that scary a picture. It's also a little unbelievable that, as an intelligent agent, she doesn't just disguise herself fully and act in a more calculated manner. One could also argue that the trauma of being questioned by Agent Pierce has, indeed, driven her around the bend.

Part of acting like normal kids involves relationship exploration. "Crazy" really highlights the difference between Michael and Maria's relationship and Max and Liz's. Liz gets gifts and romantic dinners from her considerate boyfriend. Maria just wants to be able to hold hands and kiss in public. When the two couples double date, however, the differences are glaring. First of all, I can't imagine that Michael is so dense. He obviously wants to make an effort or he wouldn't have asked Max for advice. So where did this whole performance come from? Not only that, but why *does* Maria want to be with him if Michael really can't give her what she wants? Still, these two manage to have their tender moments, and obviously do care for one another.

The mounting tension between Max and Michael comes to a head in this episode. Michael breaks Max's trust, which provokes Max, and yet Max refuses to listen to Michael's instincts, which have proven to be right in the past. Maria makes the statement that is essentially Michael's biggest issue: "It's not just about you! What you do affects me. That's how relationships work." These words could just as easily have come from either Isabel or Max. Seems Michael's lesson in life is to stop and consider the people around him before acting on impulse.

Then there's the new element: Tess. A sexy blond who knows it, Tess reads Isabel like a book. Right from the start it's apparent that Tess is going to be an interesting character. Her predatory looks aimed at Max only confirm it. With the sheriff's new insights, Topolsky's paranoid ramblings, and the appearance of Tess, "Crazy" shows us that it's no longer clear who to trust.

FLASH: Alex telling Isabel he'd do anything to protect her.

IRKS: Liz's parents have disappeared once more. Considering their daughter is out all night with Max, one would think her parents wouldn't be too keen on Liz kissing Max during work, then ditching her shift to go be with him. Liz takes off her apron and leaves, but when did waitresses start taking off before cashing out?

DOUBLE TAKE: When Michael is cooking in the Crashdown kitchen, there's another guy in there with him. Suddenly, the guy is no longer there, and we never actually see him leave.

ALIENISMS: The orb Max and Liz discover in the desert is apparently a communicator that only works when it is paired with a second one . . . which the FBI has.

SODA MOMENT: Maria refers to Liz and Max as "Gidget" and "Moondoggie," which are characters from the 1959 surf movie *Gidget* starring Sandra Dee and James Darren. Dark-haired Moondoggie saves Gidget's life twice, causing her to fall in love with him. *Gidget* then became a television series from 1965–66 starring Sally Field.

MUSIC: When Max arrives at the Crashdown, Angela Via's "Picture Perfect" is playing. "Take Your Time" by Lori Carson plays in Michael's apartment while he makes out with Maria. "Gypsy Queen" by 7th House is on when Tess joins Isabel and Alex for lunch. "Don't Stop" by Radford plays when the flowers arrive at the Crashdown for Liz. Finally, we hear "She Gave Me Love" by Get Away People on the double date at the Mexican restaurant.

1.18 Tess, Lies & Videotape

ORIGINAL AIR DATE: April 17, 2000
WRITTEN BY: Richard Whitley and Toni Graphia
DIRECTED BY: Paul Shapiro

GUEST CAST: Jim Ortlieb (Ed Harding), Michael Chieffo (Mr. Seligman), Kevin Cooney (Dr. Margolin)

Max starts having sexual fantasies about Tess that are out of his control, while the gang starts to suspect Tess isn't what she appears to be.

While "Tess, Lies & Videotape" provides us with more questions and few answers, it still has a great suspenseful element. When it rains, it pours. Not only is the FBI back in the picture full force, but the army is mentioned, and the sheriff has the orb/communicator. Not to mention the appearance of Tess and Ed Harding, who are obviously up to something. And just two episodes ago their biggest problem is finding different places to make out!

It seems the group isn't following their own advice. Last episode, Max makes the statement that Michael's apartment is the only safe place to discuss alien-related issues. The Crashdown Café is now the latest home base. Interesting choice, considering it is a public diner and anyone can hear them . . . like Tess for instance. Tess plays innocent, but almost *too* innocent, which of course, makes her seem guilty. Emilie de Ravin puts on the sugar when Max is around, but it's apparent that there is some serious manipulation going on.

Tess and Ed Harding's behavior feels straight out of *The Twilight Zone* or *The Stepford Wives* when Liz is at their home. Their almost comically false sincerity is so creepy, you expect them to bash Liz over the head and drag her off somewhere. Jim Ortlieb does a fabulous job of making Ed Harding feel threatening while wearing a smile. One minute he's acting like a sitcom dad while inviting Liz to dinner, and the next he's harshly telling Liz to back off, and glaring suspiciously when the doorbell rings. And the huge mound of mashed potatoes on his plate only enhances the disturbing image. All in all, if the writers are striving to show Tess and Ed as suspicious, possibly dangerous characters, they succeed admirably.

Jason Behr makes Max's emotional torment completely believable as he struggles with his compulsive attraction to Tess. Sometimes, as much as a person loves someone, they feel connected to someone else, which completely tears them apart. When talking to Michael, Jason really conveys how ashamed Max is for these fantasies he's having. Max comes to Michael, desperately torn, looking for a friend. Their relationship is damaged, however. Max's news about Tess only causes him to lose Michael's admiration. Considering Max is always trying to do the right thing, it's an interesting change to see him screw up.

Liz proves herself to be an honorable character in "Tess, Lies & Videotape." She defends Max right from the start, even when Maria notes the strange sexual tension between Max and Tess. Obviously upset by the new circumstances, it doesn't stop her from stepping up to the plate to help discover the truth about the Hardings. So much of Max and Liz's relationship has caused them to be isolated from the group, so it's nice to see Liz's commitment to the group goes beyond her feelings for Max.

"Tess, Lies & Videotape" is an important episode because it opens up a whole new can of worms, giving the actors a lot to work with. While there are still many questions floating about, the compelling new elements make the answers worth waiting for. Normalcy just left the building.

FLASH: The gang watching Tess recreate the Buddha statue.

IRKS: If he knows the FBI is after Max, why would the sheriff return the orb to Max in broad daylight in a public place? It's also a little weird to see him taking photographs at the end. Are we to assume that he might still be a bad guy? That's not the impression we've gotten from the previous few episodes. The army crew storming into the house is a bit strange and never explained, even if Ed Harding does work for the military.

DOUBLE TAKE: The news tells us that six people die in the fire — in total. Later, the Sheriff refers to Pierce killing "Topolsky and six innocent people."

ALIENISMS: Max has flashes of the large hieroglyphs and of himself with Tess in the desert when he looks at her in the Crashdown and later when he kisses her. Tess repairs the broken Buddha statue using her powers.

SODA MOMENT: The title is a play on the Steven Soderbergh film *Sex, Lies & Videotape* starring James Spader, Andie MacDowell, Peter Gallagher, and Laura San Giacomo. The film looks at intense, powerful, forbidden attractions between people. Appropriate reference? I think so. Also, Max puts up the sign "TRUST NO ONE" which is a reference to Mulder's motto on *The X-Files*.

COOL FACTS: The news reporter is the *Roswell* writer/co-executive producer Thania St. John.

MUSIC: When Tess arrives at the Crashdown, "Everlong" by the Foo Fighters is on. "6 Underground" by the Sneaker Pimps plays in Max's fantasy when he makes out with Tess in the science classroom. We hear Lit's "Zip-Lock" when Michael, Max, and Isabel discuss the miniature camera. "Voodoo" by Godsmack plays when Michael makes the "new girlfriend" comment.

1.19 Four Square

ORIGINAL AIR DATE: April 24, 2000
WRITTEN BY: Thania St. John
DIRECTED BY: Jonathan Frakes

GUEST CAST: Jim Ortlieb (Ed Harding), Mary Ellen Trainor (Diane Evans), Henriette Mantel (Secretary), Daniel Hansen (young Max), Zoë Nutter (young Isabel), Nicholas Stratton (young Michael)

Believing Tess to be Nasedo, the group keeps a close watch on her actions. Meanwhile, Isabel and Michael find themselves plagued by strange dreams.

"I mean, did you feel like something inside of you was changing . . . like waking up?" Isabel's comment sums up the themes in "Four Square." Suddenly, Max, Isabel, and Michael are awakening to their alien sides, and are not sure they are ready for it. Like a teenager on the brink of adulthood, there may be some hesitation to let go of childhood, yet a simultaneous compulsion to move forward. This episode can be considered a metaphor for puberty: it's awkward enough to change, but in their case, they don't know what comes next. After all this time of wanting answers, Isabel, Michael, and Max are about to get them. The question is, do they still want them?

After witnessing Tess's powers, it is assumed that she is Nasedo, the shapeshifter. If only things were that easy. Isabel comes forth, claiming that she too, feels that Tess has some sort of control over her. It's Michael who seems the most willing to trust Tess, and yet, ironically, in Max's vision later on, it is Michael who is first to leave the cave, with Tess behind them. No wonder Tess feels the need to belong when Max had chosen Isabel and Michael over her so long ago.

The question still hangs in the air — is Tess a friend or foe? She's certainly a foe to Liz — she openly declares to Isabel that she feels she is "destined" to be with Max. And just when we think Michael is impervious to Tess, she shows him the four-square symbol, and he has a vision of leaving Pohlman Ranch as a child. This episode really plays with reality, leaving the audience to scratch their heads and ask, "Just what is she doing?"

"Four Square" spends a lot of time in the dream world, exploring an inner history that Isabel and Michael specifically, aren't prepared to deal with. When the dreams become too realistic, Isabel and Michael are faced with a possible problem that cannot be ignored. The writers do a good job of bringing them together to console one another, and the dream sequences are sensual and visually compelling. Giant hieroglyphs mark the yellow sand. Isabel stands in the desert wearing a black taffeta strapless ballgown, and is beckoned by Michael, looking dark and brooding as always. Stunning.

It seems the further we go into season one, the more the teens remember of their first days. Max remembers both Isabel and Michael in the chamber, which is different from what he says in "The Balance." Isabel's visions of the present-day Michael begin with him in that same position, defiantly standing on the edge, watching her. While more is being revealed to the teens, less is being shared. Both Max and Michael lie to each other regarding alien information, and Isabel and Michael keep the details of their dreams from Max. Michael accuses Max of being afraid of being "alien," while Max turns the tables, accusing Michael of being afraid of being human. Isabel stands up to them both, putting her own needs on the table. Katherine does a great job in this episode, showing both her confusion and fear due to her dreams, and her awkwardness at being unable to share with the guys. Michael and Max don't show her the sensitivity they should, although Michael does redeem himself later in the episode. Max struggles to maintain control over the group, which foreshadows season two.

Liz, Maria, and Alex obviously have no place in this alien journey, even though Max, Michael, and Isabel want them to be part of it. The question is, how much of their desire to hold on to their human relationships has to do with wanting to feel "normal"? Both Michael's and Isabel's actions towards Maria and Alex seem to come from desperation over genuine desire. Tess may flirt with Kyle, but she's using him for her own amusement. Liz stays by Max's side, yet the minute she isn't there, he takes off with Tess. This makes us wonder, will following their destiny force them to let go of their human relationships?

"Four Square" takes the show into an entirely new realm, where science fiction has a more important role than before.

FLASH: Liz's reaction to Tess's grade point average.

IRKS: We have such a brouhaha when Max and Liz stay out all night in "Sexual Healing," and yet Isabel, Alex, and Maria are out all night in this episode and no one seems to care. I would have thought at least Isabel's parents would be on her case. We also delve into the sci-fi mythology a little too quickly, even though adding more science fiction was part of the agreement with The WB if they took the show back on. How do Isabel and Michael know where to find Tess and Max at the end of the episode?

DOUBLE TAKE: Young Isabel's hair is much longer than it is in the previous flashbacks.

ALIENISMS: Tess seems to have a mindwarping power, though how it works isn't clear. She is able to manipulate molecular structures like the rest of the aliens. Isabel and Michael have the same dream.

COOL FACTS: Liz and Max investigate the constellation of "Aries the Ram." Of the 12 Zodiacal Constellations, Aries is the first. It marks the Vernal Equinox, which is also the start of spring. The First Point of Aries is where the sun crosses the celestial equator. Now, however, the point has moved into Pisces due to the shift in the Earth's orbit. The constellation of Aries is in view during its opposite season, autumn. The most compelling part of the constellation is the triangle created by the principal stars.

MUSIC: When Maria and Liz talk about Tess in the Crashdown, "No Need to Worry" by Folk Implosion is playing. "Automatic" by Collapsis plays when Liz warns Kyle about Tess.

1.20 Max to the Max

ORIGINAL AIR DATE: May 1, 2000
WRITTEN BY: Toni Graphia
DIRECTED BY: Patrick Norris

GUEST CAST: David Conrad (Deputy Fisher), Jim Ortlieb (Ed Harding/Nasedo), Jason Peck (Deputy Hanson), Stephen O'Mahoney (Agent Norris), Jacob Bruce (Agent Samuels), Drinda La Lumia (Woman at the Carnival), Gordon Haight (Announcer)

Nasedo shapeshifts into Max and kidnaps Liz in order to trap Agent Pierce and kill him.

The tensions are mounting, and "Max to the Max" once more reminds us that appearances can be deceiving. As Nasedo says, "Don't believe everything you see."

This episode builds up from the previous one, starting right where "Four Square" leaves off. The alien teens not only discover that Tess is one of them, but that they were genetically engineered, rather than born. While the book remains a mystery, one thing is clear: the pictures show that Isabel and Michael are meant to be together, just like Max and Tess. Nasedo is not their father, but a protector. And, unlike them, he has no human elements to him whatsoever. Some answers seem to come into the picture, but there's still a long way to go.

The chase in this episode feels a lot like the one in "285 South," with one pair leading the way, and the rest following one after another. This time, however, the leaders of the pack are Liz and Nasedo. Then, of course, we have the rest of the Pod Squad, the sheriff, and the oh-so-conspicuous FBI agents. The FBI agents continue to have a limited wardrobe as they wander around in their black suits and ties. When will they learn?

One theme that is continually explored is the need for the alien teens to find out who they really are. Who am I? Will I grow up to be like my parents? Or can I change that? The human teens will explore the whole "who am I?" question in season three. Also, with all the internal changes happening to the alien teens, there are continual comments of not "knowing" someone anymore. This is alluding to the all-too-common discovery that people change and no one can truly understand why. It's an aspect of life that the teens are now starting to face. As much as they want to fight it, change is part of *human* nature. And the teens, of course, are half-human. In contrast to their need to discover who they really are is the need to hide *who* they really are, which makes their situation all the more complicated.

The whole concept of having a "destiny" is introduced in "Max to the Max," and later fleshed out in the season finale. At this point, it is a huge matter for the alien teens, who keep getting reminded of it from both Tess, and their dreams. Max believes people make their own destinies, while Tess feels strongly that it's predetermined. Isabel and Michael still haven't decided what they believe. The question of fate or destiny is an interesting debate. Is our life in our hands, or guided by someone else? Ironically, Max is the one who fights it the most, and yet he is the one who ends up right back where he's "supposed" to in season two.

The whole double Max concept puts a twist on the original Dr. Jekyll/Mr. Hyde idea. Dr. Jekyll and Mr. Hyde represent two sides of one person: one has self-control and good intentions, while the second is selfish and violent. In this case, Max is the Dr. Jekyll element, while Nasedo/Max is the Mr. Hyde. Jason Behr really shines in "Max to the Max," managing to mirror Jim Ortlieb's creepy performance as Nasedo. At times he is cold and ruthless. Other times he plays with Liz like a cat would with a trapped mouse. His laissez-faire attitude when he dumps the agent's body by the side of the road is great; and while he may seem casual at times, there is no doubt that he is a threat. Meanwhile, Jason also conveys Max's fear for Liz, and determination to save her, no matter what the cost.

Michael's human side continues to grow. He shows great sensitivity towards Isabel and her potential pregnancy even though he is discouraged at the lack of answers and confused by newfound feelings. At the carnival, he is the first one to reach out and hold Liz when tragedy occurs. Maria and Alex show a maturity beyond their years. The "Maria" from the beginning of the season would have completely flipped upon hearing of Isabel's pregnancy. Instead, she approaches Michael calmly and directly. Instead of getting angry, Alex immediately goes to Isabel to offer his support, no questions asked.

While being dragged around by Nasedo/Max, Liz stays fairly calm. Her dialogue tends to be pretty hokey, however. Telling Nasedo/Max that "you don't even know what Max and I have — we saw into each other's souls" seems utterly pointless. She's justifying her relationship to an alien who has kidnapped her and has no interest about her personal safety. Does she expect to reach him emotionally? Not likely.

"Max to the Max" introduces us to the sheriff's new deputy, Fisher, played by David Conrad. David had a main role in Jason Katims's short-lived series, *Relativity*. *Roswell* was the perfect opportunity for them to work together once more. Fisher comes across as a hardworking young cop, bonding with Jim over a father/son relationship discussion. Considering that every new person that has come to Roswell so far has been a threat, why would Fisher be any different? The stakes keep getting higher, which keeps us on the edge of our seats. The final episodes are building nicely as we head towards the season finale. "Max to the Max" has some great, intense moments, and a fabulous cliffhanger ending.

FLASH: The Mirror Maze hunt.

IRKS: Considering all of the alien topics that have been discussed in Michael's apartment since the camera has been there (apparently, since "Sexual Healing"), why would Isabel's conversation with Michael about Liz's visions ("Sexual Healing") be the one the agent would focus on? While Maria's plan to tell the sheriff that it was Max who kidnapped Liz is a good call, how would they explain it later when they were caught? And how is it that the Crashdown stays in business when the waitresses are constantly leaving? Finally, why would Nasedo even consider handing Liz over to Pierce when that would mean blowing Max's cover?

COOL FACTS: The maze, or labyrinth has existed for over 5,000 years. The first recorded maze was the Egyptian Labyrinth located above Lake Moeris, in the 5th century, B.C. It also served as a temple, and burial site for the rulers of the twelve kingdoms of Egypt.

ALIENISMS: The "Destiny" book has pictures etched in of the teens as they look now, suggesting they were "engineered." Liz has black and white flashes (very cool) of violent images when she kisses Nasedo/Max, helping her tell the difference between the two. Nasedo kills a man with his hand, heats up a gas pump causing it to explode, creates a huge "bat" signal (of the Whirlwind symbol) to attract the FBI, and transforms once more.

SODA MOMENT: It may not have been intentional, but it certainly works. When Nasedo shapeshifts into a clown, he appears quite evil. One of the most famous evil clowns comes from Stephen King's 1986 novel and 1990 television movie *IT*. The story takes place in Derry, Maine, where a group of friends battle a creature that lives in the town sewers, and takes on the shape of their worst nightmares. His most common form, however, is that of a clown called Pennywise.

MUSIC: When Maria hears Michael mention Isabel's pregnancy, 8Stops7's "Question Everything" is playing. "Open Your Eyes" by Guano Apes plays when Nasedo/Max takes Liz from the Crashdown. Beth Hart's "Just a Little Hole" is on when Alex approaches Isabel at the Crashdown. When Max, Michael, and Isabel figure out Nasedo has Liz, "Wave Good-bye" by Chris Cornell is playing. "Aliens" by Tam! is on at the carnival when Liz and Nasedo/Max arrive. Finally, Filter's "Welcome to the Fold" plays when Max follows Liz and Nasedo/Max in the Mirror Maze.

1.21 The White Room — Part One

ORIGINAL AIR DATE: May 8, 2000
WRITTEN BY: Jason Katims, Thania St. John
DIRECTED BY: Jonathan Frakes

GUEST CAST: Jim Ortlieb (Ed Harding/Nasedo), David Conrad (FBI Agent Pierce), Jason Winston George (Agent Mathison), Stephen O'Mahoney (Agent Norris), Jacob Bruce (Agent Samuels), Gunnar Clancey (Agent Bello), Gordon Haight (Announcer)

Max is viciously interrogated in a white-tiled room by Agent Pierce. Isabel, Tess, and Michael attempt to save him, with Nasedo leading the charge.

Every now and then an episode arrives that isn't just great, it's brilliant. "The White Room" is one of those. An edge-of-your-seat episode, it has all the best *Roswell* elements in it — suspense, science fiction, and of course, intense character moments. With a tight script, excellent acting, and funky camera shots, the *Roswell* team has really shown us how inhumane humans can actually be.

The camera work really enhances this episode, from using a handheld camera in the opening sequence to accentuate Max's mounting fear in the white-tiled room, to the fisheye lens used whenever Isabel dreamwalks into Max's mind, enhancing the surreal aspects in the room. The direction and photography support Max's horrible journey as he desperately tries not to go insane.

This has to be Jason's best performance to date. He conveys all the levels of anguish, fear, and terror, with the emotion being unique to each scene. His follow-through with Max's character arc in this episode is outstanding. When Max wails at the image of Liz on the virtual reality screen, it is heartbreaking: he's not leaving this place without severe psychological damage.

There was such a build-up to Agent Pierce, I was concerned that whoever took on the role wouldn't be able to live up to it. David Conrad certainly holds his own, however. His relentless questioning and casual cruelty work nicely opposite Jason Behr's performance. Pierce comes across as a man who truly believes he is ridding the world of an evil. His lack of compassion for Max's human side is brutal, and becomes even worse when Pierce uses it to break Max. The parallels between Nasedo and Pierce really shone through as well. Both Pierce and Nasedo are equally ruthless and cold, each with a single-minded purpose. And of course, each of them feels as though they are justified in their efforts. Both are killers, with a complete distaste for the opposite life form. And both are obsessed with each other for personal reasons. While there is constant reference to the teens having "two sides," Jason Katims is also showing us how aliens and humans are really not that different after all.

Katherine Heigl and Brendan Fehr also give stellar performances in this episode. Isabel's anguish at her brother's pain is heartwrenching. When she reaches out to him, it's as though she physically undergoes his torture. Brendan conveys Michael's frustration well when he struggles to control his powers at Nasedo's demand, and his tenderness shines through when he says goodbye to Maria.

It is pretty apparent that while Tess and Liz are united in their feelings for Max, they are meant to represent two worlds — one human and one alien. While Tess has special powers that can aid in the actual break-in, Liz has powers of her own. She is the one who calls on Valenti. In fact, it is the sheriff who swoops in like Han Solo at the end of *Star Wars* to help the teens. It's a fabulous touch, showing once more that human effort is just as valuable as alien powers.

What Jason Katims really accentuates in this episode is that these characters are all just *kids*. They aren't equipped to deal with extremes like this. And yet, many teenagers grow up learning to cope with horrific situations because they have no choice. These teens are forced to grow up fast, and the characters are dealing with the loss of innocence. Max's situation is obvious, but Isabel's and Michael's more subtle. Isabel, who longs to tell her mother the truth, sees how cruel humans can be when they are driven by fear. Michael finally sees Nasedo for the killer he is and knows he is not the father figure he had longed for.

"The White Room" hits a home run on so many levels. With this kind of quality, it's no surprise the fans rallied to keep the show going.

FLASH: Sheriff Valenti saving the day.

IRKS: Wouldn't the Evanses be concerned about where their son is? While the parent issue obviously can't be dealt with all the time, this could have been an interesting scene for Isabel. How does she lie to them, and more importantly, does she consider telling them the truth? Interesting how alcohol has an extreme effect on the aliens, but Max doesn't react strangely to the drugs Pierce gives him. Perhaps they know better from their experiences with aliens from 1947. The white makeup used to make Max pale doesn't work. Either they should put it on his neck and chest as well, or lose it altogether. It looks strange to have it only on his face. It's also pretty amazing how a simple comb can turn spiked hair into a coifed hair-do, especially if it's under dire circumstances! After undergoing such extreme torture, there could have been more exploration in season two of the psychological after-effects. It's touched upon at times, but for the most part, abandoned.

ALIENISMS: Isabel dreamwalks. Michael changes his fingerprint to match that of a dead agent's. Nasedo apparently boils the insides of individuals to kill them. Tess has the ability to warp minds, making individuals believe they are seeing one thing, when, in reality, it is something different.

SODA MOMENT: "Emotions are a weakness, Michael. Focus." These are Nasedo's words as Michael tries desperately to control his powers. While it isn't a direct reference, the teaching mirrors that of Yoda's in *The Empire Strikes Back* (1980). In order for Luke to access the "force," he needs to focus his energies, letting go of anger, fear, and all other emotions.

MUSIC: Grassy Knoll's "Safe" plays when Isabel first dreamwalks with Max, and we hear Remy Zero's "Yellow Light" when Valenti talks to Liz, Maria, and Alex at the Crashdown.

1.22 Destiny — Part Two

ORIGINAL AIR DATE: May 15, 2000
STORY BY: Thania St. John
WRITTEN BY: Jason Katims; Toni Graphia
DIRECTED BY: Patrick Norris

GUEST CAST: David Conrad (FBI Agent Pierce), Jim Ortlieb (Ed Harding/Nasedo), Genie Francis (Alien Mother), Gunnar Clancey (Agent Bello), Richard Dorton (Agent Levin), Howie Dorough (Man in Car)

The group run from the FBI, *come up with a plan to get rid of Agent Pierce, and take their lives back. Then, their true destiny is revealed . . .*

"The White Room" sets the pace for this episode, which starts off at a breakneck speed and doesn't let up until the end. Fumbling out in the darkness, the gang quickly separate into three cars, agreeing to meet at an old abandoned silver mine in Galitas. The sheriff takes off alone, with Liz and Max in the Jetta, and the others pile into the jeep. Suddenly, shots are fired at the Jetta, forcing Liz and Max off the road. Liz and Max manage to escape, finding solace in an abandoned bus. And that's only the opening!

"Destiny" forces the characters to open their eyes, metaphorically speaking. The personal revelations that come to them throughout this episode will dictate each character's motivations from here on in. "Normal" really doesn't exist anymore. The subtlety involved with each moment is well done: the sheriff taking off his badge, studying it, and then putting it in his pocket; Michael's reaction at his own lethal powers, then his emotional confession to Maria;

Max discovering he is actually a leader with greater responsibility; Liz recognizing she cannot interfere with destiny and backing off. Forced to see the truth of the situation, they don't fight it, but accept it quietly.

Another interesting note is how all of the Pod Squad's actions in this episode foreshadow the end comments from the hologram in the pod chamber. Max, weak as he is, takes on the leadership role once more. Michael stands by his side, acting as his right hand man, and protecting him. Isabel supports her brother, of course. Tess almost seems to lead Isabel, which is an interesting twist. Obviously their previous characteristics are slipping into their new lives.

The sheriff really grows in this episode, with Bill Sadler giving an outstanding performance. From his absolute amazement at seeing Michael's powers to his devastation at Kyle's injury, every moment is strong. Even better are the moments when he approaches Pierce. There are some great bonding moments with both Michael and Max, and his love for Kyle really comes through.

The role-reversal of Max and Pierce works extremely well, with Max coldly repeating Pierce's threats back to him. The whole concept of having the slide show reflecting off him is also a nice touch. Physically, Max recovers quite quickly, though there are serious hints of emotional pain coming through as he grills Pierce. Max's nasty tone is the only hint thus far of potential psychological damage received due to the torture session. In fact, it is Michael who demonstrates more hatred towards Pierce than Max.

Having Mrs. Jonathan Frakes (Genie Francis) play the Alien Mother is a fun idea. Does that mean Will Riker is their Dad? Now that could be interesting.

The season finale of *Roswell* is suspenseful, touching, wraps up a lot of different storylines, and leaves us desperate for more!

FLASH: The *beeping* sound spanning the country, and Howie's line: "It has begun." And Max and Liz's confession in the bus. And Michael's confession to Maria. So many!

IRKS: When did school end? Also I'm really surprised Michael and Isabel (especially) let Max take off with Liz in the Jetta. I would have thought they wouldn't want him out of their sight. And for some reason, Max is able to heal Kyle without asking Kyle to look into his eyes. Nice to see that the FBI is as predictably incompetent as always! Also, it seems that Nasedo has given up his pill-popping habit in the last couple of episodes.

DOUBLE TAKE: Generally, when someone jumps into a river, they get wet. Somehow, Liz and Max manages to stay dry.

ALIENISMS: Tess uses her mindwarping on two different people at once. Isabel manages to dreamwalk without a photo, and with Pierce being awake. Michael uses his powers to stop a Hummer, and to kill Pierce. Max heals Kyle. Using the stones, the four teens heal Nasedo. They also get the communicators to work.

SODA MOMENT: The bluish white projection that appears to the teens in the pod chamber is very reminiscent of a scene from the classic 1978 film, *Superman*. An alien is stranded on earth as a young boy, is aware that he has special powers but has no idea why until he discovers a special chamber, a crystal communicating device, and suddenly is faced with a hologram (bluish white) of a man claiming to be his father. Even the wording feels similar. In both cases, the holograms provide the teens with answers — who they are, why they are where they are, what they need to do next. The same idea applies to them both: they have a greater purpose to fulfill on earth.

COOL FACTS: *Roswell* is one of Howie Dorough's favorite shows. The Backstreet Boy only has one line, but the possibility of him returning had been entertained. Also, the day after the *Roswell* season finale aired, The WB put out an official press release stating that 13 new episodes of *Roswell* had been picked up by the network.

MUSIC: The title song, Dido's "Here With Me," plays at the end when Liz runs off, and the Pod Squad are standing on the rock formation.

SEASON TWO (OCTOBER 2000 — MAY 2001)

2.1 Skin and Bones

ORIGINAL AIR DATE: October 2, 2000
WRITTEN BY: Jason Katims
DIRECTED BY: James A. Contner

GUEST CAST: David Conrad (Nasedo/Agent Pierce), Jim Ortlieb (Nasedo/Ed Harding), Gretchen Egolf (Congresswoman Vanessa Whitaker), Jeremy Davidson (Grant Sorenson), Jason Peck (Deputy Hanson), Sara Downing (Courtney), Austin Tichenor (Dr. Bender), Phil Abrams (Max's Therapist), Dennis Lipscomb (John Shanahan), Kenneth Choi (Engineer #2), Bill Glass (Mitch, Crashdown Tourist), Daniel Fester (Security Guard)
A geologist discovers Agent Pierce's bones out in the desert. Congresswoman Whitaker investi-

gates the strange skeleton, causing the team to band together to fix the problem. It seems a danger-ous new alien group has arrived in Roswell . . .

The much-anticipated season premiere begins at the end of the summer. The teens have had a relatively normal vacation from both school and alien dramatics. Max anxiously awaits Liz's return while Maria attempts to get Michael back into her life. Isabel tells Alex they cannot have a relationship, and yet seems very interested in the (much older) hunky geolo-gist, Grant Sorenson. Nasedo, disguised as Agent Pierce, has disbanded the special FBI unit, which we can only hope means no more nasty FBI investigations in Roswell. Grant's bone discovery causes some ears to perk up, however, namely those of the young, ambitious congresswoman who was once allied with Agent Pierce. So much for normal.

The season premiere introduces some new elements. First is Sorenson, a potential love interest for Isabel (who would immediately be arrested for statutory rape if he even touched her). Second is Congresswoman Whitaker, another sexy, young, ambitious powerhouse who is a threat to the aliens (remember Agent Topolsky?). Then there is Courtney, a young blond-haired waitress at the Crashdown who seems to have a thing for Michael (sound like anyone else we know?). Whitaker seems to be an interesting addition, though having yet another alien-obsessed female out to uncover the truth seems a bit repetitive. We don't know much about Grant or Courtney yet, only that they are here to disrupt the love lives of the teens. Tess shows up to interfere with Max and Liz, so it's fitting we have two more characters to disrupt Michael and Maria and Alex and Isabel.

After finally hearing the "L" word in the season finale, it's a bit upsetting that the couples aren't together. Michael's excuse has changed from needing to be a "stone wall" to the fact that he's "destined to be [a] soldier, and a soldier can't have some chick at home waiting for him." Not terribly original. Then, there's Liz and Max. In season one, Liz is the one who wants a relationship, while Max hesitates. Now the tables have turned: Liz wants to put the past behind her while Max tries to rekindle the flame of their relationship. The problem with Max and Liz is that they are constantly changing their minds, even when they do want to be together. But then again — teenagers do that.

The sheriff is the one who is now most dedicated to the aliens' cause, which is an inter-esting twist. Lying, helping hide a body, faking police reports, and coaching Michael on how to react, he becomes deeply involved, and there's no going back for him. Michael and Jim have a great scene as Michael pours his heart out to Jim in the jail cell, and Jim really takes on a "protective parent" role. Michael also continues to be tormented by his actions in "Destiny," whereas Max appears to have recovered. Aside from the opening scene at the psychiatrist's office (a nice way to remind us of season one events), Max makes no reference to his torture experience; his biggest torture now is being without Liz.

Some other new elements come into play. We hear about the isotope Cadmium-X. The new aliens — the "Skins" — are potentially creepy, and the director uses funky, *Predator*-style visual effects when the Skins are spying on the alien teens. Life in Roswell is returning to its usual chaotic state. Who knows where things will lead? One thing is for sure — we can expect more sci-fi elements and fewer relationship-driven episodes, as ordered by the heads of The WB. The season premiere has its moments, ending with a great cliffhanger, as usual, but it could have been stronger.

FLASH: Maria giving Max a little pep talk about Liz. Nice new blonde locks, by the way.

IRKS: Where is Kyle? Considering the emotional state he must be in, audiences are anxious to see what happens to him, but have to wait another week to find out. Max being in the cyclotron is a bit ridiculous, too. An active cyclotron involves the acceleration of positively charged particles in a *vacuum*, so Max wouldn't have been able to breathe. It's also unbelievable that the computers don't pick up on his presence. His hand is in the beam, and he does have a human skeleton. And why does Nasedo care so much about Max and Tess, but not Isabel and Michael? Why would Nasedo warn the teens that they have enemies, yet tell them nothing about them? Considering he's there to protect them, it seems rather ridiculous he would leave them in the dark about their foes.

ALIENISMS: Michael is learning to smash rocks. Tess uses her mindwarp powers. Nasedo shapeshifts, and refers to the teens as the "Royal Four." Max breaks into the cyclotron, ages the skeleton, and removes any traces of Cadmium-X. The enemy aliens, or Skins, seem to shed human skin.

MUSIC: When Grant shows up at the Crashdown, "Soul Girl" by Stone Temple Pilots is playing. Later, when Nasedo/Pierce shows up at the Crashdown, we hear "Kryptonite" by Three Doors Down. "Lucky" by Bif Naked plays when the gang is gathered at the Crashdown, following a pre-school tradition. Finally, Richard Ashcroft's "Brave New World" plays when Liz and Max talk outside the café.

2.2 Ask Not

ORIGINAL AIR DATE: October 9, 2000
WRITTEN BY: Ronald D. Moore
DIRECTED BY: Bruce Seth Green

GUEST CAST: Desmond Askew (Brody Davis), Gretchen Egolf (Congresswoman Vanessa Whitaker), Jim Ortlieb (Nasedo/Ed Harding), Sara Downing (Courtney), J.G. Hertzler (Mr. Lafeber)

In the wake of the Skins crisis, Max looks to John F. Kennedy's actions for answers. Meanwhile, a new owner has taken over the UFO *Center, and Tess moves in with the Valentis.*

"Ask Not" was obviously written to parallel JFK and the Cuban Missile Crisis, and while the comparison provokes some interesting moments, the final message isn't clear. Are they saying that Max is a leader who may succeed in some areas, but certainly isn't perfect? Max is more reluctant to be a leader, while President Kennedy signed up for the job. JFK had a choice; Max has a destiny. As far as I am concerned, the best comparison made is Maria's, when she notes that Liz and Tess are Max's "Jackie" and "Marilyn."

The Cuban Missile Crisis of 1962 really began after the failed U.S. invasion of Cuba's Bahia de Cochinos (Bay of Pigs) in April of 1961. The plan was to overthrow Cuban dictator Fidel Castro with the help of U.S. backed Cuban exiles. While the plan was created by President Eisenhower, it was approved by his successor, President John F. Kennedy. Within the first hours of the fight, it was clear that the exiles were not going to win and Castro's army consequently stopped the invasion, with 90 exiles killed. The whole situation was quite an embarrassment for the Kennedy administration.

The invasion forced Castro to look for ways to keep the U.S. out of Cuba, and he turned to the U.S.S.R. Since the Soviets were behind in the cold war arms race in 1962, Soviet Premier Nikita Khrushchev suggested placing intermediate-range missiles in Cuba that could deter any potential U.S. attacks on the U.S.S.R. Fidel Castro approved the plan, and the Soviets quickly and quietly built up military installations in Cuba. Then, on October 15, 1962, U.S. reconnaissance photos revealed the Soviet missiles being constructed on the island, and President Kennedy was thrown into seven days of debate with his 12 key advisors as to what the next steps would be. On October 22, Kennedy informed the American public of the situation, then executed his decision to quarantine Cuba. After a declaration that any attack from Cuba would be considered an attack from the U.S.S.R. and action would be taken immediately, Kennedy demanded the missiles be removed. The tensions grew until Kennedy had the military declare DEFCON 2 (with 1 meaning active war). Finally, in the final hours, with excellent advice from his brother, General Robert Kennedy, President Kennedy and Soviet Premier Khrushchev were able to come to an agreement, and thus averted a nuclear war. The Cuban Missile Crisis of 1962 was the closest brush with nuclear war that the world had ever seen.

So what does this have to do with *Roswell*? The first parallel in Mr. Lafeber's history class describes JFK as a young man who would "rise to the occasion" by resolving the situation with the U.S.S.R. and therefore avoid nuclear war. He asks the class to think of JFK not as a president, but as a man with the "fate of an entire nation in [his] hands" whose next decision could lead to the destruction of the world. With Nasedo dead and an unknown enemy on the loose, Max is a young leader forced to take on a situation that seems too big to handle. Michael, thinking like the soldier he was in his former life, argues that taking the inactive approach is a mistake, that they shouldn't just "lay low." Max just wants to keep everyone safe. The nation in this instance could refer to his home planet, where the very lives of the inhabitants are reliant on the return of the Royal Four. Unless, of course, the Skins are going to take over planet Earth, in which case the nation refers to the world that Max, Michael and Isabel live in now.

The second parallel is the fourth day of the Cuban Missile Crisis, when Kennedy dealt with pressure from everyone. The military was pushing for an attack while the diplomats wanted to take the blockade route. Kennedy hadn't made a decision, but knew he had no time. He had to take action before the missiles became operational. Max's big choice involves breaking into Brody's new office to find out what is going on, even if it means risking exposure to a possible Skin. Michael obviously represents the military and Isabel is the diplomat of the group. As for operational missiles, one can only assume that those are the Skins, who could attack at any time.

The final parallel involves the American spy plane that was shot down over Cuba, the dead pilot, and the pressure for Kennedy to take action. Pummeled with different opinions, and with Bobby having doubts about him, Kennedy had no choice but to make the call and let history be "his final judge." Michael is knocked out from a beam shooting out of Brody's strange alien pentagonal device, suggesting that Brody is out to kill the teens. Michael wants to take action, and Isabel finally stops backing Max and agrees with Michael. Maria's only advice to him is to follow his heart. As the three of them enter the UFO Center to deal with Brody, Max finally realizes the right course of action. The irony is, it was Bobby Kennedy who came up with the plan that actually averted disaster, not JFK. So, if we were following the analogy correctly, it should have been Isabel's realization.

The concept of "Ask Not" is interesting, if not subtle.

FLASH: Every time Kyle quotes Buddha.

IRKS: Congresswoman Whitaker tells Liz that she has a "paid staff" in "Skin and Bones," and yet it appears that Liz is the only one working for her in *Roswell*. I'd also like to know how a U.S. congresswoman has enough time to get drunk and shred files during business hours. Also, for all the talk of being careful about using powers, it's rather ridiculous of Isabel to use her powers to play CDs when the Café is unlocked and Liz's parents are upstairs. And why don't the teens ply Nasedo with questions about their other world? Considering they spend an entire season looking for answers, it's not very realistic for them to ignore a major resource when it is available to them. It's also a little odd that Tess has nothing to do with the Brody situation.

DOUBLE TAKE: When Max runs down the Roswell streets towards the Crashdown, there is a smear of blood on his chest. When he bursts into the Café, it has become a perfect red handprint.

ALIENISMS: Nasedo's body returns briefly to its alien form before becoming dust. Tess admits to having some "memory retrieval techniques," along with being able to heal. Max creates a green force field. Isabel acts as the DJ, using her powers to play CDs. Brody's alien device emits a strange blue wave that knocks down Michael, but it does not react to Max. Brody's cancer was healed after being abducted by aliens.

SODA MOMENT: Maria accuses Max of playing "patty-cake" with Tess. The reference comes from the 1988 film *Who Framed Roger Rabbit?* For the cartoon characters, playing "patty-cake" is the equivalent of having sex.

COOL FACTS: "Ask Not" is the first episode written by new co-executive producer Ronald D. Moore. Ron Moore has been a writer/producer for *Star Trek: The Next Generation*, *Star Trek: Voyager*, and *Star Trek: Deep Space Nine*, along with screenplay credits for *Star Trek: Generations* and *Star Trek: First Contact*.

MUSIC: "Be Ya Self" by Tarsha Vega plays in the beginning as the girls dance. When Kyle returns from football camp, "Bohemian Like You" by The Dandy Warhols is playing. We hear Amanda Ghost's "Idol" when Liz and Maria see Max walking with Tess. "867-5309 (Jenny)" by Crease (original song by Tommy Tutone) comes on when Kyle's alarm clock goes off. Trinket's "Superhuman" plays at the Crashdown after Max tells Liz how he feels.

2.3 Surprise

ORIGINAL AIR DATE: October 16, 2000
WRITTEN BY: Toni Graphia
DIRECTED BY: Fred K. Keller

GUEST CAST: Gretchen Egolf (Congresswoman Vanessa Whitaker), Sara Downing (Courtney), Jeremy Davidson (Grant Sorenson), Mary Ellen Trainor (Diane Evans)

Isabel's surprise birthday party gets disrupted when she has violent images of Tess and she leaves to search for her.

Finally, an episode that showcases Katherine Heigl. The main plot follows Isabel as she hunts for Tess, and the sub-plots involve the Courtney/Whitaker mystery. "Surprise" is a coming-of-age story in the alien sense. Celebrating her eighteenth (human) birthday, Isabel becomes an adult. But it's not her age that propels her into the world of adulthood; it is her actions.

Isabel has obviously matured from the glam-girl she is in season one. She comes across as very self-possessed, and is no longer afraid of standing up to her brother, regardless of his "ruler" status. She stays strong when facing the enemy, and makes Tess her first priority. While the intent behind her actions is honorable, the results are devastating. Isabel is forced to come to terms with her own "loss of innocence," but not only does she have blood on her hands, she discovers her past "persona" was not so innocent. Isabel, who really began to show her feelings of isolation in season one, now has an even bigger burden on her shoulders. Katherine does a good job with her monologue in the pod chamber, conveying Isabel's frustrations at not having an alien mother figure in her time of need. The writers are certainly taking Isabel's character on an interesting ride.

The use of color in this episode is deliberate. Red is prominent, first in Isabel's flashes, and in the intensity of her red dress. Later, the intense light coming into Whitaker's office from the street bathes Michael in red. Then, in contrast, we have the dark blues and blacks of the power plant. Yellow appears at the beginning of the episode in the light shining in the doorway of the plant. Later, there's the yellow glow from behind the pod. And, of course, a green glow from the pod chamber later colors Isabel's face. Considering the change that she undergoes in this episode, the deliberate use of complementary colors — opposites — is a smart touch. Red represents her human personality at the start. Green complements the changed woman at the end, as Isabel starts to look at her alien nature.

All three alien teens are hunting in "Surprise." The scenes in the power plant are excellent as Isabel searches through the maze of machinery to find Tess. Michael rifles through

Katherine Heigl at the 2001 UPN All-Star summer party

(Photo by Christina Radish)

Whitaker's office as a consequence of Liz's earlier discovery. Finally, Max and the sheriff find a possible suspect in Grant Sorenson. Like vigilantes, they head off to break the law by breaking into his apartment without a warrant.

The human teens are supporting characters in this episode. Maria's confrontation with Courtney has a great comic touch, but Liz is becoming a bit of an enigma. First of all, she's been alone in Whitaker's office at night filing reports, but after Whitaker locks a drawer, and leaves to freshen up, Liz is suddenly breaking into it. Why doesn't she do it before if she suspects Whitaker? And even stranger, she's caught with the CD and the drawer open (we didn't see her close it, anyway) and *nothing happens*! Whitaker is a whole other issue. She doesn't appear to have any other staff, and records Liz's phone conversations. She gives Isabel the whole *Murder, She Wrote* confession speech, completely unprovoked, which immediately tells me the writers just wanted some method to throw more details our way. It also shows that Nasedo was rather inept as a protector if he couldn't even identify the enemy he was sleeping with. Thank God for Kyle and Alex: they keep us sane. Kyle's reaction to Mrs. Evans after she catches his crude comment is great. Alex, of course, really can shake it down. Even Mrs. Evans had some zinger lines of her own.

Katherine does some excellent work in this episode, which makes up for some of the problems. I know the writers have been instructed to add more sci-fi, but do they need to pile it on us all in one episode? The Granilith, husks, Skins, Vilandra, and past battles . . . it's a lot to take in. I'm beginning to miss the FBI!

FLASH: Michael's Tabasco birthday cake. And Officer Whitman's dance, of course.

IRKS: The whole Grant Sorenson element to the story is a bit off. First of all, it's really pushing it that he goes on a date with Isabel. Secondly, he only just meets Isabel, so how can he know Tess? And how does he get Tess's number? And how can Tess know Isabel's favorite flower, considering she and Tess aren't really even friends? And why does Tess leave without her cell phone? Whose car is she driving? There are a lot of holes in this particular storyline. On another note, why doesn't the group just tell Courtney the truth, because they are always talking about business when she is in earshot. So much for secrecy! Finally, Grant must be a hemophiliac, because he cuts himself during the day, and he's still bleeding that night.

DOUBLE TAKE: Isabel holds a full glass of pop. When she drops it and it shatters on the floor, it's empty.

ALIENISMS: Courtney fills up the glasses using her hand. Isabel has urgent flashes of Tess, melts metal, and uses a force field to reflect the bolt of electricity back at the Skin.

SODA MOMENT: Grant refers to Max as "Deputy Dawg." *The Deputy Dawg Show* was a popular cartoon in the sixties. The title character, an actual dog, was totally inept as a lawman. He preferred sleeping over catching the bad guys. The sheriff, his human boss, was always getting on his case about it, but the deputy kept falling back into his old ways.

MUSIC: "Boom" by Trinket plays when Isabel first walks into her party. When Liz is in Whitaker's office, she's listening to "Wish (Komm Zu Mir)" by Franka Potente and Thomas D. from the *Run Lola Run* soundtrack. "Come On 'N Ride It (the Train)" by Quad City DJs is the song Alex strips to. Later, when Michael and Courtney are in the kitchen, Neve's "Digital On" is playing. Finally, when Isabel opens her presents, "One Planet People" by Fishbone is on.

2.4 Summer of '47

ORIGINAL AIR DATE: October 23, 2000
WRITTEN BY: Gretchen J. Berg, Aaron Harberts
DIRECTED BY: Patrick Norris

GUEST CAST: Charles Napier (Hal Carver), Eric Saiet (Teacher), Tom Kenny (Pete), Michael Roddy (M.P. #1), Finn Curtin (Male Bar Patron), Lisa Kaseman (Female Bar Patron), Jeff Johnson (Army Bus Driver)

Michael is forced to interview a former Air Force Captain as a history assignment on World War II, but ends up hearing a story that changes his life.

Gretchen Berg and Aaron Harberts have given us a terrific episode with compelling parallels, a tight story, and great character moments. While the main plot follows Hal's story, it's nice to see that the issues of Whitaker and the Granilith are at least touched on. "Summer of '47" feels a touch like Dickens' *A Christmas Carol*, where Scrooge has to learn about life from three ghosts in order to become a changed man. In this case, our alien Scrooge (Michael, of course) has to learn the truth — that he owes a lot to the humans in his life — from an older soldier.

Using the main actors as the characters from Hal's 1947 flashback is a great idea and is borrowed from the 1939 film, *The Wizard of Oz*, where the actors playing the Kansas roles played similar counterparts in Oz. Not only do they shine in their new roles, but the characters they play are very appropriate. The 1947 relationships also parallel the present day ones. Fehr plays the young Hal Carver, a rebellious captain who disregards rules and gets himself into trouble; Jason Behr plays Captain Richard Dodie, a friend of Hal's who tends to get his "skivvies all up in a bunch" and longs for the ideal "normal" life including a wife and white picket fence. He and Hal end up arguing a lot, and, of course, Richie ends up putting Hal in his place for Hal's own good. Surprise, surprise.

Delfino plays Betty Osario, a spunky reporter for the Fort Worth *Star-Telegram*. While she clashes with Hal, they also have amazing chemistry. Older Hal's message to young Michael as he reflects on Betty is to seize the moment and have no regrets. Isabel plays Rosemary, Hal's sophisticated bed buddy. As Hal says, she is very much a "woman." Isabel, too, has become more of a woman this season, considering the age of the men she's dating.

The other characters include Bill Sadler as Colonel James Cassidy, a tough, no-nonsense character that has elements of the Sheriff Valenti we know at the beginning of season one. De Ravin plays Dixie, the Colonel's ditzy secretary. Appleby takes on the role of Yvonne White, a very scientifically minded nurse and witness to the alien autopsy who just wants to get the hell out of Roswell. On an interesting note, in season three, Liz's actions as Yvonne mirror her flight from Roswell. Hanks plays Captain Sheridan Cavitt, a.k.a. "Mr. Brain." Wechsler plays Kyle's own grandfather, Deputy James Valenti.

What really works with this episode is the fact that the writers allude to the true events of the Roswell incident, while using fictional characters. Major Jesse Marcel, the weather balloon, Glenn Dennis from the funeral home, and the coffins are all mentioned (see "The Roswell Incident" chapter for more details). Hal was a member of the 509th Bombardment group, like Maj. Marcel. Only two of the characters in "Summer of '47" are based on real individuals: Captain Sheridan Cavitt and Yvonne White. Glenn Dennis was the one who spoke with the young nurse about the alien autopsy, and she drew a sketch for him, just as Yvonne does for Hal. She was also transferred immediately afterwards, and the last address Glenn Dennis found was in London, England. The real nurse's name was never revealed to the public. It's also a nice touch that the histories of two *Roswell* families are included through Kyle's character and through the bar (Parker's) run by a relative of Liz's.

The whole idea of the old embittered soldier opening up to the young embittered soldier (in theory) is a great concept. Charles Napier is wonderful as Hal Carver, conveying the tough guy with a good heart who tried to do the right thing. Brendan Fehr gives a solid perform-ance as young Hal, the devil-may-care captain who likes the ladies. Of the "1947" characters, the one who really shines, however, is Majandra Delfino. Pulling out her best Southern accent, she sasses her way through each scene. Michael's final scene with Hal undoubtedly causes a few lumps in the throat. His efforts to make amends remind us once more why

Michael is such a great character.

Gretchen J. Berg and Aaron Harberts have done a fabulous job on their first *Roswell* episode.

FLASH: Michael revealing the truth to Hal.

IRKS: Since both Hal and Richie saw the sacks in the back of the truck, why wouldn't they take a closer look at them?

DOUBLE TAKE: Hal enters the morgue building empty-handed. Suddenly, in the morgue, he has a camera.

ALIENISMS: Michael smashes bottles using his powers and makes a lighter of his thumb. Hal sees eight pods and two glowing white aliens with dark eyes. He also has a piece of metal that, when crumpled up, immediately slides back into its original form (taken from the actual Roswell incident).

SODA MOMENT: Maria refers to Hal as "old man river." "Ol' Man River," the famous soulful song, is from the musical *Show Boat*. It was composed by Jerome Kern, with lyrics by Oscar Hammerstein II.

MUSIC: "Drawing Board" by Mest plays when Michael and Max walk through the school hallways. Frank Sinatra's "Fly Me To The Moon" plays when Hal is at Parker's bar. When Hal is at Rosemary's, we hear "In the Mood" by Glenn Miller. Later, at the Crashdown, Vast's "Free" is playing. Finally, "Mack the Knife" by Jimmy Dale Gilmore plays when Hal gets the key from Pete at the bar.

2.5 The End of the World

ORIGINAL AIR DATE: October 30, 2000
WRITTEN BY: Jason Katims
DIRECTED BY: Bill Norton

GUEST CAST: John Doe (Geoff Parker), Sara Downing (Courtney), Winnie Holzman (Madame Vivian)

A future version of Max travels to present-day Roswell through the Granilith. In order to save the planet, future Max needs Liz to help his present self fall out of love with her. Michael's investigation of Courtney causes major problems with Maria.

If it is Jason Katims's goal to break the hearts of every *Roswell* dreamer fan, he succeeds. In the tradition of *Romeo and Juliet*, "The End of the World" is definitely tragic.

The episode opens in the Granilith chamber in 2014, where the world is about to end, and Max and Liz (Max looking older, Liz definitely *not* looking 31) rush in to send Max back to the year 2000. They share a rushed, painful goodbye, before Max is pulled into the large cone, and poof. Gone.

In the present day, Liz, Alex, and Maria are all off to Madame Vivian to have their futures read. All looking for answers in their romantic lives, it's Liz who receives the shock — Max will choose love over all. They will be together. She goes home, elated, and then a rugged, long-haired, leather clad Max arrives to crush all of her dreams. When a couple breaks up, it can feel like the end of the world. In this case, the couple needs to break up or it *will* mean the end of the world.

With Tess's arrival and the whole destiny thing thrust into the picture, it's obvious that problems would arise. In the future, Tess will grow frustrated with Max's disinterest in her and will leave town. The break-up of the "Royal Four" means disaster for Earth when the enemy aliens attack. According to Future Max, the problem can only be fixed if Tess stays. This means Max must embrace Tess and not Liz.

Shiri really does a great job in this episode. Every time she attempts to cut Max off, it's obvious that it's killing her inside. When she initially approaches Tess about Max, you really have to admire her for keeping it together. Jason does the love-sick boy routine extremely well, too. His passion in Whitaker's office is intense and almost desperate. He pulls off both roles well, with Future Max coming across as an older, wiser version of Max. Future Max has suffered and understands regret. This episode is one where you want to reach into the television screen, shake the characters, and scream out the truth. The heartbreak both actors convey is amazing.

The heroes of this episode, however, are Kyle and Alex: Kyle for his hilarious and brilliant Buddhist philosophies that bring joy to an otherwise depressing episode, and Alex for standing up for Maria and doing to Michael what many may have wanted to do to him after this episode — nail him with a solid right hook!

While "The End of the World" really goes to an extreme, the cast does a thorough job of tugging at our emotional heartstrings. Even though it's painful to watch, it's an excellent episode, and is regarded by fans as one of the best of season two.

FLASH: Liz's wedding dance.

IRKS: If the only issue is keeping Tess in town, there could be better solutions to the problem than the one chosen. And while sweet, it feels out of character to have Max singing with a mariachi band. That's something Alex might do. Also, does Michael have amnesia? He goes from thanking Maria to acting like a complete jerk within one episode. Does he learn nothing from his experience with Hal?

ALIENISMS: The Granilith is manipulated to work like a time machine. Michael sends out a blast of energy, shattering his television set.

SODA MOMENT: Not so much of a pop culture reference as a cool inside joke. As Maria talks to Liz, she states that Michael is the "world's worst boyfriend. I know that. You know that. America knows that." Nice acknowledgement of the audience!

COOL FACTS: The same day that this episode aired, Crashdown.com received its four millionth hit.

MUSIC: "Save Me" by The Pierces plays when Alex, Maria, and Liz drive to Madame Vivian's. Later, Jason Behr serenades Liz with "Tres Diaz." Liz has her wedding dance with Future Max to Sheryl Crow's "I Shall Believe."

2.6 The Harvest

ORIGINAL AIR DATE: November 6, 2000
WRITTEN BY: Fred Golan
DIRECTED BY: Paul Shapiro

GUEST CAST: Miko Hughes (Nicholas Crawford), Gretchen Egolf (Congresswoman Vanessa Whitaker), Sara Downing (Courtney), Chris Ellis (Walt Crawford), Holmes Osborne (Mr. T. Greer), Jenny O'Hara (Ida Crawford), Joshua Wheeler (Willie), Bella Shaw (Newscaster)
  The team discovers that a group called the Universal Friendship League in Copper Summit, Arizona, has covered up the congresswoman's death. Liz, Max, Isabel, and Tess decide to visit the town. Meanwhile, Michael and Maria try to find out more about Courtney.

"The Harvest" is extremely plot driven, providing more exposition about the Skins, their history, and their intentions. While it has some interesting elements, it also has a lot of holes. Like "Surprise," it tries to introduce too many new elements at once.

After discovering that Courtney is a Skin, Maria and the Royal Four get together in an empty classroom to discuss their next steps. Just then, they see a news report on the television (why is there a television set on in a classroom?), stating that Congresswoman Whitaker died in a car crash in her home town of Copper Summit, Arizona. Obviously, someone is covering up the situation, considering she actually dies by Isabel's hand two weeks earlier. Still heartbroken, Max realizes the next step is to talk to Liz. In Whitaker's office, Liz fields phone calls while the gang searches for clues. Tess finds a letter postmarked Copper Summit (with a year but no date!) from the Universal Friendship League. From this point we separate into two plots — the main plot involving the team in Copper Summit, and the sub-plot involving Michael, Maria, and Courtney.

"The Harvest" is influenced by both *Invasion of the Body Snatchers* (1978) and Stephen King's *Children of the Corn* (1984). *Invasion of the Body Snatchers* involved aliens using pods to suck the lives out of humans. Emotionless aliens with a human image would then grow from the pod, taking over the human's life. *Children of the Corn* starts with a young couple stopping in a ghost town where there are no adults, and the children worship a god that lives in the corn. Their leader is an intense-looking teen named Isaac Chroner. In "The Harvest," the town of Copper Summit appears completely devoid of life, and the people who do live there seem rather odd. Whitaker's parents are strangely friendly, inviting the four teens to stay over. A multitude of human husks are kept vertical in glass containers, having been cloned and nurtured over 50 years. The Skins seem to be run by a very intense young teen named Nicholas. The lighter *Twilight Zone*-style soundtrack helps create a very bizarre and almost amusingly creepy atmosphere.

Miko Hughes is great as Nicholas, conveying both a young teen who is grieving for his sister and later an intense powerful man trapped within a younger body. His chemistry with Katherine Heigl is fascinating. The Liz and Max moments still tug at our heartstrings. Tess continues to work hard to gain the trust of the other aliens, as well as gain the sympathy of the audience. Courtney's story is interesting, and I'm glad to finally see her character have strength, rather than just a hyperactive sex drive. Jenny O'Hara and Chris Ellis are appropriately eerie as Vanessa Whitaker's parents. My only question is, how could the Skins have been competent enough to take over a planet, when they stupidly place all of their husks in one open area? We also discover that Michael, like Isabel, has an interesting past "persona" on their still-anonymous home planet.

"The Harvest" at least deals with the Congresswoman Whitaker situation, but a whole new set of questions arise as a consequence. It has its moments, but it also has flaws.

FLASH: Nicholas taking on Isabel in the husk chamber.

IRKS: How on earth do they get permission to drive 400 plus miles out to Copper Summit, Arizona? If they follow the New Mexico 75 MPH speed limit, the trip would take around five and a half hours. Also, what is the threat in the Universal Friendship League letter to Whitaker referring to? And wouldn't the Skins know that Max and the group are the Royal Four if Whitaker was reporting back to them? Why don't Greer and the other Skins just blast through Max's field right at the start? Doesn't Isabel think to use her powers against Nicholas? Isn't it a tad convenient that the first husks in the chamber are all the characters Isabel has met? Also, why does Isabel get to be Vilandra, while Max, Tess, and Michael keep getting referred to as the king, his young bride, and the second-in-command?

DOUBLE TAKE: When Courtney approaches Michael and Maria at the apartment, she tells them that she follows Michael "in the . . . political sense." Michael's response is "Our leader?" Obviously there is a cut somewhere because his response doesn't fit with her comment. Also, the Alien Mom Hologram from 1947 confirms the enemies were also on the planet in 1947, and yet Courtney mentions they all came down in 1950.

ALIENISMS: Nicholas uses a blast of power to knock out Isabel. Michael blasts Nicholas backwards. Max creates a force field, and Tess melds her energy with Max's to hold it up. Greer uses his power to knock down Liz, Tess, and Max, and drag Max back towards the coffins. The Skins live in ageless husks resembling human beings, but have a parasitic relationship with them. The husks only last 50 years.

SODA MOMENT: "It's Graceland . . . and you're Elvis!" is Maria's response to Courtney's altar of Michael.

COOL FACTS: On November 6, the *Daily Variety* announced that The WB had picked up four more episodes of *Roswell*. This brought season two to a total of 21 episodes. On Courtney's altar are Michael's Metallica T-shirt (Brendan's favorite band), along with Doc Marten boots (also Brendan's fave). And finally, in the *Roswell High* books, Nikolas was the name of Isabel's alien boyfriend.

MUSIC: Cleopatra's "U Got It" plays when Liz and Maria arrive at school. Later, at the Crawford home, we hear Gene Autry's "Back in the Saddle Again."

2.7 Wipe-Out!

ORIGINAL AIR DATE: November 13, 2000
WRITTEN BY: Gretchen J. Berg, Aaron Harberts
DIRECTED BY: Michael Lange

GUEST CAST: Sara Downing (Courtney), Miko Hughes (Nicholas Crawford), Jenny O'Hara (Ida Crawford), Mary Ellen Trainor (Diane Evans), David Batiste (Skin Tour Guide)
Using a special device, the Skins cause all the humans of Roswell to vanish in a time warp as the aliens hunt down the Royal Four.

"Wipe-Out!" (sharing the same name as the '60s song by the Surfaris) is a compelling concept with some interesting moments, but like its preceding episode, leaves the audience with a *lot* of questions.

Using a special device (which happens to be very phallic and is conveniently located in the anatomically correct location on the alien billboard), Nicholas creates a time displacement field over Roswell that causes the humans to disappear. Conveniently, Liz, Maria, the sheriff, and Kyle are all out of town when it happens. When they return to town, they hook up with the alien teens and Courtney to try to come up with a solution. Unfortunately, a busload of Skins is wandering around town and the humans don't have long before the time warp causes them to disappear with the others.

It's nice to have Miko Hughes back for another episode. He does a superb job as Nicholas, exhibiting boyish impatience and true evil power. His scene with Isabel on the bus is great, showing his frustration with his small awkward body and his desire to feel like a man once more. I love the fact that they have him playing with an electronic car. Jenny O'Hara has some nice moments, especially when scolding her leader as though he really is her son.

Like "The Harvest," "Wipe-Out!" is plot driven, yet it sets up some nice issues for the characters to deal with in the following episodes. Isabel and Michael's secrets are revealed by Nicholas in front of Max, causing future rifts in the trust the three share. Liz's longing to tell Max everything is nice, as is Michael's reassuring words to Maria. Tess really comes to the rescue a few times in this episode, which makes her a more sympathetic character. At this moment, her powers seem to be the strongest of the four. Even though she has had difficulties fitting in, it seems very apparent that she will fight to the death for all of them.

While the whole concept of the time warp and human disappearance could have been more complicated, Berg and Harberts make it fairly simple to comprehend. What works well is the parallel battle going on — namely, the humans battling against time to save the day while the aliens battle to survive the Skins. In both cases it's a great choice to have two of the less obvious characters save the day.

There's a big show of increasing maturity in "Wipe-Out!": Isabel puts the others before her own life, Max puts his issues with Kyle aside and offers Tess emotional support, and Kyle, in a comic turn, defies Buddha. Furthermore, Maria manages to keep her head in a crisis, Tess pulls a heroic maneuver, and Courtney makes a major sacrifice in order to keep Michael's secret. The sheriff opens up to Kyle on an emotional level. The fact that they all pull together in "Wipe-Out!" is great, considering in the last few episodes the humans haven't had as much of a role in the fight.

"Wipe-Out!" is an interesting follow-up to "The Harvest," although there are still many questions about the Skins that are never addressed.

FLASH: Maria's reasoning behind her vitamin collection.

IRKS: When does Nicholas stick the rod in the sign? Also, I can't imagine that the entire town of Roswell is at home during this event. Surely more humans would be heading into town. And where do they keep the moisture chamber? Why does the skin dissolve in Liz's hand, but not in Maria's? The powers that the Skins possess seem a bit vague. And why don't the Royal Four at least attempt a fight when Nicholas and the Skins appear in the school? It can't be due to the energy field over Roswell because Isabel uses her powers earlier, as does Tess.

DOUBLE TAKE: The Café is empty, then suddenly the sheriff is there with a gun. He just "appears."

ALIENISMS: Tess uses her mindwarp power to create a wall and mirror where the bathroom door usually is. She also creates a wave of fire, annihilating the Skins. Nicholas is said to have a thousand times the power that the teens do. He motions with his hand, making Isabel's handcuffs disappear. He can read through people's memories by touching their heads. The Skins can be killed through a trigger in their lower back.

COOL FACTS: Miko Hughes was only three years old when he landed the role of baby Gage Creed in the 1989 film *Pet Sematary*. He also acted with Majandra Delfino in the 1997 film *Zeus and Roxanne*. At six years of age, he was the youngest actor to ever be interviewed by Johnny Carson on *The Tonight Show*.

MUSIC: When Mrs. Evans presents her frittata to Isabel and Max, "Complicated" by Good Charlotte is playing. "The Itch" by Vitamin C plays in the Jetta as Maria and Liz return to

Roswell. Elvis Costello's "Alison" is on in Liz's bedroom when she talks about her mother. Finally, "Next Year" by the Foo Fighters plays when the humans of Roswell have returned.

2.8 Meet the Dupes — Part One

ORIGINAL AIR DATE: November 20, 2000
WRITTEN BY: Toni Graphia
DIRECTED BY: James A. Contner

GUEST CAST: Desmond Askew (Brody Davis), Garrett M. Brown (Philip Evans), Michael Chieffo (Mr. Seligman), Sean Allen Rector (Guy with basketball), Steve Picerni (Carjacked Driver)

The second set of alien teens, duplicates of the Roswell aliens, show up in town. They intend to bring Max back with them to New York to attend the summit meeting with the ruling families of the five neighboring planets.

Seems we've moved from Copper Summit to an interplanetary summit in New York. "Meet the Dupes" takes us away from the Skins and into a whole new story concept. The second set of pods end up in New York, creating physical duplicates of the Roswell teen aliens, but only these four are truly as opposite as opposite gets. Street punks with no conscience, or concern for human life, these four are out for themselves, and good luck to anyone who stands in their way.

The whole metaphor for this episode stems from science class. Mr. Seligman brings up the recent death of a red giant that broke astronomical records by burning out in its prime. This led to a violent explosion in a "supernova of a hundred million degrees," which disappear[ed]. This process usually takes thousands of years. Instead, it happened unexpectedly, leaving a black hole.

The metaphor is an obvious one for Max and Liz's relationship. Has Max's love for Liz truly been destroyed, leaving a void? The whole exploding star metaphor for a broken heart is a cute touch; based on Max's general mood, it's completely believable that he is caught in an emotional black hole. There's an interesting significance to the moment when Max returns the pen knife Liz gave him as a gift. In many European and Asian countries, it's bad luck to give someone a knife as a present: it is interpreted as "cutting off a relationship." The proper way to do it is to ask the gift receiver for a penny, thus making it a "purchase." Liz didn't follow this tradition and now Max is cutting his ties to her.

The star metaphor can extend to Max, Isabel, and Michael's relationship as well. With the new information on their history surfacing, all three find themselves keeping secrets. Max feels betrayed by both Michael and Isabel: Michael for revealing information to Courtney, and Isabel for not telling him about Vilandra. When Max confronts "Isabel" and she lashes out, with "Michael" rushing to her aid, he's quick to believe they are against him, causing him to break out on his own. Obviously he's truly caught up in his emotional wounds if one fight causes him to do something spontaneous like go to New York.

The "Dupes" are an interesting trio, with great punk outfits and New York accents. (It's too bad we don't get to see more of Zan, simply because Jason makes him a compelling character.) Brendan does a great job as the hell-raiser Rath. An extreme version of Michael, Rath tosses loyalty to one side, more interested in running the show. Meanwhile Katherine is fabulous as Lonnie (Vilandra). Lonnie is a nasty manipulative woman who truly knows how to play people. Her subtle threats to Ava in the car are brilliant, along with the false sincerity she shows both Max and Mr. Evans. Her personality is more along the lines of what we have heard thus far about the original Vilandra. Ava is interesting because she is the most compassionate of the four, with some scruples. She actually comes across as human, while Tess does not embrace her human side at all. While there are a lot of things about the Dupes that have not been addressed, the actors are doing such a great job and the characters are so wild that the problems are covered up.

A lot of different shows use the whole "evil" clone story. "Meet the Dupes" may not be working with an original concept, but the characters are so great we can't wait to go to New York with them.

FLASH: Liz's reaction to "Michael" kissing her.

IRKS: Considering this is the first time the Dupes are meeting the Roswell teens, it's pretty impressive how well they know them. First of all, Lonnie and Rath know exactly where Max's bedroom is. Secondly, Rath somehow figures out that Liz and Max are no longer together. Finally, how does Lonnie possibly know that Max is involved with Liz Parker, and that it's causing problems with the alien trio? Finally, why is Tess going with Max to NYC when Max is the only one invited?

DOUBLE TAKE: When Max drives up to Isabel, stopping her from jogging, he has his seatbelt on. For his close-up, it's off. Long shot, it's on. Close-up, it's off. Finally, it's on again as he drives away.

ALIENISMS: Zan causes a fruit stand to collapse. Rath accelerates a truck and changes a license plate with his hand.

SODA MOMENT: Lonnie refers to Alex as "Opie." Opie (played by Ron Howard) was Sheriff Andy Taylor's young son on *The Andy Griffith Show* (1960–1968). The show looks at small town life in the virtually crime-free town of Mayberry, North Carolina. Essentially, Lonnie is calling Alex a small town hick boy.

COOL FACTS: This is the third episode in a row where someone comments on Michael's hair. First it's Hal in "Summer of '47." Then, it's Nicholas in "Wipe-Out!" Finally, Brody makes a comment about Rath's hair in this episode. This could very well be because Brendan Fehr has a fixation with his hair. He likes to do his own hair on set, and yet "it just looks funny when [I'm] doing it, especially being a guy. So on one of the last days of the season, I'm sitting on the couch doing a scene and a director comes up to me and he's like, 'Are you ready?' and I'm like, 'Yeah, let's shoot it.' And he's like, 'Oh, wait just one second.' Suddenly, everybody in the room — grips, electrics, camera department, directors, producers — whips out a tiny pocket mirror with my picture on it, flips it open and starts fiddling with their hair."

MUSIC: Linkin Park's "With You" plays at the beginning as the Dupes walk down the New York streets. "El Cu Cuy" by Coal Chamber plays when the Dupes steal the car. When Maria talks with Michael in the Crashdown, Imani Coppola's song "You Stole My Fun" is on. "Rhinestone Cowboy" by Glenn Campbell plays in the car as Rath, Lonnie, and Ava drive to Roswell. Then, "Lovely" by F.O.S. plays when the sheriff pulls the Dupes over. When Liz approaches Max at the Crashdown, "Don't Leave the Light On Baby" by Belle & Sebastian is playing. "Shine A Light" by Apples in Stereo plays during Brody's breakfast with Maria. Finally, "What Am I Supposed to Do?" by Papas Fritas plays when Max, Tess, Rath and Lonnie leave for New York.

2.9 Max in the City — Part Two

ORIGINAL AIR DATE: November 27, 2000
WRITTEN BY: Ronald D. Moore
DIRECTED BY: Patrick Norris

GUEST CAST: Desmond Askew (Brody Davis), Miko Hughes (Nicholas Crawford), Jerry

Gelb (Emissary), Marji Martin (Hanar), David Reivers (Sero), Faline England (Kathana)

Max represents the Royal Four at the summit meeting of the five planets. He is forced to make a major decision that could affect his, Isabel's, Michael's, and Tess's lives forever.

While "Meet the Dupes" touches on the destruction of bonds, a large element of "Max in the City" deals with mending relationships. The title is borrowed from the film *Babe: Pig in the City*, where the hero (a reluctant pig) leaves his small town to head to the big city to help save the farm. In this episode, Max (reluctant alien) leaves the smaller town of Roswell to head to New York to help save his planet. In both situations, trouble ensues in the city. Max's ending may not be as joyous as Babe's, but it certainly has positive moments.

This episode introduces a whole gambit of elements, making it more than a little confusing. Everyone wants the Granilith. My issue with this comes later on ("The Departure") when we see it used as a "one time only" travel device. Is that all it is? A glorified spaceship? If that is the case, why does Kivar want it so badly? And why are the other four planets looking to Max for peace when it is apparent that Kivar is the problem? Also, it is stated that the "V" shape is made up by five planets. In "Four Square," we discover that in order for the constellation of Aries to get that shape, it aligns with Venus. Does that mean that one of the warring planets is Venus? The purpose of the summit is to create peace among the planets, with the ambassadors hoping that Max will make a deal with Kivar. Kivar is running Max's planet, and Max has no power whatsoever except for the Granilith. Does that mean that Kivar will stop the war with the other four planets if he gets the glorified spaceship? So many questions, so few answers.

Miko Hughes at Bogart Backstage
(Photo by Christina Radish)

The problems arising in this season's storyline are due to the scattered science fiction elements that keep getting thrown in. Several details are overlooked in the hopes that the audience won't care, or will just resort to suspension of disbelief. First the Skins, now the summit, five other planets, the Dupes, the Dupes making plans with the Skins, the Granilith. . . . Nothing is terribly clear. How is it that Nicholas knows Lonnie and Rath? Do they meet before or after the Roswell crew take them on? We are left trying to put pieces together instead of enjoying the acting and storyline.

There are some interesting moments, however. Once more we get to enjoy Katherine as

Lonnie and her dynamic with Nicholas is just as excellent as Isabel's. The Dupes really come across as selfish, sex-addicted punk criminals with absolutely no redeeming qualities, but tough as they are, anyone who grows up in a nasty atmosphere has to have been affected emotionally. It's nice, at least, to see some humanity in Ava as she bonds with Liz. The Liz/Ava storyline is an interesting addition, considering Liz's tumultuous relationship with Tess. Tess is also becoming more sympathetic as she stands by Max. One thing Jason does extremely well is balance Max's responsible leadership side with the part of him that is an insecure teenager, and the dichotomy really comes across in this episode.

While "Meet the Dupes" separates friendships, "Max in the City" brings people together. Brody and Maria are forming a nice bond. Isabel and Liz's betrayals are the push Max needs in order to make this journey, and it's effective having Isabel and Liz work together in order to save him in his hour of need. Ava comes through for Liz and Max as a way to make peace for betraying Zan. A bittersweet exchange between Max and Larek reveals more about Max's own history, causing him to suddenly recognize Tess's dedication to him.

Once again, there are some wonderful moments in "Max in the City," but too much of this episode is overloaded with new, complicated elements. All in all, however, the moments outweigh the confusion.

FLASH: Rath's reaction to pastrami with mayo.

IRKS: See main description above.

ALIENISMS: The emissaries and other rulers use humans as puppets/communicators on Earth. Lonnie manipulates a CD like Isabel has done in the past and she causes a window washer platform to crash. Alien sex is apparently quite exciting. Tess manages to fight off mind-reading powers, but isn't sure how she does it. Isabel and Liz manage to project an image of Liz to Max. Liz is able to see what is happening as though she is actually in New York. Ava makes a comment about Liz "changing" due to Max's actions, which foreshadows season three.

SODA MOMENT: Up at the top of the Empire State Building, Max quietly says, "I'm the king of the world." Most recently, those words were uttered by Will Smith in Michael Mann's 2001 film *Ali* (Muhammed Ali happens to be the originator of the comment). The line is also associated with Leonardo DiCaprio in James Cameron's 1997 film *Titanic*. So, is Max a champion who stands up against a war, and takes on a new name and identity for himself, or is Max an artist who follows his heart and falls madly in love with a woman which leads to tragic circumstances? Tough choice.

MUSIC: "Passing Me By" by The Pharcyde plays when Rath and Lonnie take Max and Tess to their "crib." Later, as Max is tested by the Emissary, we hear "How to Disappear Completely" by Radiohead. Finally, when Max talks with Liz at the end of the episode, the song is Lifehouse's "Everything."

2.10 A Roswell Christmas Carol

ORIGINAL AIR DATE: December 18, 2000
WRITTEN BY: Jason Katims
DIRECTED BY: Patrick Norris

GUEST CAST: Desmond Askew (Brody Davis), John Littlefield (John Sutton), Garrett M. Brown (Philip Evans), Mary Ellen Trainor (Diane Evans), Diane Farr (Amy DeLuca), Adeline Allen (Sydney Davis), Madison McReynolds (John's Daughter), Whitney Weston (John's Wife), Kelly Hill (Pediatric Nurse), Biff Wiff (Security Guard), Holly Gray, Joshua Kranz, Jeni Wilson, Christine Noh, Jaquita Ta'Le, and Jordan Smith (Carolers), Joseph Williams, Amye Williams, and Jason Schef (Choir members)

It's Christmas time in Roswell, with Isabel running everything! Meanwhile, Max fails to heal an accident victim and finds himself haunted by his ghost.

This is the first Christmas episode we have on *Roswell.* The title is from Dickens's *A Christmas Carol,* which is the story of Ebeneezer Scrooge discovering the true meaning of Christmas, and consequently, of life. While he certainly isn't cantankerous, Max is the one who is haunted in this version. Max's lesson leads him to discover the religious side of Christmas. And, like Scrooge, three people — John, Liz, and Michael — manage to touch Max, allowing him to open his heart.

The ghost to visit Max is John, a young father who is killed by a car while saving his daughter. Max witnesses the event, but does not take the risk to heal John as he did with Liz. We finally see how the events of "The White Room" have taken their toll on Max. Fearing for his own safety, Max watches John die. From that point on, he suffers from guilt. The question is, is John simply Max's guilty conscience surfacing, or is he actually a ghost? It's easy to believe that John could just be Max's subconscious. After all, John is pretty aggressive about the situation, angered and wanting retribution. And yet, that theory is later contradicted when Max arrives at Brody's home to discover John. John claims Max needs to "restore the balance." It's not clear why the balance has been disrupted, though. John is killed before his time, which had been Max's reasoning for healing Liz, and while Liz helps him to "restore the balance" she makes a very strong point afterwards, relaying Max's words from "Leaving Normal" back to him: "You're not God, Max." That being said, if John is a ghost, is he the one who decides that the balance has been disrupted? Or does he speak for a "higher power"?

Michael is the third person to reach Max. Michael's moment with Max is an especially nice touch considering how much these two fight. It's always a welcome change to see them bond.

It seems that Roswell gets a break from all the alien chaos at Christmas time, allowing the teens to embrace their human sides. Isabel is truly hilarious as the "Christmas Nazi" with her compulsive need to have the "perfect" Christmas. In the book series, Isabel would continually organize and reorganize things compulsively in order to deal with stress. In this case, Isabel has taken on the town, organizing everything possible in order to have a "normal" Christmas. The best subplot, however, involves Tess and the Valenti boys. How perfect to have the alien teen rekindle a human tradition for the Valentis.

Keeping a nice balance between drama and comedy, "A Roswell Christmas Carol" is a truly touching "holiday" episode.

FLASH: Jim attempting to use Buddhist meditative techniques to help the football team score.

IRKS: While Isabel's compulsive organizing is great, don't these events she's been involved with take up a lot of time? She's been very busy these last few episodes with alien business. And I can guarantee if Maria's been talking about Tess to her mother, she isn't passing on positive comments. Also, where's Alex? This is a full cast episode, and he isn't around. Finally, while having snow fall is always a nice Christmas touch, it really seems a bit much, considering we are in New Mexico.

DOUBLE TAKE: When Michael talks about God to Max, if you look closely over Michael's shoulder, a crew member moves in the laundry room of the Evanses' home.

ALIENISMS: Max heals a bunch of children in the pediatric oncology ward at the hospital. He also fixes a light on the tree. Tess uses her powers to carve the turkey.

COOL FACTS: This episode touched *Roswell* fans so much, they ended up donating thousands of dollars to the Pediatric Cancer Foundation in order to help grant the wish of a boy with cancer who wanted to visit the *Roswell* set and meet the cast.

MUSIC: When Max and Michael pick out a Christmas tree, "Santa Swings" by Swingtips is playing. "I Want An Alien For Christmas" by Fountains of Wayne is the song in the Crashdown as Michael and Maria discuss gifts. Lucious Jackson's "Let It Snow" plays while Isabel shops with Michael. The carolers sing "Jingle Bells" and "Deck the Halls." We hear "Babybird" by The Wallflowers in the park when Maria tells Liz about Sydney. When Tess confronts the Valenti boys, "Have a Holly Jolly Christmas" by Burl Ives is on. Later, during dinner with Amy, "Everything's Gonna Be Cool This Christmas" by the Eels plays. The song playing when Max heals the kids is "Calling All Angels" by Jane Siberry. "Hello Mr. Kringle" by Kay Kyser plays when Michael gives Maria her gift. When John leaves Max, we hear "Silent Night" by Angie Aparo. Finally the choir at midnight mass sings "O Come, All Ye Faithful."

2.11 To Serve and Protect

ORIGINAL AIR DATE: January 22, 2001
WRITTEN BY: Breen Frazier
DIRECTED BY: Jefery Levy

GUEST CAST: Keith Szarabajka (Dan Lubetkin), Jeremy Davidson (Grant Sorenson), Jason Peck (Deputy Hanson), Devon Gummersall (Sean DeLuca), Allison Lange (Laurie Dupree), Robert Katims (Judge Robert Lewis), Breon Gorman (Judith Foster), Sebastian Siegal (Brad), Woon Park (Buddha), Sage Kirkpatrick (Melissa Foster)

While dreamwalking, Isabel's mind is infiltrated by a terrified young kidnap victim, and Sheriff Valenti's lawlessness starts to catch up to him.

First, it was the Skins, but they've been dealt with. Then, we had the Dupes, but they seem to have disappeared. Now we have more new characters to contend with, only these characters come to the teens in a human form, or so it seems. The next few episodes are referred to as "The Hybrid Chronicles." "To Serve and Protect," the first of the series, deals with the consequences that can come with having powers, as well as keeping secrets.

In "To Serve and Protect," Isabel's recreational snooping into the minds of others has "curiosity killed the cat" results, with the eventual victim being someone the teens care for. Bored, Isabel finds herself wandering through Kyle and Liz's dreams. Liz's PG-13 dream of "Brad" in the Crashdown is amusing. Still bored, Isabel channel surfs to Kyle's dream. Buddha informs Kyle that Max's healing has "changed" him. Kyle screams in comic horror at his lizard-like arm. Things then take a dark turn as Isabel finds herself standing alone in a forest clearing, under eerie yellow light. Quick jerky shots show a faceless man dragging a black body bag across the ground with a young woman inside, screaming. David Lynch's *Twin Peaks* immediately comes to mind.

Sheriff Valenti is in a tough spot in "To Serve and Protect." The enemy seems to have come in the form of a human once more, and that human is his friend Dan. In town to investigate Hubble's death (remember "The Convention"?), Dan continues to ask his friend for answers. Jim has two issues to deal with. First of all, he knows what the law has done to the teens before, and longs to protect them. The "father" parallel comes up once more, however, as Dan reminds Jim of James Sr.'s blatant disregard of the law. Jim spends season one walking down the same path as his father to prove him wrong, and Hubble's death helps change that. Both Jim and his father killed a man outside of duty, and now, he joins his father in having to hand over his badge as a consequence of his actions. Jim has thrown caution to the wind this season, acting rather than thinking things through. He's also playing the "Max" card by taking all the responsibility onto his own shoulders. By putting his complete faith in the alien teens at all costs, Jim puts his life on the line. And like his father before him, Jim forgets to consider the fate of his son.

We see some new faces in this episode. There's Dan, an employee of the State Police Board who obviously has greater motives than investigating Hubble's death. Then we have Sean DeLuca, Maria's older cousin, fresh out of jail, who has returned to town for awhile. Finally, we have Laurie, our kidnap victim. With some daunting situations in the town of Roswell, comic relief is a necessity. Cue Tess and Kyle, our new favorite clown pseudo-siblings. Kyle's obsession with changing into an alien is priceless, especially when he tries eating Tess's sweet and spicy pancake dish, and decides he likes it.

While Sheriff Valenti seems to be serving and protecting the aliens, he's certainly stopped doing so for himself. "To Serve and Protect" is intense, dark, and definitely stirs up the pot, leading us all in a new direction.

FLASH: Kyle changing the television channels with his "newfound power."

IRKS: The sheriff really has been reckless since he found out about the alien teens. I'm surprised that Max would even think to approach the sheriff about the final vision, considering the trouble Jim is in. Why doesn't Isabel dreamwalk Melissa's picture in the sheriff's office? That way she could save everyone a lot of trouble. It's also a bit surprising that Max has difficulties sustaining the force field for a few bullets, when in "The Harvest," he held it up for quite some time against the strong powers of the Skins.

DOUBLE TAKE: If someone intends to eat a burger, they should *eat* a burger. Sean takes three bites, but the burger remains whole. Also, why is Liz Parker on the same yearbook page as Cheryl Cain (who incidentally wrote the episode "River Dog")?

ALIENISMS: Isabel dreamwalks and receives visions of a distressed woman (as she does with Tess in "Surprise"). Max creates the force field to deflect the bullets. Isabel has a flash of an internal cellular structure when she touches Laurie.

MUSIC: "Fallen Icon" by Delirium (featuring Jennifer MacLaren) plays during Liz's dream. "Amongst the Ruins" by Delirium plays during Kyle's dream. Collective Soul's "Turn Around" is on at the Crashdown when Kyle and Tess eat breakfast. Later at the Crashdown when the sheriff talks to Mrs. Foster, we hear "Duck and Run" by Three Doors Down. "Into the New" by Vallejo plays when Maria gives Sean the "rules." Then, when Sean comes in to ask for fries, "Innocent" by Fuel is playing. Finally, "Trip Like I Do" by Crystal Method plays when the Sheriff, Max and Isabel find Laurie.

2.12 We Are Family

ORIGINAL AIR DATE: January 29, 2000
WRITTEN BY: Gretchen J. Berg, Aaron Harberts
DIRECTED BY: David Grossman

GUEST CAST: Erica Gimpel (Agent Suzanne Duff), Keith Szarabajka (Dan Lubetkin), Diane Farr (Amy DeLuca), Allison Lange (Laurie Dupree), Robert Katims (Judge Robert Lewis), Devon Gummersall (Sean DeLuca), Jason Peck (Deputy Hanson), Rachel Winfree (Customer), Shana O'Neil (Store Clerk), Seema Rahmani (Nurse)

The Town Council comes together to make a decision on Jim Valenti's future, while Laurie Dupree's paranoia reaches an all time high when she sees Michael. A strange blue crystal grows at the burial site.

"We Are Family's" power lies in Jim Valenti's story. Right in the opening we see just how lying catches up with you and can lead to devastating consequences.

Rumors circulate around town about the sheriff's relationship with the town teenagers, insinuating some pretty nasty behavior. His humility while dealing with Agent Duff is difficult to watch, knowing the authority he once had. His final decision to protect Laurie cements his fate. The hardest scene to watch involves Jim sitting in a dark and empty courtroom, with the day's proceedings echoing around him. His loyalty remains intact, even at such a high cost. Knowing that he cannot speak the truth makes it so tough to watch as Jim undergoes the judgment. Sadler gives a very strong performance in this episode, holding no grudge against the teenagers whose secret has put him in this position. Sheriff Valenti is arguably the one character on the show that has grown the most. He starts as a villain and grows into a true hero. While Valenti's choices haven't always been lawful, they still manage to seem "right." After all, justice isn't black and white.

The Pod Squad's behavior in this episode is extremely disappointing. Max and Isabel's actions are the major catalyst for Jim's suspension, and yet they can't seem to do anything productive except feel guilty. Instead of going to the sheriff to apologize, Michael risks more trouble for Jim by digging around the crime scene. In a less than sensitive moment, Max approaches Kyle about removing the crystals from his father's desk, claiming it will spare both them and the sheriff from more trouble, even though he's really only thinking of himself. Finally, after Isabel and Max find out about the town council verdict, all it takes is a rather callous statement from Michael to have them back at work, causing more trouble. After everything that Jim has done for them, their character reactions are not only cold, but unbelievable. Guess that's teenage insensitivity for you. Of all the alien teens, Tess is the most sympathetic in this episode as she comes to Kyle's aid, then bonds with him in the Valenti kitchen.

The humans are starting to realize they are missing out on being normal teens. When Alex returns from a month's exchange in Sweden, he returns with a new outlook on life, which causes Liz to realize there's a world out there to discover.

The Laurie Dupree story and the alien crystal don't make too much sense yet. Allison Lange does a good job portraying Laurie as a paranoid schizophrenic, but it's not clear why an FBI agent would be sent to deal with Laurie's situation. While Erica Gimpel is a great fit for the honest, hardworking Agent Duff, it's yet another new character we have to figure out. Somehow the main story seems to be losing its focus as more and more elements enter into the picture. "We Are Family's" best moments are the human ones, and that is what makes this episode memorable.

FLASH: Amy DeLuca defending Jim's name in the convenience store.

IRKS: Liz seems pretty casual about Sean breaking into the Crashdown storeroom to eat at his leisure. I'm surprised there are no guards at the burial site considering the amount of investigation into it. Also, it would have been very easy to mention earlier that Alex was off in Sweden, but it looks like even the writers weren't sure about his whereabouts until now and have inserted it as a convenient plot point. Sure, he's not really in Sweden, but the others think he is, so it could have been mentioned. Finally, why was Laurie's file empty, yet her personal stuff left behind?

DOUBLE TAKE: Alex sets up his slide show for Maria, Isabel, and Liz the same night Isabel needs to leave to look after Laurie. When we next see Alex and Liz on the balcony, still watching the slide show, she tells Alex he was pretty cool with Isabel "yesterday." Are we supposed to believe that the slide show went on for two days?

ALIENISMS: Michael knocks a door open, then later breaks a window with his power (when he could've easily kicked it). Tess uses her mindwarp power to make Agent Duff and Kyle believe they are looking at a report card. It seems that Laurie Dupree's grandfather is a doppelgänger for Michael.

SODA MOMENT: Kyle calls Tess "my favorite Martian," referring to the television series *My Favorite Martian* (1963–66), or the 1999 movie of the same title. The alien Exodus comes to earth to live with Timothy O'Hara, and takes on the guise of his "Uncle" Martin. It seems Martin spends most of his time trying to solve problems his presence has caused.

MUSIC: When Alex first talks with Maria and Liz, "King Of All The World" by Old 97's is playing. Later, during the 'Swedish Night' on Liz's balcony, we hear "Best I Ever Had (Grey Sky Morning)" by Vertical Horizon. Travis's "Turn" is on when Liz and Alex look at the slides and discuss traveling. When Sean shows Liz his mustard trick, "Bring Your Lovin' Back Here" by Gomez plays. Finally, when Jim kisses Amy in the Jetta, James Taylor's "Her Town Too" is in the background.

2.13 Disturbing Behavior — Part One

ORIGINAL AIR DATE: February 5, 2001
WRITTEN BY: Ronald D. Moore
DIRECTED BY: James Whitmore, Jr.

GUEST CAST: Desmond Askew (Brody Davis), Allison Lange (Laurie Dupree), Jeremy Davidson (Grant Sorenson), Diane Farr (Amy DeLuca), Erica Gimpel (Agent Suzanne Duff), Devon Gummersall (Sean DeLuca), Heidi Swedberg (Meredith Dupree), Dennis Christopher (Bobby Dupree), Rosana Potter (Carmen), Wendy Speake (Reporter)

    Michael and Maria rescue Laurie and take her to her grandfather's home in Tucson, Arizona. In Roswell, Liz, Isabel, and Michael investigate the strange crystal while Jim Valenti and Agent Duff look for Laurie's kidnapper.

This episode is a nod to David Nutter's 1998 film *Disturbing Behavior*. Taking the concept from *The Stepford Wives* and putting it into a high school, the film follows the new kid in town, who befriends two of the less desirable teens, then uncovers the secret as to why so many of the kids are disturbingly "perfect." In the *Roswell* episode, Grant Sorenson appears to switch personalities, Jim Valenti's moods become a little odd, and Michael and Maria have to deal with the bizarre personalities of Laurie's aunt and uncle. The range of "strange" behavior is quite interesting.

"Disturbing Behavior" uncovers more about Laurie Dupree, yet she still remains a mystery. She flips out on Michael in the last episode, screaming "You're dead!" only to lead Michael and Maria to her grandfather's home as though he is alive and well. Is Laurie really insane? Allison Lange portrays a character who, if not crazy, is terrified and desperate. There are some nice moments as Michael and Maria deal with Laurie, tossing barbs back and forth. While Michael may have some issues as a boyfriend, Maria can be downright abusive to him. Some might consider Michael and Maria's behavior stranger than Laurie's.

Dennis Christopher and Heidi Swedberg are great as the self-serving children of Laurie's grandfather. The writers are setting up a big conspiracy-style situation here at the Dupree home. Her relatives don't seem to know she was committed, yet they somehow know of her paranoia about aliens. Uncle Bobby and Aunt Meredith's cool, yet polite reactions to Michael are great. Poor Michael, who has been constantly looking for some sort of family, finally finds one — and they turn out to be nuts.

Bill Sadler once more gives a subtle yet strong performance. Jim struggles with his new situation, trying to keep himself busy. Caught in a self-confessed "dark place," he tries not to break down in front of Kyle. When Jim asks Kyle to bear with him, it's a lovely father/son moment. While Jim's reaction is obviously out of the ordinary, it's not only justifiable, but evokes sympathy. I'm also glad to see Agent Duff actually investigates Jim's lead. It gives him back a sense of dignity.

Isabel and Max still don't apologize for everything that has happened to Valenti, and make no efforts to actually do something about the situation. Instead, they blow off the sheriff to deal with the crystals. The crystal storyline seems to be the most complicated of the lot, involving ecosystem issues and alien parasitic behavior. It's still not clear exactly what these parasites are or what they want. While it would make sense to ask Tess about them, seeing as she's spent her life with their alien guardian, they instead attempt a dangerous maneuver which could destroy another life. Max and Isabel don't appear to be thinking too clearly these days.

Finally the writers address the whole parent situation. Amy's freak-out session is brilliant, combining the right amount of exaggerated humor, emotional concern, and strong parental authority. Her conversation with both Maria and Michael shows how desperate she is not to have her daughter turn out like her.

"Disturbing Behavior" has some intense moments, and opens quite a few different and complicated story threads, but is weak overall.

FLASH: Maria's commentary to Michael as Laurie tears apart the Jetta.

IRKS: The fact that Tess has little to no involvement with the crystal investigation doesn't make sense. Maria's description of the Roadhouse doesn't quite fit. She describes it as a hole, when it fact it looks like a well-kept diner. And why doesn't Isabel just give Agent Duff the same excuse that she gives Brody — that she is psychic! That would solve a major problem, with Agent Duff understanding why Jim is protecting her. Forgive me if I'm wrong, but I haven't heard of any FBI agents kidnapping *psychics* in order to study them.

DOUBLE TAKE: Usually people don't have to walk through the kitchen of a restaurant to head to the washroom, which is what Laurie does in the diner.

ALIENISMS: The Gandarium are alien parasites that are possibly water-borne. Michael uses his powers to cause a car explosion and to keep Laurie locked up in the Jetta. Isabel uses her powers to communicate with Larek through Brody.

MUSIC: When Michael and Maria spy on the police station, "Sometimes" by Nine Days is playing. "Quasimodo" by Lifehouse is playing when Sean shows up at the Crashdown. Jesse Dayton's "The Creek Between Heaven And Hell" plays in the Roadside café. Finally, "Throw the Brick" by Palo Alto is on at the Crashdown when Isabel talks with Grant.

2.14 How The Other Half Lives — Part Two

ORIGINAL AIR DATE: February 19, 2001
STORY BY: Gretchen J. Berg, Aaron Harberts, Breen Frazier
TELEPLAY BY: Jason Katims, Ronald D. Moore
DIRECTED BY: Paul Shapiro

GUEST CAST: Desmond Askew (Brody Davis), Jeremy Davidson (Grant Sorenson), Allison Lange (Laurie Dupree), Heidi Swedberg (Meredith Dupree), Dennis Christopher (Bobby

Dupree), Erica Gimpel (Agent Suzanne Duff), Rosana Potter (Carmen), Antonio Vega (County Clerk)

While the team hunts for the Gandarium Queen, Kyle and Alex get trapped in the nest. Michael and Maria continue to protect Laurie — this time from her own relatives!

"How The Other Half Lives" is a great title considering the references — how the rich live versus how the crystals live. The rich need money to feed their lifestyle while the crystals need oxygen to survive. An alternate title for this episode could be "Alex and Kyle Save The World." This episode is the last of The Hybrid Chronicles, tying up both the Gandarium and Laurie Dupree storylines. While a lot of questions are left unanswered, we still have some great moments to keep us happy. This episode also plays a large part in Michael's seasonal story arc, giving him one more reason to connect to his human side.

Today's "Hybrid" awards come courtesy of me. Alex and Kyle are the recipients of the Golden Hybrid for their accidental discovery while singing "American Pie" in the Gandarium nest. Whoever came up with the idea to trap Alex and Kyle together in a cave deserves serious accolades. All of their moments are great, from their discovery to their sing-a-long, to surfacing from the slime. Even though it's by force, Kyle has finally joined in with the group activities, though neither he nor Alex is 100% thrilled by the situation.

The Silver Hybrid award goes to Maria and Michael. Maria shows excellent leadership skills in this episode. She comes up with the plan to take on Bobby and Meredith, finds condemning evidence against Laurie's "guardians," and gets a lawyer involved at the end, making Michael feel better. Maria has proven herself to be a strong, cool head under pressure. Michael's sensitive side comes out in this episode. He and Laurie share a nice "Grandpa" moment. Michael also comes through as a hero in the end, though taking credit for Maria's work loses him a few points. Maria and Michael are hilarious as they take over the positions of master and mistress of the house. They've gone from no relationship to acting like an old married couple. They may bicker, but all in all this Mutt and Jeff couple fits together perfectly.

Jim and Agent Duff get the Bronze Hybrid award for coming to the rescue. Agent Duff looks beyond Valenti's previous actions and relies on him. After all, Agent Duff is an officer of the law who can now at least partially understand Jim's predicament. Special Mention goes to Isabel for her attempts to help Grant and her touching scene with him in the bunker.

As for the "other halves" . . . rich Uncle Bobby and Aunt Meredith keep up their amusing, manipulative fronts, but give up too easily. Considering the trouble they go through to get Laurie out of the picture, they certainly don't make too much of an effort to deal with Maria and Michael. Greedy as they are, they obviously aren't terribly intelligent.

Then, there is the Gandarium storyline. A lot of questions are left with this one. Grant goes from nice guy geologist to possessed pod person. Where does he find Laurie exactly?

How does the Gandarium Queen go about finding an individual with Laurie's particular genetic defect? Why are the Gandarium starting to attack people now, when they've been around since 1947? Grant may have been digging in the area, but Jim, Michael, and Max were digging there first. It's also pretty convenient that of the one in 50 million people who have the genetic defect, Laurie just happens to live fairly close to Roswell, New Mexico. How the Gandarium would be lethal to the human race once mutated is something I guess we'll never know . . .

If you ignore all the questions, "How The Other Half Lives" is a strong episode with suspenseful and quirky moments. The characters all learn that sometimes you make friends in the strangest of circumstances. And it's always great when a group of teens saves the world. Just ask anyone who watches *Buffy*.

FLASH: Michael and Maria in robes on the lounge chairs by the pool commenting on the shallow behavior of rich people.

IRKS: In "To Serve and Protect," Laurie claims that she is on her way to Roswell to visit with her grandparents when she is kidnapped. Then, in the following episode we discover that she escapes from Pinecrest Psychiatric Hospital, she's terrified of aliens, and that her grandfather is dead. In "Disturbing Behavior," she makes it sound as though her grandfather is alive (he's not), and that her grandfather sees aliens just as she does. Finally, in this episode, we discover that Laurie is not crazy. I beg to differ.

ALIENISMS: The Gandarium are used to bridge the gap between alien and human cells, which means that the alien teens have some inside of them. Alien powers do not work against the crystals. Michael uses his powers to suck the air out of the bomb shelter and kill the Queen.

COOL FACTS: Created in the early 20th century, Mutt and Jeff were comic strip characters. One was tall, the other short. These two were working-class Everyman-type characters who liked to drink, gamble, and tended to get into hot water with their spouses. How does that relate to Michael and Maria? First, Michael is tall and Maria is short. Second, both are working-class characters who gamble in situations, bicker, and definitely get into hot water either in general, or with each other.

MUSIC: "Lying in the Sun" by Stereophonics plays when Michael and Laurie talk. Colin Hanks and Nick Wechsler sing Don McLean's "American Pie" when trapped in the nest. "So Nice (Summer Samba)" by Bebel Gilberto plays when Maria and Michael lounge by the pool.

A favorite photo among many fans, Brendan Fehr gives girlfriend Majandra Delfino a smooch at the premiere of The In Crowd

(Photo by Christina Radish)

Later, "Taste of Honey" by Herb Alpert & The Tijuana Brass plays over dinner. Finally, when Michael and Maria look at Laurie's picture, we hear "Everything" by Jill Phillips.

2.15 Viva Las Vegas

ORIGINAL AIR DATE: February 26, 2001
WRITTEN BY: Gretchen J. Berg, and Aaron Harberts
DIRECTED BY: Bruce Seth Green

GUEST CAST: Eileen Galindo (Senora Villa), Samuel Ball (Dave the Best Man), Linda Pine (Traci the Bride), Gregory Saites (Glenn the Groom), Howard George (Sonny Glass), Ken Cook (Dealer), Phil Nelson (Stickman), Ned Schmidtke (Pit Boss), Michael Bailey Smith (Security Guard), Deondray Gossett (Bellhop)

Michael and the gang head to Las Vegas to spend the Dupree money.

"Viva Las Vegas" is a wonderful break from the heavy stories we've had lately. It takes us back to the good old days when *Roswell* was about teenagers just trying to figure out who they are and how they fit in. This episode allows the gang to finally act their age, and comes with a lesson about responsibility to boot.

Gone are the Liz/journal framework days. Now, in order to sum up the plot to new viewers, the writers have introduced the Maria/blackboard monologues. In the classic Maria DeLuca style, she gives us a play by play of events past in order to bring new audience members up to speed. These are the aliens, these are the humans . . . are you following? Things have gotten complicated for the long-time viewers lately, so it's no wonder the writers are trying to make things easier on new ones!

Haunted by nightmares of being shot, Michael makes the decision to take Max on a "guys only" trip to Las Vegas in the hopes of "clearing out the cobwebs." Max agrees in order to appease Michael, but the trip doesn't stay exclusive for long. Soon Isabel, Tess, Kyle, Maria, Alex, and Liz have heard about the trip. It's nice to see the good old high school rumor mill still works as fast as e-mail.

Michael's desire to bond with Max is intriguing, considering how much their friendship has suffered due to their "responsibilities." Max, however, isn't the type to embrace rebellious behavior just for the sake of it. Even if it had just been the two of them in Vegas, odds are conflict would still arise. Michael's need to be a normal guy is interesting considering he's the one desperate to find out more about their alien history. Max could have relaxed, but Michael's irresponsible behavior forces Max to always be ready for the fallout. Their fight in the jail cell reminds us how opposite they truly are. We are also reminded of the fact that Michael had no role models growing up, while Max did. They have difficulties understanding each other simply because they come from different worlds (earthly worlds, that is). In order to bridge the gap, each one needs to take a few steps into neutral ground.

"Viva Las Vegas" takes a closer look at the dysfunctional relationship between Maria and Michael. Michael brushes her off, while she puts him down. And then Michael does something sweet and everything is fine again. Michael has been this way with Maria throughout the series. One minute he's understanding, and the next he reverts back to his bad behavior. The same goes for Maria. Having expectations going into a relationship can be detrimental, but when respect is tossed out the window, it's time to re-evaluate things.

Max and Liz continue to dance around each other. Liz stands alone next to an Elvis wedding chapel poster, which only makes things worse as she reflects on the wedding that never was. When Max and Liz are in the arcade, and she throws out a question about an "Elvis Chapel" wedding, she is left disappointed. In classic high school style, her "fishing" for a response is not dissimilar to asking someone out on a date in the roundabout, less humiliating fashion. Considering these two used to talk things to death, it's rather sad that it's lack of communication that is destroying their relationship.

The best part of this episode involves Sheriff Valenti. Jim brings a terrific twist to this episode that people had been noting (but not seeing) since the beginning of season two. Suddenly the free-spirited vacation takes on a whole new slant. It feels straight out of William Goldman's *Lord of the Flies* when, after pretending to be adults for so long, the boys suddenly find themselves in the presence of real adult soldiers. Jim Valenti is that soldier. "Viva Las Vegas" is a fabulous episode that shows us even heroes are far from infallible.

FLASH: Michael's arrangement in the dinner club. That, and the names chosen for the fake I.D.'s.

IRKS: The trip begins with Max and Michael, and quickly spreads to the others — but how do they all manage to get flights arranged so quickly, especially since Liz decides to come only two minutes before they leave for the airport? If Maria wants Liz to go in order to be her "gal pal" for the trip, why does she abandon her right at the start? It's also pretty impressive that Max gets their names on the debate team list, considering he doesn't know who is going! Why does Isabel go from one cradle robber to another? Yes, Katherine Heigl does look more mature than the other teens, but does she have to be set up with men who look thirtysomething?

DOUBLE TAKE: Michael tosses out six bundles of money. There are seven recipients.

ALIENISMS: Michael uses his powers to change everyone's I.D.'s and to "load" the dice. Isabel clears a stain off Traci's wedding dress. Max has a vision of Liz and himself married in Las Vegas.

SODA MOMENT: At school, Alex tells Liz and Maria "I love the smell of formaldehyde in the morning." This is a spin on Robert Duvall's classic line from Francis Ford Coppola's Vietnam epic *Apocalypse Now,* "I love the smell of napalm in the morning."

MUSIC: When Maria begs to join Michael and Max on their trip, "Chemistry" by Semisonic is playing. "Viva Las Vegas" by ZZ Top plays during the stock shots of the Vegas strip. Morcheeba's "Be Yourself" plays when Michael lays out the rules in the hotel suite. Majandra Delfino sings "I've Got The World on a String" during her audition, then later sings "I've Got It Bad (And Ain't That Good)" at the dinner club. Dido's "Thank You" can be heard when Isabel dances with Dave in the suite. Finally, Shawn Colvin's version of "Viva Las Vegas" plays when Michael and Max share a coffee the next morning.

2.17 Heart of Mine

ORIGINAL AIR DATE: April 16, 2001
WRITTEN BY: Jason Katims
DIRECTED BY: Lawrence Trilling

GUEST CAST: Diane Farr (Amy DeLuca), Devon Gummersall (Sean DeLuca), Taran Killam (Malamud), Scott Clifton (Evan), Michelle Moretti (Allie), Mya Michaels (Juanita)

Prom fever hits Roswell leading to unexpected results.

"Heart of Mine" explores the one time of the school year that can either be blissful or hellish. That is, of course, the PROM. Maria refers to it as that evil four-letter word. No enemy Skins or FBI agents come barging in to mess up things. The only one to blame in this episode is "change," which happens in the human world *all the time*. All the characters are discovering new things about themselves, leading them to either embrace change reluctantly or gracefully.

Liz and Max are moving into different directions, as Liz's voiceover informs us (yes, the journal is back). Max is unearthing memories of a life that has nothing to do with Liz, while Liz needs support and security that Max cannot give her, even though she still loves him. After all she has done to push Max away, she's angry at Max for even getting close with Tess. Max, on the other hand, thinks that Liz slept with Kyle, but he's willing to get close again as we see at the prom. Liz once more has to tell him she's suffocating in their non-relationship. She leaves him sitting alone while she dances away enthusiastically with Maria. And we're supposed to feel badly for her when she sees Max and Tess together in the school hallway? Some teenagers aren't exactly rational, and Liz needs to work out what she wants.

Isabel is also changing. While she previously rejected the idea of getting close to anyone, she now longs to do so. Whether it's loneliness, sentimentality, or honest desire, she reaches out to Alex. Alex, in turn, has also matured significantly thanks to Sweden, and makes it perfectly clear that he's not prepared to turn into an emotional wreck once more.

Michael and Maria continue to work on their rocky relationship. Michael has made some changes over the season, but as we've seen, change doesn't happen overnight, which is what makes Michael's character believable. Now it's Maria's turn to learn some trust. Kyle is wonderful, as always, in this episode. Gone are the days when sex was his first priority. Sure, he mentions watching porn every other episode, but his relationship with Tess has allowed him to get close to a woman without relying on sex. It's so great to see Kyle come to Tess's defense when Malamud makes his lewd comments. Even better is Kyle's own reaction . . . to his reaction.

As Liz notes in the Crashdown when everyone has their photo taken together: "And there we were. All together, with everything we'd all been through over the last two years. And somehow in this moment I had this really strong, really upsetting feeling that this was the last time we'd all be standing together." In "Heart of Mine," Jason Katims has truly caught the bittersweet feeling that comes with growing up, and in a lot of cases, growing apart.

FLASH: The shots of the bowling alley at the beginning and end as Liz dances down the lanes, and Maria's reaction to Michael's comment that proms are "unnatural": "You know what? I find it to be really unnatural that you're half alien warrior and half Grandpa Dupree! But I make do."

IRKS: Liz tells Max about how this prom is so special to her, and how she's been planning for it since last year. And yet, Kyle tells Tess he went to the prom last year with Trudy MacIntire. Kyle and Liz are the same age, so why didn't Liz and Max go to the prom last year? Also, why is it that all of *Roswell*'s teens prefer to knock on people's windows rather than their front doors? Finally, where does Liz get socks to slide down the lanes with Sean?

DOUBLE TAKE: Maria manages to break into Michael's apartment with a fake cardboard MasterCard. Nice job.

ALIENISMS: Max remembers swimming in Jell-O-like water on his planet, as well as a burnt orange sky with three moons. His clearest memories involve Tess, including remembering their first kiss at a party. Tess helps Max to remember using her "memory retrieval" techniques.

COOL FACTS: During episode #54 ("The Prom") of *Buffy the Vampire Slayer*, Angel broke it off with Buffy because he knew they would never have a normal life together. He did give her one last dance at the prom, however. Seems Liz and Angel have the same thoughts.

MUSIC: When Sean makes a move on Liz in the VW Bug, "Catch the Sun" by Doves is playing. Later, "Don't Panic" by Coldplay is on when Sean drives Liz to school. At the bowling alley the first time, we hear Josh Rouse's "100m Backstroke." Josh Joplin Group's "Camera One" plays at the Crashdown before the prom. As people arrive at the prom, "Rock DJ" by Robbie Williams is playing. Max and Liz dance to "Worry About You" by Ivy. Liz and Maria later dance to "Slide" by L7. When Michael arrives, the song changes to Nelly Furtado's "I'm Like A Bird." Musiq's "Girl Next Door" is playing when Isabel kisses Alex. Finally, Ivy's "Undertow" plays at the end of the episode when Liz sees Max and Tess.

2.18 Cry Your Name

ORIGINAL AIR DATE: April 23, 2001
WRITTEN BY: Ronald D. Moore
DIRECTED BY: Allan Kroeker

GUEST CAST: Mary Ellen Trainor (Diane Evans), Jo Anderson (Nancy Parker), Diane Farr (Amy DeLuca), Jason Dohring (Jerry the Delivery Boy), Jason Peck (Deputy Hanson), Hawthorne James (Ed the Truck Driver), Ted Rooney (Charles Whitman), John Doe (Geoff Parker), Garrett M. Brown (Philip Evans), Devon Gummersall (Sean DeLuca — uncredited).

Alex's tragic death affects everyone differently, with Liz refusing to believe it is anything other than murder.

This is Ron Moore's most emotional episode, without question. An extremely powerful hour, "Cry Your Name" explores how teenagers deal with the death of a friend.

In Alex's room, Maria and Liz coach Alex playfully on his budding relationship with Isabel before heading off to work. None of his actions seem extremely out of the ordinary except for his moody conversation with the delivery boy. Later, Alex's teachers claim that Alex is "moody" and "sullen" and at other times over-confident, even "cocky" — surely warning signs for what is about to happen. Valenti's words hit the nail on the head: "Sounds like every teenager I ever met." Sometimes, there are no answers, no matter how much we want to understand "why" something happens. "Cry Your Name" really makes that clear.

Liz's reaction is one of denial and fury, and is painful to watch. Liz bottles up her emotions so tightly she physically makes herself ill. Forever the scientist, she puts aside any horror she might experience by dissecting the elements until a logical conclusion is formed. Her need to "not be alone" is the closest she gets to reaching out. Her tunnel vision prevents her from seeing anything but what she believes to be the truth. While many would see her behavior as harsh, her reaction is completely believable under the circumstances. Sometimes, however, death just doesn't make sense. Her refusal to let go, along with her compulsive sorting of the photos shows just how desperately she is trying to keep it together. Major kudos to Appleby for her acting in this episode.

Maria's reaction is the opposite of Liz's: she falls apart completely. It's exhausting watching her. Even her moving version of "Amazing Grace" at the funeral is choked by emotion. Maria's horror at Liz's actions is a further demonstration of the different reactive paths they are on — Maria is consumed by her emotions while Liz tries so hard to keep focused on other things, she doesn't mourn his death. Considering all that we know of these two characters, their reactions suit them.

Isabel takes the guilt route. After all, this is the second guy who has died on her. Her goodbye scene in the Crashdown with Alex is a major emotional moment and both Colin and Katherine do a lovely job. While Isabel feels responsible, she also toys with the idea that perhaps his death is due in part to their alien background. Her pain triggers her final decision to leave Roswell: she will deal with her grief by running away.

Michael's behavior makes up for just about every episode where he's been a jerk. He takes on the caregiver role, immediately going to Maria's aid and not leaving her side. It's the little things he does that make his character so charming, like knowing Maria doesn't like barbeque at the Whitman home, and yet making sure she eats. He stops being argumentative for an episode, instead sheltering Maria from any brewing storms. He also takes care of Amy, knowing what she needs even when she doesn't. Their scene together at the DeLuca home shows us that Michael comes through when it counts. Michael's way of dealing with grief involves taking care of everyone else.

Max is once more reminded that he is not "God." While he feels guilty about not being able to revive his friend, he feels even worse when he realizes he doesn't want to touch Alex's body. His insecurity about how to react to the people around him works well, considering Liz's aggressive actions. Later, when Liz pushes his buttons, he fights back. The question is, does he do it because he believes she might be right? Liz's cruelty is a product of her grief, just as Max's reaction is a product of his. In a situation like this, it becomes very difficult to say just who is right and who is wrong.

One of the most compelling elements of this episode is the use of the Robert Frost poem, "Stopping By Woods On A Snowy Evening." The fact that the concert tickets (which represent Alex's desire to live) are by that poem is interesting, considering some believe the poem to be about suicide.

The narrator speaks of knowing the owner of the woods, and how "lovely, dark, and deep" they are. The owner would be God, with the woods representing death. The "promises" the author must keep include the people in his life. The repetition of the final line, "And miles to go before I sleep," can show a double meaning, with "sleep" being literal in the first stanza, and representing "death" in the second. What does this have to do with Alex? Even if Alex *was* suicidal, this suggests that he would not give in to it, having too much to accomplish first. Having Liz repeat the final line shows that she understands the journey she has ahead of her as well, and that it will be a long and exhausting one.

"Cry Your Name" is an excellent, emotional, and thought-provoking episode. Alex is a wonderful component to the show, and will be missed.

FLASH: Michael and Max arguing over *The Matrix* versus *Crouching Tiger, Hidden Dragon*. And of course, all of Alex's scenes.

IRKS: Valenti hasn't gotten his job back, yet in this episode he's acting like the sheriff again.
DOUBLE TAKE: Liz keeps flashing back to memories of Alex doing the striptease for Isabel. Problem is, Liz wasn't there when it happened. She was in Whitaker's office.

ALIENISMS: Max attempts to heal Alex, but fails.

COOL FACTS: The title comes from the Beth Orton song "She Cries Your Name" which is played at the end of the episode. Alex bought two tickets to a Beth Orton concert in Roswell taking place on the day of his funeral.

MUSIC: When Alex talks to Isabel on the phone, "Storybook Life" by Blessed Union of Souls is playing. "I Quit" by Meat Puppets plays when the gang are at the Crashdown looking at prom photos. When Isabel first dreams of Alex, we hear Emer Kenny's "Light of You." Emer Kenny's "Heaven" plays the next day at school when Liz sees Alex's locker. "Human" by Fisher plays during the memorial service in the football field. Isabel's second dream involves "Nothing" by Peter Searcy. Majandra Delfino sings "Amazing Grace" for Alex's funeral. When Liz looks at the prom photos, Beth Orton's "She Cries Your Name" plays in the background.

2.19 It's Too Late and It's Too Bad

ORIGINAL AIR DATE: April 30, 2001
WRITTEN BY: Gretchen J. Berg and Aaron Harberts
DIRECTED BY: Patrick Norris

GUEST CAST: Diane Farr (Amy DeLuca), Devon Gummersall (Sean DeLuca), Jason Peck (Deputy Hanson), Ted Rooney (Chuck Whitman), Michael Caldwell (Florist), Jeremy Guskin (Derek), Per Bristow (Mr. Stockman), Alison Ward (Deb the Yearbook Editor), Antoinette Broderick (Bank Teller), Brendan Pontzell (High School Security Guard), Stephen Kupka (Cab Driver), David Schwartz (Flight Crew Member)

Liz's obsession with Alex's death and Isabel's decision to attend college in San Francisco drive further wedges into the already unstable group.

Liz as a selfish obsessive fanatic? Max acting like a nasty control freak? Isabel turning from her family? Michael becoming a sensitive boyfriend? The characters of *Roswell* have been possessed! The death of Alex has turned the world of *Roswell* upside down, accelerating the changes which began in "Heart of Mine." Continuing on from "Cry Your Name," this episode looks at the aftermath of tragedy. It also teaches the lesson that you can never go back, only forward.

The alien teens seem to be drawing closer to their "past life" personalities. On their home planet, Rath was loyal, Vilandra put her own needs first over family, and Zan forced change upon a planet too fast, which led to rebellion. In this episode, Michael spends his time looking after Maria, being sensitive to her needs. Isabel puts all her efforts into getting out of Roswell, refusing to listen to Max. Finally, when pushed to the wall, she uses her powers in public as a sign of her defiance. Max is so desperate to maintain control he threatens Isabel and almost forces Liz into his car. And then, there's Tess. Quietly waiting in the wings, Tess has conveniently slithered her way into Max's life. Just watching her walk off with Max is a sign of Max's growing isolation from Isabel and Michael.

Liz and Max are on parallel journeys. Both of them are completely focused on one issue, and aren't taking anyone else's feelings into consideration. Liz refuses to stop her obsessive investigation, ignores her best friend's needs, puts Sean's freedom on the line, and breaks the law (rather sloppily, too. Ever heard of gloves, Liz?). Max won't let Isabel go to San Francisco, and refuses to support Liz's investigation into Alex's death. Liz is hurt that no one believes her. Max is hurt that he's lost all the people he cares about. Both are desperately yearning for comfort, and are acting like stubborn children. Maria and Michael seem to be the only sane characters in Roswell at the moment, which is rather frightening when you think about it. Max and Liz acting irrationally, and Michael and Maria as the model couple? Who would've thought?

The whole Alex/Sweden mystery continues to intrigue as more and more clues pile in. Liz's detective skills are far superior to those of the FBI agents in Roswell, that's for sure! With a few compelling, creepy moments (Leanna is not Leanna), it's pretty obvious that Liz is onto something. Liz may be uncovering the truth, but at what cost? She's completely alienated herself from the others. In fact, of all the episodes in season one and two, this is the one where almost every character finds themselves alienated from the group.

Michael's words best sum up the moral of this episode: "Don't make a huge decision right now. Not when your emotions are still running high." As seen in "It's Too Late and It's Too Bad," doing so can lead to unfortunate conclusions.

FLASH: The garbage-disposal-and-Amy as a metaphor for Maria and Michael's relationship.

IRKS: Liz has turned her room into a bizarre shrine of information on Alex, and her parents haven't noticed? It's also a little far-fetched for her to buy a ticket to Sweden in the hopes of uncovering more of the mystery. What does she expect to find there? She already knows that the number she has for the Olsens is wrong. How does she expect to find Leanna (who is not Leanna) in a country whose population is close to nine million people?

ALIENISMS: Michael fixes the DeLucas' garbage disposal. Isabel uses her powers to send a jock flying back into a set of lockers.

SODA MOMENT: This is the first episode to use the term "Pod Squad." Maria uses it in her blackboard introduction. The term is a play on the title of the funky 1968–73 cop show *The Mod Squad*. *The Mod Squad* was also a 1999 film starring *My So-Called Life* star Claire Danes.

COOL FACTS: The Roswell Observatory is actually the famous Griffith Observatory that resides on the southern slope of Mount Hollywood and was established in 1935. The 1955 film *Rebel Without A Cause* immortalized both James Dean and the Griffith Observatory.

MUSIC: When Liz and Maria are in Alex's room, "Whatever Gets You True" by Paddy Casey is on. "Perfect Place" by Pancho's Lament plays when Michael talks to Isabel about staying in Roswell. Later, Jim White's "Handcuffed to a Fence in Mississippi" plays at the yearbook staff meeting. Finally, we hear "I Will Love You" by Fisher when Tess and Max are together at the Observatory.

2.20 Baby It's You

ORIGINAL AIR DATE: May 7, 2001
WRITTEN BY: Lisa Klink
DIRECTED BY: Rodney Charters

GUEST CAST: Michael Chieffo (Mr. Seligman), Jeff Wadlow (Ed the College Student), Sean Dwyer (Percy), Jodi Ann Paterson (as herself), Jeremy Guskin (Derek), Lauren Roman (Bonnie), Nicole Brunner (Leanna/Jennifer), Nelly Furtado (as herself)

Maria and Liz get to the bottom of the Alex mystery with Michael's help. Max deals with the ramifications of his one-night stand with Tess, and Isabel and Kyle hook up to use her powers for a little recreational fun.

It's always fantastic to watch an episode that addresses past and present issues, and does it with such flair. "Baby It's You" incorporated mystery, emotional character journeys, and threw in a bit of comic relief as well. The build towards the season finale is excellent, and keeps us guessing at each turn.

Liz actually manages to find proof that Alex was murdered, and enlists Maria's help in the investigation. As they work to unravel the mystery at Las Cruces University . . . they stop briefly to listen to a free Nelly Furtado concert. This scene is nothing but a cheesy plug for Nelly, and an even cheesier way to get people to watch the show. It's entirely unrealistic that a huge pop star would be giving a free outdoor concert in the middle of a campus with no security and a small audience. And Maria's response to seeing Nelly is even worse: "Oh my god, it's Nelly Furtado. Please, one, one song?" Okay, so they're teenagers, and seeing a free concert has appeal, but Liz has killed friendships over this investigation! Stopping to listen to Nelly sing seems so contrived, it's ridiculous. (Yes, it's also a little unrealistic that Liz would manage to get a student to open up Alex's files on the supercomputer, but at least there is a significant plot point to it!)

Just when we think Michael can't get any better, he ups the ante. Considering how immature Max is lately, Michael does a complete 180, turning into Mr. Sensitivity. First, he respects Maria's decision to go to Las Cruces with Liz but insists she contact him if there is any danger. He's obviously thrown his loyalty into the human court, which is interesting considering Michael's always been the one to hammer home the alien/human division. How he finds Max and Isabel in the park is a mystery, but then Michael seems to have the ability to show up when needed, and save lives. Michael's da man!

Kyle and Isabel team up in this episode, and play very well off each other. Nick once more displays his comic sensibility as Kyle tempts Isabel to have some fun. Kyle's love of porn is one of the most consistent elements of the show, and the Playmate scene is brilliant as he explains to Jodi Ann with a goofy expression, "I'm the towel boy." Isabel finds herself getting sucked into childish pranks as a way of getting back at Max. One of her pranks, however, turns out to be one of the more heartbreaking moments of the episode. The look that transpires between Max and Isabel as he sits in class desperately untying his shoes is devastating. It's a strong reminder of how close these two were. Isabel learns that her pranks don't make her feel better, and ultimately trades the childish behavior for childhood memories.

Once more Behr comes through with an excellent performance. First of all, his awkwardness with Tess after their night together is completely appropriate. While many teenage guys become boastful after their "first time," Max yearns for his innocence. Isabel offers him a nostalgic glimpse later when she makes it snow, but as we learn in the last episode, you can never go back. Max is dealing with the consequences of his rash actions. He desperately wants to reach out to Isabel, but his cruel words to her in the last episode have taken their toll. Michael isn't terribly supportive, and is even surprised that Max wasn't more careful about the situation (considering Michael's reputation, that says a lot). In a well-crafted scene, Max breaks down while putting out the garbage. We see him once more as the kid that he is, completely confused and torn just as any teenage father-to-be would be.

While there are still questions to be answered, "Baby It's You" is a strong lead-up to the season finale.

FLASH: Max touching the little glowing baby hand.

IRKS: This is a pretty elaborate setup Alex was caught in. My nitpicks really have to do with the outcome of this situation. Reflecting back on the "responsible party," it must have kept this individual incredibly busy, which requires a lot of suspension of disbelief. The perpetrator also had to keep maintaining Alex while somehow being in Roswell the entire time. It also requires some serious suspension of disbelief when Michael finds the letter from the property board. Why does Liz come to ask Tess about her mindwarp powers?

ALIENISMS: Isabel dreamwalks a Playmate, bringing Kyle along. She replaces Max's yearbook photo with an alien image. During a fire drill, she makes Max's feet stick to the floor so he can't leave. She also makes it snow. Michael uses his powers to hurtle a bomb out of the window. Max touches Tess's womb, is able to see his son, and discovers what the problem is. It seems the gestation period for an alien baby is one month.

SODA MOMENT: Isabel makes the comment "I'm gonna have to read *Backlash* twice after

Emilie de Ravin at the premiere for Original Sin (Photo by Christina Radish)

this!" as Kyle drools over *Playboy* playmate Jodi Ann. *Backlash*, a book by prize-winning journalist Susan Faludi, addresses the post-'80s backlash against feminism. Basically she creates an argument for the validity of feminism in today's society.

MUSIC: When Max and Tess wake up together, "Fade Into You" by Mazzy Star is playing. "Another Pearl" by Badly Drawn Boy plays when Max and Tess walk down the school hallway together. When Max looks at his yearbook, "I Want To Destroy You" by The Soft Boys is in the background. Nelly Furtado sings "I'm Like A Bird" at the University. Lifehouse's "Only One" plays at the Crashdown when Isabel tells Kyle the pranks are over. When Max breaks down by the trash, we hear "Wednesday's Child" by Emiliana Torinni. Finally, "Atmosphere" by Landing Gear plays when Isabel comforts Max.

2.16 Off The Menu

ORIGINAL AIR DATE: May 14, 2001
WRITTEN BY: Russel Friend, Garrett Lerner
DIRECTED BY: Patrick Norris

GUEST CAST: Desmond Askew (Brody Davis), Diane Farr (Amy DeLuca), Devon Gummersall (Sean DeLuca), Jason Peck (Deputy Hanson)

After receiving an electric shock to the head, Brody accesses Larek's memories and holds Max, Tess, Amy, Maria, Sean, and Liz hostage in the UFO Center.

"Off the Menu" is literally an episode that was taken off the menu. The 16th episode filmed, it was slotted in the #20 spot. It answers a lot of the questions that come up during "Heart of Mine" and actually fits better where it was originally supposed to be. Placed where it is, it takes away from the tension built up in "Baby It's You," but the producers moved it to slot #20 because they were concerned audiences would forget the finger-drumming clue that is essential to understanding "The Departure." Maria states in the opening that this episode will provide the key to everything, but that isn't true; the key doesn't become apparent until the following episode. While "Off The Menu" isn't the best of the *Roswell* episodes, at least it clears up a few issues.

Determined to remember what happened to him during his abductions, Brody tries working with a high-tech virtual reality program. The program helps him recall Max's image at the summit, but an overload causes a massive power surge that sends an electric shock to Brody's brain. Presto — instant Larek memories. The aliens have powers because they access a higher percentage of their brain. So, when the aliens use the humans as their "cell phones," they tap into an unused part of the gray matter. The shock sends Brody into a state of confusion about his identity. Motivated by fear and newly aware of Max's secret, he traps Max and Tess in the UFO Center. Maria, Amy, and Sean wander into the center with the hopes of making a sale . . . and end up remaining as hostages. The rest of the town is busy dealing with the power outage.

"Off The Menu" introduces the concept of virtual reality as memory therapy. When computers began to advance technologically and the graphics became more sophisticated, virtual reality was able to emerge. The flight simulator program used to train pilots on land was an instrumental predecessor to present-day virtual reality technology. Both the military and the entertainment industry pumped money into the advancement of computer graphics, but it became more accessible to the public with the advent of video games in the 1980s. The "dataglove" started as an interface device sensitive to hand movements. Now there are datagloves, cybergloves, powergloves, and the Dexterous Hand Master, all of which are operated through hand movement. The development of high performance computers allowed for greater animation advancement. Soon, visual headpieces were created, allowing the player to view the world in a contained unit and experience the game three-dimensionally. The head-mounted display uses separate screens for each eye and incorporates a head-tracking device. This device works with a computer graphics workstation so that the image displayed is consistent with the direction of the user's view. Virtual reality simulators have been used to help conquer different phobias through exposure therapy, and have been used specifically to help Vietnam veterans overcome their traumatic experiences. Their use in the psychological field continues to grow.

As stated, this episode addresses some of the questions that come up during "Heart Of Mine." First of all, it becomes clear why Liz goes out on a date with Sean. Secondly, the whole Tess/Max memory regression concept starts to make sense: Max has some flashes of his former life with Tess while healing Brody. It's a little unrealistic, however, that Larek would have *human* images of Max and Tess together. Max realizes Tess isn't lying about their past, and therefore is inspired to start doing memory work with her. The device first seen in "Ask Not" is given a name and a function. The Trithium Amplification Generator (TAG, a.k.a. the pentagonal thingy) can prevent aliens from using their powers when it is activated — it's like kryptonite for the Pod Squad.

Another issue that is cleared up involves Jim Valenti. It seems as though Jim has been reinstated as the sheriff in "Cry Your Name," but we discover Deputy Hanson is the new sheriff and Jim is still unemployed. Why someone hires Deputy Hanson to take over Jim's job is beyond me. They must be pretty desperate for good help these days in Roswell. Even though he's lost the title, the previous episodes make it clear that Jim still has a lot of authority with the Roswell Police Department.

Sean really comes through in this episode as an admirable character. The scene when Sean attacks Brody is reminiscent of the classic scene in *Romeo and Juliet* when Mercutio attacks Tybalt only to be thwarted by Romeo's efforts to stop the fight. Both Mercutio and Sean also suffer stab wounds. While he seems very weak at the start, he certainly recuperates enough to help dismantle the security system and face Deputy Hanson later on. Talk about a miraculous recovery! Desmond Askew has some good moments in this episode as he battles to discover his true identity. His fear is real and understandable; like a sufferer of Alzheimer's, Brody wants so much to remember who he really is, and is frustrated by his inability to do so. Brody also has a lovely moment with Max when he relays the story of how Zan and Ava first met.

"Off The Menu" is an interesting concept, but is badly placed in the episode schedule. Seems like a metaphor for the actual series and its scheduling problems on The WB.

FLASH: Michael and Isabel's response to Liz's question regarding Maria's cryptic message.

IRKS: As noted earlier, this episode answers questions surrounding "Heart of Mine," but requires us to really think back to the world at that time. So much has happened since, it's a bit challenging. It's also nice to see that while the sheriff is no longer the sheriff, he still somehow finds a way to access the department's equipment!

DOUBLE TAKE: When Brody's bullet hits the REFUGE sign, it takes out a chunk of the paint. When Hanson later inspects it, the paint is intact.

ALIENISMS: Max uses his force field to deflect Brody's bullets, and later heals Brody of Larek's memories. The TAG device prevents aliens in the vicinity from using their powers. Isabel heats her burger, and later Michael and Isabel help cook the burgers and fries with their powers. Tess uses her mindwarp powers to make Amy forget what happened.

COOL FACTS: The night this episode first aired, Majandra Delfino posted on her Fan Forum board as Nephelite for the first time.

MUSIC: When Maria talks to Brody at the Crashdown, "Follow Me" by Uncle Cracker is playing.

2.21 The Departure

ORIGINAL AIR DATE: May 21, 2001
WRITTEN BY: Jason Katims
DIRECTED BY: Patrick Norris

GUEST CAST: Diane Farr (Amy DeLuca), Garrett M. Brown (Philip Evans), Mary Ellen Trainor (Diane Evans), Devon Gummersall (Sean DeLuca), Nicole Brunner (Leanna/Jennifer), Nicholas Stratton (young Michael)

The Royal Four activate the Granilith, giving them 24 hours to say goodbye before leaving for their home planet, Antar.

Wow. Jason Katims makes up for just about every mediocre episode in this season with a stunning season finale! Okay, so there are still a lot of questions, but it doesn't take away from this episode one bit. "The Departure" not only satisfies us on so many emotional levels, it leaves us desperate for more! The finale of both season one and two brings us to the pod chamber and the rock formation in the desert. Both finales also pose the now famous question — "What happens now, Max?" At least Max has an answer at the end of *this* season.

Giving the teens 24 hours to say goodbye to the only home they know is a great tension-building scenario. There are so many loose ends to tie up, but the biggest one involves finding Alex's killer. One thing that season two has demonstrated is that the human teens are just as important in the grand scheme of things as the alien teens. Sure, the alien teens have powers, but Alex is the one who decodes the Destiny book, while Liz is the one who discovers it, saves Leanna/Jennifer's life, and clues in to the evil plot behind Alex's death. And let's not forget that Alex and Kyle save the world! (Okay, so Liz does it first, but still . . .)

We catch a glimpse of the old active Liz/Max team at Las Cruces. Season one ends with their separation, season two sends their relationship through the ringer, and "The Departure" gives us a satisfying conclusion. The truth comes out but it doesn't hinder their reconciliation. Things aren't going to be easy for them, however. While many of the characters endure a loss of innocence this season, Liz arguably suffers the most. She is denied the chance to start afresh all year. She is forced to break Max's heart, forced to watch him with Tess, continually pulled back into the alien issues, and then, just as Sean enters her life, she loses one of her best friends. Max and Liz have connected once more, but as she says to Sean, "Max Evans broke [my] heart." The next season will show us the repercussions of his transgression.

Michael's character arc has come to a fitting conclusion as he breaks down the wall and embraces his human side and Earth as his home. Maria's character has also been rather erratic, but she has matured in the long run. In a beautiful moment, Michael shares his inner self with Maria, allowing her to "see" what she was denied in season one.

Isabel's inability to tell her parents her secret is heartbreaking. When we have to let go of loved ones, it's the little moments that really hit us, like silly conversations over Chinese food. Isabel has finally grown into a woman, standing up for her own rights. Regardless of the divisions created this season, Isabel puts loyalty to her brother first, making up for Vilandra's betrayal. Katherine does a wonderful job in this episode, really showing the emotional torture that can come with saying goodbye.

It's easy to get choked up during Jim Valenti's final goodbyes with the teens. Our hearts race when Kyle has his first memory flash of Alex, when Amy taps the stove, and when the mirror reveals the truth. When Michael sends the jeep off the cliff with Coldplay's "Trouble" playing in the background, we are reminded of how music can truly enhance a scene. With a title like "The Departure," it's hard to figure out just what could happen to the Pod Squad, or even to the series. Thankfully, UPN had announced *Roswell*'s move to their network four days earlier. Not only do we get fantastic performances and a fabulous script, we also get a funky-looking spaceship that resembles the craft from the 1986 Disney film *Flight of the Navigator*. "The Departure" is, without a doubt, one of the best episodes of season two. "What happens now, Max?" Now? We've got a new network, and it's time to anticipate the arrival of season three!

FLASH: Michael letting his guard down so Maria could "see" him. And Tess getting her comeuppance, of course.

IRKS: While "The Departure" really is a great episode, we're still left with a lot of questions. If Alex manages to translate the Destiny book by January, why are we only seeing it now? Does that mean Alex e-mails it to the "Leanna" address just before he dies? And how on earth does Tess manage to orchestrate this whole thing? She fools the school, Alex's parents, Alex, and Jennifer; creates photos and two months' worth of false memories; and keeps him at the University? Does she do it alone, or is she in kahoots with the Skins? She's obviously powerful if she can do all of that alone. In "The End of the World," Future Max tells us that the four have to stick together or it would mean the end of the world. And yet, Tess is now otherwise occupied. Does that mean we're in for an apocalypse? I somehow doubt it.

DOUBLE TAKE: The shot we first see of Jennifer pricking her finger and grabbing a tissue is different than the shot Liz flashes back to of the same moment. In the first one, we never see the blood on her finger.

ALIENISMS: Tess is a busy girl! She's mindwarping everyone these days. Michael uses his powers to send the jeep over the cliff, causing it to burst into flames. Max starts to heat up the wire system in Jennifer's dorm room, intending to set it on fire.

SODA MOMENT: Kyle refers to Max and Michael as "Heckle and Jeckle." Heckle and Jeckle were two black magpies, identical and inseparable. While they looked the same, their person- alities were quite different. Heckle had a New York accent, while Jeckle had a more cultured voice. Using their wit, they spent their time conning food and shelter from the rich. These two cartoon characters first appeared in 1956 on CBS Cartoon Theater, and they later had their own show in 1979.

COOL FACTS: The dates on Alex's grave read June 21, 1984 to April 29, 2001. That would mean that Alex was sixteen when he died. Isabel turned 18 in 2000. That makes Isabel two years older than Alex. She's a year older than Max.

MUSIC: "Here It Comes" by The Doves plays when Maria, Liz, Kyle, and Sean are at the Crashdown. Remy Zero's "Perfect Memory" plays when Isabel visits Alex's grave. When Max and Liz say goodbye, David Gray's "My Oh My" is in the background. "Blackbird" by The Doves plays when Michael tells Maria he's leaving. When the Pod Squad say goodbye to Jim, the song is "Trouble" by Coldplay. Finally, U2's "Walk On" plays at the end.

SEASON THREE (OCTOBER 2001 — MAY 2002)

3.1 Busted!

ORIGINAL AIR DATE: October 9, 2001
WRITTEN BY: Jason Katims
DIRECTED BY: Allan Kroeker

GUEST CAST: Garrett M. Brown (Philip Evans), John Doe (Geoff Parker), Jo Anderson (Nancy Parker), Mary Ellen Trainor (Diane Evans), Michael Chieffo (Mr. Seligman), Phil Reeves (Judge Davi), Yorgo Constantine (Agent Burns), Joey Ferrini (Dayton Callie), Jeannetta Arnette (Delores Browning), John Bisom (McGregor), Glenn Brown (Security Guard), Michael Earl Reid (Harlan), Gilbert Joshua Drennen (Officer), Randy Thompson (Tytell), Joseph Williams (Singer)

Max and Liz are arrested for armed robbery in Utah. Isabel continues her secret affair with Jesse Ramirez, and Michael attempts to get his school life in order.

Well, we're not in Roswell anymore: literally. With the move to UPN, we expected there would be some changes to the show, but whoa! Max and Liz as fugitives? Michael taking responsibility for his education? Isabel's short coif and illicit affair? Okay, the latter two were feasible, but . . . Max and Liz as fugitives? What happened to the calm, rational alien we all knew and loved? Where did the perky, responsible Crashdown waitress disappear to? Who are these people waving guns around and playing at being Bonnie and Clyde? Okay, so we know the characters tend to change a little over the summer, but this is *huge*.

One of the first notable differences is the filming style. The present-day sequence in Utah looks like an episode of *NYPD Blue*, with hand-held camera shots and a bleached appearance. It's a bit jarring to watch at first, since the style is so different from the *Roswell* we had seen before. The flashback shots are done in the more traditional style, with fresh-faced characters and brighter colors. In a lot of ways, it feels as though the "flashbacks" represent the old network, while the present-day grittier shots are representative of *Roswell*'s new home at UPN.

As we ponder the fate of Max and Liz in Utah, we are thankfully brought up to speed through the flashbacks, allowing us to adjust to this new, rebellious version of our favorite couple. Liz goes from pastels to black, both in her clothing and make-up choices. Max not only has major bags under his eyes, but a five o'clock shadow. And a new black leather jacket. There's no question that these two are getting a sexual kick out of breaking the law . . . even if it is for a "greater" cause. Initially, it seems a bit illogical that Max and Liz embraces their rebellious natures so quickly, but then again, when we leave Max last season, he isn't exactly

Mr. Responsible. Liz also has her irrational moments. So, even though armed robbery seems far-fetched, considering their behavior in season two, it's plausible. Throughout the series, Max and Liz have continually been wrapped up in each other so much so that no one else seems to count, and this episode is no exception.

Max and Liz aren't the only two rebels in this episode. Isabel, we discover, is having a secret affair with Jesse, a young lawyer at her father's firm. Adam Rodriguez is a welcome addition to the cast, fitting right in with the more "mature" look that this season seems to be taking on. Michael, on the other hand, goes from the troublemaking alien to the domesticated, rational one. Continuing from where we leave off in season two, Michael embraces Earth as his home, and is actually interested in bettering himself by finishing high school. Even with a crisis at hand, Michael continues to negotiate with Mr. Seligman in the hopes of getting through Biology 101.

Considering all the parents were AWOL in season two, it's nice to see them return to their duties this year. The Parkers finally rein in Liz, establishing some serious ground rules for a change. Meanwhile, Mr. Evans swoops in as the hero to save the day — a role once belonging to Jim Valenti. With the Skins gone and the general sci-fi elements being downplayed, it appears as though the parents have returned to thwart the actions of our teenage friends.

In one scene, Liz is goaded into skinny dipping with Max. First, she hesitates as she watches him dive in. As she clues in that he is drowning, she dives in to rescue him without any hesitation. If that's not a metaphor for season three, I don't know what is. Throughout the season, Liz continually dives right in to save Max, never thinking of herself. The scene introduces her major character arc for the season.

FLASH: Maria's line as she arrives in Salina: "Why can't these aliens ever get in trouble somewhere decent? Like Graceland or Tahoe or New Orleans. No, Utah. Mormons and mountains."

IRKS: Considering the amazing schemes Max and the team come up with to break in to various different buildings, why such a stupid one this time? There are so many options for them, but they choose the whole Bonnie and Clyde armed robbery one? Not very believable considering the characters we're talking about. The diamond theft is also very far-fetched. A diamond that size would be enclosed under glass. Also, wouldn't the alien crew have gone through Tess's things already? I'm also not too sure on this new "dark circles/pale skin" look for Max. He's become a rebel, not a drug addict.

DOUBLE TAKE: Delores Browning has champagne thrown on her face, hair, and presumably her dress, but somehow manages to stay dry.

ALIENISMS: Max causes a video camera to break, unseals and seals a wall a few times, causes a gun to melt into the car floor, lights up a harbor à la "Blind Date," has a flash of his alien son, activates the "door" on the spaceship, and breaks the lock on Sam's Quick Stop. Isabel heats tea with her hand. The diamond is actually a key to their spaceship.

COOL FACT: The 1967 film *Bonnie and Clyde* was based on the true story of bank robbers Bonnie Parker (a distant relative of Liz's perhaps?) and Clyde Barrow. In the film, Bonnie is a bored, sexually frustrated waitress. When they meet, Clyde has just been released from prison for armed robbery. While Bonnie gets aroused by the crimes, Clyde is unable to satisfy her needs. Instead, he appeals to her sense of adventure and desire to skip town. Once on their way, they become almost like Robin Hood and Marian, with their own band of Merry Men. They botch up a few robberies to start. Their crime spree continues, but their actions slowly catch up to them. They finally make the decision to go clean, but they are too late, and are both shot to death. In the case of Liz and Max, the parallels are clear. Fortunately for Liz, Max is perfectly capable of keeping her satisfied. The movie parallel continues throughout the season as Liz and Max continue on a rebellious path. In the series finale, Liz's premonition mirrors Bonnie's in the film.

MUSIC: Sugar Ray's "Under the Sun" plays when Max and Liz are outside the Quick Stop. In the flashback, "Choked Up" by Minibar is playing when Max gives Liz the flowers. Later, "Whalebones" by Preston School of Industry is on when Michael talks about Biology 101. We hear "Where Happiness Lives" by Evan Johansen outside the museum as Max and Liz take off. Sense Field's "Here Right Now" is the background music when Max gives Liz the gun. When Max returns to the Quick Stop, Blur's "Trimm Trabb" is playing. Finally, "The Last Laugh" by Mark Knopfler featuring Van Morrison filters through the night while Max stares at the stars.

3.2 Michael, the Guys, and the Great Snapple Caper

ORIGINAL AIR DATE: October 16, 2001
WRITTEN BY: Ronald D. Moore
DIRECTED BY: Paul Shapiro

GUEST CAST: John Doe (Geoff Parker), Jason Peck (Sheriff Hanson), Michael Peña (Fly), Earl C. Poitier (George), Martin Starr (Monk), Terence Quinn (Carl), Steven Roy (Steve),

Kathy Byron (Bartender), Joseph Williams (Singer)

Michael gets a job at Meta-Chem Pharmaceuticals and makes trouble for his new co-workers, while Kyle confronts his father about their financial difficulties.

We've gone from armed robbery in "Busted!" to the theft of fruity drinks in this episode. The underlying theme of taking responsibility in life links all three storylines together. With a nice balance of humor and drama, "Michael, the Guys, and the Great Snapple Caper" is an episode worth watching.

Michael gains a sense of morality. With the bills mounting, Michael gets himself a job on the graveyard security shift at Meta-Chem, and the opening cutaway shots during Michael's interview are priceless, showing the truth behind his answers. The journey of personal growth Michael embarks on is intriguing. Brendan Fehr is in his element here, and is obviously enjoying himself. Michael not only starts to recognize that his actions affect other people, but he actually begins to feel badly about them. Even more surprisingly, Michael apologizes and puts his neck on the line to help out a friend. Considering Michael has always been a loner, it's great to see him become one of the "guys." Throughout the seasons we have witnessed the evolution of his "human" side, and his behavior in this episode is one more step in that direction. Michael's storyline has some hilarious moments ("We all drank of the Snapple") as he grapples with his newfound conscience. Fly, George, and Monk are all nice additions, sharing some resemblance to the "geek" gang from *Buffy*. And let's not forget that allusion to *The Breakfast Club* as Michael crawls through the air duct and falls through the ceiling. Judd Nelson would be proud.

For Kyle and Jim, the question of responsibility has more serious implications. It appears Kyle has been working part time as a mechanic to pay off the mounting household bills. Jim is still dealing with losing his job, and his solution to the financial problem does not meet Kyle's expectations. In a great role-reversal scenario, we get to see the child acting as parent, and the strain that it can cause. This situation is certainly a common one in many households, and both Nick Wechsler and Bill Sadler do a wonderful job as always. Kyle is obviously frustrated, while at the same time attempting to be understanding. Jim comes across as an insecure teenager, hesitant about sharing his new business venture for fear of the lecture to come. The Jim/Kyle segments of this episode take a more serious look at the realities of both financial and emotional responsibility.

And what's with those crazy Evans kids? Isabel keeps her relationship with Jesse a secret just as Max blatantly disregards Mr. Parker's rules about seeing Liz. Rebellion seems to be as much of a theme this season as responsibility. The teens are breaking away from their previous identities, and forging new ones for themselves. "Michael, the Guys, and the Great Snapple Caper" or "Busted, Again!" is a good follow-up to the season premiere.

FLASH: Kyle's reaction to catching Isabel and Jesse: "Ho ho." Also, when Kyle starts clapping along to his father's band.

IRKS: I may be wrong, but it's very hard to believe that the guys could get away with smoking cigars in a pharmaceutical lab, even if they are only in the security room. And could Max shave? Or at least get some sleep? Please? Let's hope he finds a razor at Michael's. Considering Max's recent arrest, it's rather ridiculous that he's giving Michael a hard time about not having a plan. Also, based on where Mr. Parker is sitting in the Crashdown, Max and Liz would have seen him when they came in.

DOUBLE TAKE: At one point, when Isabel is talking with Kyle in the Crashdown, she rests her hand on her neck. It cuts to Kyle, and Isabel is eating a fry. It's too fast for her to have picked one up.

ALIENISMS: Max manipulates the wall mural in the Crashdown, then later creates a breeze to lift the glider into the night sky. Michael breaks into Meta-Chem using his powers, causes a part of the ceiling to fall (we think), and later fixes a VHS tape.

SODA MOMENT: Liz's "Superman" fantasy is in reference to the first film when Superman takes Lois on a joy-flight through the night. Who could forget the infamous internal monologue "Can you read my mind?" This, of course, was an ironic touch considering how *Smallville* kept overriding *Roswell* in the ratings. Does that mean Liz is really dreaming of flying away with another dark-haired alien?

COOL FACT: The third "Save *Roswell*" campaign involved fundraising for Families of Spinal Muscular Atrophy, a charity connected with *Roswell* writer Garrett Lerner. Tabasco makers McIlhenny & Co., who had been connected with the show since the first season, made a donation. The makers of Snapple, the new product of choice for season three, was approached, and they also got on the fundraising bandwagon.

MUSIC: Merrick's "Infinity" is playing when Kyle catches Isabel and Jesse kissing. When the boys mess around on their shift, "Weapon of Choice" by Fatboy Slim is on. "Have a Nice Day" by the Stereophonics plays when Liz sees the message from Max in the Crashdown. Later, we hear "Promise To Try" by Leona Ness when Isabel and Kyle talk about Jesse. Finally, we get the musical debut of Jim Valenti and the Kit Shickers at Cow Patty's when they cover the Barenaked Ladies song "If I Had A Million Dollars."

3.3 Significant Others

ORIGINAL AIR DATE: October 22, 2001
WRITTEN BY: David Simkins
DIRECTED BY: Patrick Norris
GUEST CAST: John Doe (Geoff Parker), Garrett M. Brown (Philip Evans), Mary Ellen Trainor (Diane Evans), Jo Anderson (Nancy Parker), Michael Chieffo (Mr. Seligman), Colin Hanks (Alex Whitman), Ivonne Coll (Estelle Ramirez), Michael Peña (Fly), Earl C. Poitier (George), Steven Roy (Steve), Martin Starr (Monk)

Isabel calls upon Alex for advice on her relationship with Jesse. Meanwhile, Liz discovers more about her father's past, and Michael double-books himself on "date night."

Considering the battles the *Roswell* teens are involved in last season, you would think that dealing with relationship and parental conflict should be a piece of cake. Unfortunately, while the teens have matured on certain levels, the same issues continue to follow them. Gone are the sci-fi days when the Gandarium and the Skins are the major problem. In "Significant Others," relationship commitment and understanding are the issues to overcome, and we are reminded that in order to find balance, open communication and compromise are important.

Isabel and Jesse's relationship is at a crossroads. Isabel gets the impression from one of Jesse's dreams that he is about to propose, and the idea is enough to bring forth all of her commitment fears. It's normal enough for an 18-year-old to fear commitment, and even more understandable if that individual watched two of her boyfriends die. Isabel's fluctuating opinion on her relationship is easy to relate to, and while her final decision is not terribly practical, it is an interesting choice. And even though she already said goodbye to Alex in season two, it's great to see Colin Hanks once more as he helps her come to terms with the past that literally seems to "haunt" her.

Michael and Maria continue to struggle with their functional/dysfunctional relationship. As relationships evolve, priorities change and new ground rules have to be established. As Michael discovers that keeping mistakes secret is not a solution, Maria recognizes that Michael is growing and she needs to share him. Michael and Maria's relationship continues to be the most realistic one on the show. Maria's patience, however, is monumental considering what she puts up with to be with Michael, and it made the actors uncomfortable. Both Majandra Delfino and Brendan Fehr spoke with the writers, explaining that having Maria constantly tolerate Michael's neglect was a bad influence on impressionable audience members. Luckily, the writers listened and changes were made.

The best storyline in this episode involves Liz and her father. It's easy for teenagers to forget that their parents were once teenagers also. It's understandable that Liz's parents would be overprotective and upset with Liz after her arrest, but to link it to Geoff Parker's shady past is a great idea. Not only does he see his own mistakes in Max, but in Liz as well. Mr. Parker's touching line "You're the poem, Liz," is a lovely, understated moment.

As promised, the third season of *Roswell* is putting more emphasis on character exploration. "Significant Others" is an example of that.

FLASH: Maria's reaction to Isabel's question: "If Michael proposed, would you say yes?" And Alex, of course.

IRKS: Liz and Max really need to revisit their closets and explore color once more. The whole black clothing thing is a tad stereotypical. It's also rather bizarre to see an old black payphone in Jesse's garden. And what's with the wig in Liz's bedroom? Also, when Jesse leaves Isabel, he leaves his mother's ring with her. After her pep talk with Alex, when she dashes out of the restaurant, she also leaves the ring behind. Considering his mother is in financial debt and is considering hocking it, it's not too wise to abandon it in a restaurant.

ALIENISMS: Isabel dreamwalks Jesse.

SODA MOMENT: In Alex's first pep talk for Isabel, he uses the phrase "Eye of the tiger." That line is in reference to *Rocky III*. Rocky's coach keeps reminding Rocky to keep the eye of the tiger: namely, his edge. This led to the hit song "Eye of the Tiger" by Survivor.

MUSIC: "I Want All Of You" by The Verve Pipe is playing when Isabel and Jesse go to the movies. Later, during Jesse's dream, "Dance Until Dawn" by Emer Kenny can be heard. When Max approaches Geoff Parker, "Crashing Down" by Eagle Eye Cherry is in the background. In the bowling alley, we hear "Not Want I Wanted" by Evan Olsen. "Shattered" by Emer Kenny plays when Isabel is in the bathroom talking to Alex. When Liz talks to her father in the Crashdown, "I'll Say I'm Sorry Now" by Shawn Colvin is in the background. Finally, we get to hear Remy Zero's "Perfect Memory" once again as Isabel accepts Jesse's proposal.

3.4 Secrets and Lies — Part One

ORIGINAL AIR DATE: October 30, 2001
WRITTEN BY: Russel Friend, Garrett Lerner
DIRECTED BY: Jonathan Frakes

GUEST CAST: Joe Pantoliano (Kal Langley), Garrett M. Brown (Philip Evans), Mary Ellen Trainor (Diane Evans), Stephen Tobolowsky (Julius Walters), Stanley Anderson (James Valenti, Sr.), Eve Brent (Jane Covendall), Dayton Callie (Joey Ferrini), Adilah Barnes (Journalism Teacher), John Billingsley (as himself), Richard Eck (Detective Erlick), Rocky McMurray (Detective Kerr), Aimee Nicole (Actress), Bitty Schram (Bunny), Barry Wiggins (Deputy Brown), Jonathan Frakes (as himself — uncredited)

After hearing of the strange death of Joey Ferrini, Max heads to L.A. to search for the second shapeshifter. Kyle and Liz investigate Kyle's grandfather's past as part of a school project.

"Secrets and Lies" both amuses and confuses me. The amusement factor comes from the Hollywood segment, which incidentally could be titled "Tongue-in-Cheek" for its little digs at the Hollywood scene and at *Roswell* itself. The confusion arises from the Jim Valenti storyline as Jim once more deals with his issues regarding his father. All in all, this episode involves searching out the truth "no matter how uncomfortable or unpleasant that may be."

This episode is touted as a "cross-over" episode with the new series *Enterprise*. While we do get to see John Billingsley (Dr. Phlox on *Enterprise*) when Max auditions for a one-day role on the show, it isn't a "cross-over" in the classic sense at all. Still, it's fun to see Max audition for the part of "Korgan," and you can't help but chuckle when Jonathan Frakes stops him mid-reading to inform Max that he doesn't feel like Max is an alien. Jason Behr does a great stilted performance in the audition as well. Stephen Tobolowsky is fabulous as Julius the talent agent, bringing a lot of humor to the episode. Having Julius call Max a kid from "Kansas" is an amusing allusion to *Smallville*. Later, when informing Max that if the *Enterprise* audition doesn't work out, there's always *Buffy* is also cute (Jason Behr actually did make an appearance on *Buffy*). All in all, it's nice to see the writers having some fun while Max searches for the "truth" in L.A.

While Liz uses the information learned from Kyle's grandfather to help Max's investigation, Kyle uses it to reach out to his father. And here is where it gets confusing: when we last saw Jim with his father, he had discovered that his father was innocent of the Silo murder. At that point, Jim and James Sr. shared a couple of tender moments. Later on, Jim discovered that aliens did exist, and that his father wasn't crazy. So, why is that Jim now appears to have regressed when it comes to his relationship with James Valenti, Sr.? He won't visit his father and is quick to assume that the actress murdered so many years earlier was indeed killed by a freak lightning strike. After everything Jim has seen, it's rather ridiculous that he wouldn't give his father's theories another day in court. It's also a little far-fetched that Jim immediately takes his father's words — "They are among us" — to be the title of the movie he worked on, rather than simply assuming he was referring to aliens in general. That aside, his final scene with his father is well acted as usual. It would have held more power, however, if we hadn't already seen it before in "Into the Woods."

All in all, "Secrets and Lies" is a good episode, incorporating a mystery that feels straight out of a 1950s film. While not as strong as some of the other episodes, it has its moments. Liz and Max make a great team, and seeing them in action is always a pleasure.

FLASH: James Valenti, Sr. clutching his medals, and attempting to reach his calendar to mark the date of Jim's visit.

IRKS: See above. Also, it's a little hard to believe that if James Sr. made a mess, a family member would be required to show up to clean it. And West Roswell High must be a very wealthy school. Not only does it appear that everyone in the class gets their own laptop or iMac, but the school can afford video cameras as well. Having the video camera perspective is a nice touch, however, as Liz and Kyle make their way through the nursing home.

DOUBLE TAKE: Jim walks into the house and spies his father's medals among the photos that Liz and Kyle are going through. When we cut back to Liz and Kyle there is no sign of the framed medals on the table anywhere. Also, when Max enters the audition room, he closes the door so it is barely open. The next shot has the door half-open.

ALIENISMS: Joey gets fried by a glowing shapeshifter, and an actress working on the B-film "Among Us" died the same way in the 1950s. Max uses his powers to break into the Paramount film lot and to create a light for his makeshift projector. Kal blasts Max into the wall and sets the room on fire using his powers.

SODA MOMENT: After Max tells Julius that he wants to be an actor, Julius responds with "Hello, Stephen! Hello, Martin! Hello Francis!" He is referring to the award-winning directors Stephen Spielberg, Martin Scorsese and Francis Ford Coppola.

COOL FACT: In the opening scene, it's insinuated that Bunny has just finished performing oral sex on Joey in the car. After that, Joey's charred remains are seen. The American Parents Television Council, which had given *Roswell* a green light rating and called it "family friendly" in its first season, switched their rating to a yellow light for second season. After this episode, the council was apparently not at all pleased, and was encouraging people to write to the show's sponsors as a form of protest. Also, there's a different actor playing James Valenti, Sr. Stanley Anderson got the part in this episode because John Cullum was in a live theater production during the filming.

MUSIC: When Jesse gives Isabel the engagement ring, "The Beginner" by Miranda Lee Richards is playing. Later, "Beautiful Dreamers" by Grant Lee Phillips plays when Liz and Kyle talk with Bess Covendall about the 1950s film.

3.5 Control — Part Two

ORIGINAL AIR DATE: November 6, 2001
WRITTEN BY: Gretchen J. Berg, Aaron Harberts
DIRECTED BY: Bill Norton

GUEST CAST: Joe Pantoliano (Kal Langley), Mary Ellen Trainor (Diane Evans), Richard McGonagle (General Edward Chambers), Missi Pyle (Windy Sommers), Ron Fassler (Scott), Dylan Kussman (Brian), Julie Anne Liechty (Blond Woman), Randall Rapstine (Customer)

Max pressures Kal Langley to help him find the ship. Meanwhile, Isabel begins planning her wedding, much to her mother's disapproval.

Max and Isabel seem to be on the same path as they put their own needs first and butt heads with Kal and Mrs. Evans respectively. With powerful performances from both Joe Pantoliano and Mary Ellen Trainor, "Control" looks at the consequences that come from rash action. By taking control of a situation without considering the larger ramifications, alienating oneself can be inevitable. "Control" is easily one of the top five episodes of the season.

It seems Max is turning over a new leaf. Gone is the long floppy hair and the brooding presence of the first few episodes. After Kal sends him packing, Max returns with a new look and a new attitude, once again acting like a leader. With a terrific entrance at Kal's Hollywood party, Max and Kal begin to circle each other, preparing for a battle. As the episode progresses, Kal carefully tries to hide his vulnerabilities while Max strives to unearth them. And yet Kal is not without his own power, and in a very humorous moment puts Max in his place. Joe Pantoliano is fabulous in this episode, exuding both authority and frustration with his inability to overpower his genetic coding. Jason does a nice job portraying Max's crumbling confidence. Max recognizes the error of his rash ways, which is in contrast to his confidence at the start. The two actors have great chemistry as they delve into the strengths and weaknesses of their characters.

While Mary Ellen Trainor has appeared in previous episodes, this particular storyline really shows off her talent. It's obvious that Diane is having difficulty supporting her daughter's decision, and like many daughters, Isabel only wants her mother's support. Diane wants

Jason Behr at the 2000 Glamour Magazine *pre-Emmy party*
(Photo by Christina Radish)

Isabel to have a good life, and the rationale for her behavior is actually quite logical. Isabel, however, does not see herself as 18, but as a responsible adult who has never given her parents reason to question her decisions. The writers have done a good job with this conflict, not allowing either party to seem irrational in their arguments. Like Max, Isabel is alienated for her decision, but eventually finds comfort in the arms of a loved one.

"Control" offers strong emotional moments, fantastic lines, and excellent performances.

FLASH: It was a tough call. Max's pitch is hilarious, as is Maria's response to Liz handing over Max's package ("Are we breaking up?"). But I have to go with Michael returning Mrs. Evans's dish . . . unwashed. Brilliant.

IRKS: It's a little strange for Liz to be sending Max a care package. Where does she intend to send it? It's also harsh that Max ignores Liz's phone call in the hangar, but good for her for standing up to him later on.

DOUBLE TAKE: Kal admits to killing Joey, yet he claims not to have shapeshifted in around 50 years, so how is that possible? The man leaving the scene of the crime is definitely not Joe Pantoliano. Either the writers didn't notice that bit, or Kal is lying. I'd go with the former.

ALIENISMS: Kal puts out a fire with a wave of his hand. He also blasts Max up his staircase and later smashes a vase with his powers. He is unable to feel anything, and is only able to smell chlorine and taste lemons. He must obey Max's direct orders. He shapeshifts into his alien form, and activates the ship. Max uses his powers to break into the hangar. Isabel uses her powers to snuff out street lamps, while Michael causes one to explode.

SODA MOMENT: Kal tells Max he's on "The Zone." The Zone nutrition program was created originally by Barry Sears, PhD. Published in book form in 1995, it became a huge fad in Hollywood. Essentially, it focuses on balancing and controlling insulin production within the body, thus affecting weight, mood, and endurance.

MUSIC: "Lost In You" by Sugarcult plays when Mrs. Evans shows up at the Crashdown looking for Michael. Later, when Isabel talks with Michael in the Crashdown, "Can't Cry These Tears" by Garbage is playing. Finally, "Closer" by Better Than Ezra is on when Max returns and apologizes to Liz.

3.6 To Have and To Hold

ORIGINAL AIR DATE: November 13, 2001
WRITTEN BY: Ronald D. Moore
DIRECTED BY: Fred K. Keller

GUEST CAST: Spence Decker (Kivar), John Doe (Geoff Parker), Garrett M. Brown (Philip Evans), Mary Ellen Trainor (Diane Evans), Ivonne Coll (Estelle Ramirez), Benjamin Benitez (Louis), Chad Gabriel (Mark), Danny Seckel (Richie), Patrick T. O'Brien (Minister), Joseph Williams (Singer), Greg Zola (Karter)

As the wedding approaches, Isabel finds herself plagued with dreams of an attractive stranger. Max and Michael secretly investigate Jesse.

We first heard of Kivar in "Surprise" and since then have been constantly reminded of his history with the teens. He managed to take the throne of Antar and murder Zan, Rath, Vilandra, and Ava. Ever since, he's been searching the Earth for his reincarnated love. And since viewers first heard his name, they've been waiting for him to make his move. How perfect for him to show himself days before Isabel's wedding. "To Have and To Hold" is a great episode for many reasons, but there is no question as to who steals the show.

Katherine Heigl gives a wonderful performance in this episode. We see elements of the Christmas Nazi as she juggles everything in her efforts to create the perfect wedding. As the episode progresses, so does her nervous state. The music helps support her journey, and works especially well to enhance the transitions. After a compelling scene with Michael, the first strains of "Hava Nagila" instantly switch the mood, leading to Isabel's discovery of the microscope and Michael's hilarious response. The best moments, however, are the dream sequences. Not since Buffy and Spike has there been so much chemistry between a villain and a heroine! Spence Decker and Katherine Heigl definitely have that special something: unfortunately, their chemistry far outshines Isabel and Jesse's.

Max's investigation into Jesse's past is another example of him taking action without thought, and in doing so, Max once again fails to see that Isabel can take care of herself. Of the three alien teens, Isabel has the best track record so far when it comes to avoiding screw ups. This is an episode where the men need to let the women stand on their own. Max learns to respect Isabel's strength, while Liz stands up to her father with respect and maturity. The women pull the wedding together, while the men get caught up in petty fights.

There are actually a lot of small but special moments in this episode that are definitely worth noticing, like Michael hiding the microscope under the pillow and Isabel swatting Michael's hand off her leg, or Liz's expression upon seeing the picture of the bridesmaid dresses. What about Jim's attempt to plug his band to Maria, or his response to Isabel's wedding request? Then there's that oh-so-frightening wedding dress and Mrs. Evans's understated arrival. And let's not forget Michael and Kyle's killer pool game, all shot to the stylin' tunes of Jim Valenti and the Kit Shickers. It's also important to note the beautiful visuals in "To Have and To Hold," from the wedding to Isabel's dream world.

I really only have one thing to say about "To Have and To Hold": Kivar rocks.

FLASH: Isabel's final dance at her wedding reception.

IRKS: Max makes a strange comment in his speech by claiming that everyone in the reception knows about his and Isabel's history. Considering half of the people at the reception are Jesse's relatives, the comment seems rather silly. Also, the first guests to arrive at the wedding look more like models than real people.

DOUBLE TAKE: First, Jesse looks at his nose in the mirror and it seems straight, but purple. As the scene progresses, the bump almost . . . grows.

ALIENISMS: Kivar communicates with Isabel through her dreams and she later uses the alien symbols to recreate the dream on paper. Michael uses his powers to kick some butt at pool. Max heals Jesse's nose.

SODA MOMENT: Kyle uses the line, "And don't call me Shirley," which is from the 1980 Leslie Nielsen comedy *Airplane!* Whenever anyone would use the word "surely" in a sentence, the response was "And don't call me Shirley." Did you happen to notice that Karter was talking on the phone to . . . Shirley? Karter also makes a few different references to *The Andy Griffith Show* — calling Kyle "Gomer" and Roswell "Mayberry," for example.

MUSIC: The show opens with Souza's "Wedding March." The Old 97's "Question" plays at the Crashdown when Isabel spends the whole day working on the wedding. When Liz tells her father she is catering the wedding, "Digging Your Scene" by Ivy is in the background. "Hava Nagila" plays when Isabel is talking to Michael. An older version of "Get Me to the Church On Time" comes on just before Jim Valenti and the Kit Shickers do their numbers. Isabel walks down the aisle to "God of Love" by Alana Davis. Finally, Ivy performs "Edge Of The Ocean" at the wedding reception.

3.7 Interruptus

ORIGINAL AIR DATE: November 20, 2001
WRITTEN BY: David Simkins
DIRECTED BY: Bruce Seth Green

GUEST CAST: Spence Decker (Kivar), John Doe (Geoff Parker), Garrett M. Brown (Philip Evans), Mary Ellen Trainor (Diane Evans)

Isabel and Jesse's honeymoon is interrupted by Kivar's presence. Max and Michael head to La Jolla in order to kill Kivar. Mr. Evans begins to investigate his son.

The title of this episode is a sly reference to the Latin "coitus interruptus," a term specifically referring to the interruption of the sex act. It's the perfect title for this episode, seeing as "coitus interruptus" occurs between Isabel and Jesse, and Isabel and Kivar.

Another concept, which we have seen before, is the idea of enemies disguised as friends. This plays out in "Interruptus" on two levels. First, Kivar comes to Jesse in the form of a friend when his intentions are well known to us. Later, we realize that Kivar had been an enemy to Vilandra/Isabel while pretending to be on her side. An even better analogy is the fact that Kivar has used someone else's body to disguise himself as a "good guy." The other enemy in question appears to be Mr. Evans, who has begun an in-depth investigation into Max's past. While his motives come from love, it is clear that he is an enemy when it comes to keeping the secret buried. One thing that *Roswell* has always done well is continually alter the face of the enemy. Obviously, the ultimate enemy is exposure. We've seen the FBI, the local police force, other aliens, alien hunters, peers and now family all try to expose the teens.

The person we really feel for in this episode is Jesse. Isabel and Kivar have great moments, and even Max and Michael feel heroic as they struggle to save Isabel. Jesse, on the other hand, not only has to deal with his bride's continual rejection, but keeps getting sick or wounded. All the guy is trying to do is be a good husband, and he ends up looking like a goof. He's a brilliant lawyer . . . surely he must realize there is more to this situation than meets the eye (and don't call me Shirley!).

"Interruptus" is a nice follow-up to "To Have and To Hold," but the ending lacks, um, satisfaction.

FLASH: Kyle's comment regarding Mr. Evans: "Suppose he discovers the interstellar love triangle and the alien hit squad winging its way to honeymoon central?" That, and Michael and Max's chat regarding scuba diving.

IRKS: Why is it that Michael has only now discovered his talent to turn PAST DUE notices into first class airline tickets? If he can do that, why not cash them in for money to pay his bills? This is a massive irk that plagues me for the entire season (warning: it contains spoilers): how could they get rid of Kivar so easily? And why would the writers want to? Also, if the man is so powerful, why wouldn't he kill Max and Michael when he has the chance? How is he able to disappear/reappear in the steam room if he has borrowed a human body? Why does Kivar wait so long to go to Isabel, especially since Nicholas would have told him that Isabel/Vilandra had been found during season two? We spend so much time focused on the great enemy Kivar, so to just brush him off so easily is not only ridiculous, it's an anticlimax. It's also terribly convenient that Michael suddenly remembers what happened with Vilandra on Antar at the very moment he needed to.

DOUBLE TAKE: This one takes place on the patio when Kivar relays his story to Isabel and Jesse. The rose in front of Kivar has bloomed, whereas the same rose in front of Isabel has not. Also, watch the scene where Isabel stands with her back against the hotel door. The security swing lock is open, then closed, then open, then closed, every time the camera moves away from her and back again.

ALIENISMS: Michael changes his bills into airline tickets and uses his powers to trip Jesse with a wheelbarrow. Isabel melts the bathroom door handle, then later causes a tree branch to fall on Jesse. Her eyes go an inky black when Vilandra takes over. Kivar possesses a body, "appears" in the steam room, uses his powers to drug Jesse's drink, blasts Michael and Max into the bushes, and creates a portal.

SODA MOMENT: "You're gonna ride his handlebars all the way back to Antar, aren't you?" is Michael's line to Isabel. Michael is referring to *E.T.: The Extra-Terrestrial*, as Elliot flies past a full moon with E.T. in his basket, helping take the alien back to its home.

COOL FACT: La Jolla is Spanish for "the Jewel." Close to San Diego, it is one of the more affluent communities in the U.S. and houses the Scripps Institution of Oceanography, along with the Stephen Birch Aquarium & Museum. No wonder Michael wants to check out the scuba-diving situation.

3.8 Behind the Music

ORIGINAL AIR DATE: November 27, 2001
WRITTEN BY: Russel Friend, Garrett Lerner
DIRECTED BY: Jonathan Frakes

GUEST CAST: Clayne Crawford (Billy Darden), Mary Ellen Trainor (Diane Evans), Garrett M. Brown (Philip Evans), Matt Southwell (Mystery Man)

An old crush from Maria's past comes to town causing Michael's powers to go out of control. Mr. Evans continues to investigate Max.

It's a sad day for all of those Candy fans out there. The big "Who am I?" question the alien teens were asking in season one has shifted to the human side. Maria's situation looks at how a sense of "self" can get lost when in a serious relationship. This issue isn't just relevant for teenagers, however. As Maria uncovers more of the girl she used to be, Mr. Evans uncovers more of the truth behind Max's strange behavior.

Billy Darden is the cream in Maria's pasta sauce. While her life seems fine without him, he enhances it, giving it that extra oomph. Billy has unearthed her dreams of singing once more. It's easy to dream when we are young, but not always so easy to follow through with it. We "grow up," as Maria tells Billy, leaving our dreams behind. But, as Billy aptly shows us, it is never too late to follow our dreams. Billy's analogy, comparing Alex's guitar to Maria's talent, is an excellent one — both have been buried for too long. Clayne Crawford does a wonderful job playing the role of Billy, the prince who wakes the Sleeping Beauty. While Michael clearly loves Maria, his inability to fully appreciate her talents becomes evident in this episode, and Billy's sensitivity enhances Michael's insensitivity.

Michael is unable to deal with his insecurities, and they manifest themselves in violent explosions. While Michael tries to come to terms with his own emotions, Max faces a greater problem: his lies are catching up to him. Max can't possibly expect his parents to trust him when he cannot trust them by revealing the truth. Mr. Evans is an intriguing threat to the teens, simply because his motives are coming from a good place.

Maria is stepping into her own power and taking control of her life, soon to be followed by Liz. This episode is almost an analogy for Majandra's life: herself a budding singer, she put that on hold when she began acting and became involved with *Roswell*. Once free from the show, Majandra fully delved into her dream career, and started touring with her new CD, "The Sicks."

FLASH: Michael holding the dissolving flowers, unable to catch the ashes.

Majandra Delfino signs a poster of her album cover in Santa Barbara, California (Photo by Christina Radish)

IRKS: I'm with Isabel on this one — why can't they just tell their parents the truth? Sure, some tension might be lost, but then again it might be interesting territory to explore. Instead, it's dealt with in one episode at the end of the season, and brushed aside far too quickly. Anyone notice how Isabel's story about Max and Tess isn't that far from the truth? Also, those photos of Billy's are badly doctored.

DOUBLE TAKE: When Billy begins to play "Only When You Go" for a second time, if you look closely you can see his fingers are not on the strings.

ALIENISMS: Michael unconsciously causes eggs to burst from the carton, a salad to burst out of the bowl, sugar canisters to explode (which he can't fix), car windows to explode thus setting off the alarms, a lamp to blow up, shelves to shudder in the Crashdown, and flowers to dissolve in his hands.

COOL FACT: Liz uses the term "Alien DEFCON 5" to describe Max's reaction to the board in Mr. Evans's office. In the U.S., DEFCON stands for Defense Condition. There are five levels, with one being the highest military readiness level. The U.S. Strategic Air Command was put on DEFCON 2 (increase in military force readiness, but not maximum readiness) during the Cuban Missile Crisis, which was the first time in history for that to happen. DEFCON 5 actually means "normal peacetime readiness" although I highly doubt that that's what Liz means. Then again, maybe they do things backwards on Antar.

MUSIC: "Love is the Key" by Charlatans UK plays in the Crashdown when Billy arrives. Later, "Lies to Me" by 54–40 is on when the salad blows up in Maria's face. When Michael and Liz talk in the café after closing, "Apple Bed" by Sparklehorse is in the background. Finally, we get to hear three songs from Majandra Delfino. She sings "Only When You Go" with Billy, and "Breathing On My Own" at the end of the episode. Her song "Hell and Bliss" plays when Michael and Maria talk in the back room of the Crashdown.

3.9 Samuel Rising

ORIGINAL AIR DATE: December 18, 2002
WRITTEN BY: Jason Katims
DIRECTED BY: Patrick Norris

GUEST CAST: Gavin Fink (Samuel Turner), Sean O'Bryan (Warren Turner), Colleen Flynn (Rebecca Turner), Navi Rawat (Shelby Prine), Yvonne Farrow (Dr. Lynette Ramey), Zachary Isiah Williams (Zeke), Allison Ward (Deb), Christopher Plumley (Paul), Haley King (Other Kid), Gene Borkan (Santa #1), Cole Dodson (Santa #2), Alejandro Patino (Santa #3), Bret Loehr (Kid #1), Jenevieve Norris (Kid #2)

When an autistic child reaches out to Max, he vows to help the boy and learns the meaning of altruism.

"Samuel Rising" has all of the best elements of a Christmas episode — touching moments, life lessons, humor, a sentimental ending, and a gorgeous little boy. Gavin Fink steals the show as Samuel. With huge blue/green eyes and a sweet smile, he is the picture of innocence. Once again we are reminded of the joy of Christmas through the eyes of a very special child.

Christmas lesson number one is about sharing with others. Both Max and Isabel are so caught up in their own lives and good intentions that they fail to truly be there for their partners. Sure, Isabel's storyline leans towards the humorous side ("All Hail the Christmas Nazi!"), but the fundamental principles are the same. Her obsession with having the perfect Christmas alienates Jesse, which is rather ironic considering how much time she spends helping others. Max's lesson is two-fold. Like Isabel, he longs to help someone, but he is so caught up in his desire to save his son, he does not recognize Samuel as an individual. Liz later reminds Max that Samuel is not sick, and in a roundabout way essentially reminds him that he is not God.

Christmas lesson number two reminds us that Christmas is a time to embrace your family and put aside personal differences. Kyle struggles to understand Jim's mid-life crisis. Maria tries to put more distance between her and Michael, who in turn wants her back. Finally, Samuel's parents share the miracle they have witnessed. While it is not a Christmas lesson per se, it's a powerful element to the episode nonetheless. Unlike last Christmas, no guarantees are offered. Instead, Max learns to recognize the value in a child who just happens to be different. Sometimes holding on to hope can be difficult, yet hope keeps us going on so many levels. The shared looks between Max and Samuel remind us that children have a lot to teach us, and sometimes hope can come in the face of a stranger.

And isn't Michael just perfect as Santa Claus?

FLASH: Snowflake and Santa in the hut, and Jim Valenti stuffing the turkey with a head of lettuce. Priceless.

IRKS: Because this episode puts so much emphasis on family, it's too bad that we don't get to see the Evans family or the Parkers. Also, the final shots are inconsistent. Max and Liz are skating Christmas night, while Michael and Maria are talking on the porch on Christmas Eve. The shots of Jim and Kyle, Isabel and Jesse, and the Turners are all during Christmas morning. The timing feels skewed. Oh yeah, and it snows. I'm a huge fan of snow, believe me, but the weather has never had such great timing.

ALIENISMS: Isabel creates two stockings out of socks using her powers. She also helps Samuel's parents enter Samuel's dream. Max attempts to heal Samuel.

COOL FACT: Brendan Fehr had a hernia operation around the time this episode was filmed. Needless to say, having kids on his lap while playing Santa was a painful experience for him.

MUSIC: Michael and Max walk into the Crashdown to hear "Have a Holly Jolly Christmas" by Old 97's. When Liz and Max realize the truth behind Samuel's drawing, "Christmas Day" by Dido is in the background. Max attempts to heal Samuel to "Silent Night" by Gypsy Soul. Later, Gypsy Soul's "The First Noël" plays when Max watches Samuel with his parents on Christmas Day.

3.10 A Tale of Two Parties

ORIGINAL AIR DATE: January 1, 2002
WRITTEN BY: Laura J. Burns, Melinda Metz
DIRECTED BY: Allan Kroeker

GUEST CAST: John Doe (Geoff Parker), Eve Brent (Jane Covendall), Erin Foster (Suzie), Adam Frost (Jock #1), Jason Strickland (Jock #2), Melanie H. Gassaway (Karen), Scott Hamm (Boyfriend), Frieda Jane (Bitsy), James Ross (Daryl), Kimberly Russell (Girlfriend #1), Jennifer Humphrey (Girlfriend #2), Jon Ryckman (Party Guy), Frank Tignini (Frat Guy), Joseph Williams (Singer)

It's New Year's Eve and Maria, Michael, and Max join in the hunt to find the secret "enigma" party. Liz is stuck at the Crashdown helping to run the annual party for the local senior citizens. Isabel and Kyle go out to find Kyle a woman.

Whoa! Max with Maria? Michael with Liz? Jesse catching Kyle and Isabel asleep together? The clever opening showing "the day after" causes double-takes throughout the audience, but all is explained. New Year's Eve traditionally involves turning over a new leaf, and this includes the *Roswell* crew. While this is called "A Tale of Two Parties," the episode actually focuses on three New Year's events. The first is the hunt for the infamous party to end all parties; the second is the annual New Year's party at the Crashdown, and the third is the college party that Isabel and Kyle end up attending. While the parties are indeed a fun part of the episode, the best parts are the changes each character undergoes by the end of the show.

On a comic note, Max spends the entire episode defending his personal decision to hunt for the concert "Enigma." Does this mean that Max's New Year's resolution involves him lightening up and having some fun? Liz's resolution comes hand in hand with her father's. Geoff Parker first appears in the episode strumming away at his guitar (seems Jim Valenti isn't the only singing dad). While he begins the evening keeping Liz on a tight leash, he soon gains a new perspective. After a lovely chat with Jim Valenti (which again reminds us of how great an actor Bill Sadler is), he finds it within himself to reconsider his point of view. At the same time, Liz's evening begins on a sour note with her at odds with her father, but after a rather convenient conversation with Jane Covendall (whom we last saw in "Secrets & Lies"), Liz recognizes that perhaps she has been too hard on her father.

Michael's evening is not a terribly pretty one. It took Max getting drunk to confess his emotions to Liz in "Blind Date," and Michael getting drunk to finally hear Maria. Kyle's evening begins on an amusing note as he prays to Buddha for sex, and then takes on a very interesting and unexpected twist once he realizes what he really wants. Isabel and Kyle have wonderful chemistry, and it's too bad it wasn't explored earlier.

Each couple takes a personal journey in this episode: Max and Maria's is about taking risks and walking to the beat of their own drum, Michael and Liz's involves recognizing the needs of their loved ones, and Isabel and Kyle's looks at supportive friendship. A lighter episode, "A Tale of Two Parties" is a nice break from the alien "hootenanny."

FLASH: Kyle and Isabel. Period.

IRKS: How could so many people break into the science room of West Roswell High and not trigger any security alarms? Even without an alarm system, wouldn't the sheriff's department have found out about it? Is there really a purpose behind that blond hitting on Max at the party? Max looks like he wants to escape. While Jane's speech is great, it's one of those "too convenient" moments. And maybe it's me, but the burning cactus is a major fire hazard. Also, if the party is such a family tradition, where is Mrs. Parker?

ALIENISMS: Isabel snaps her fingers, causing the candles to light. She also gets the stereo going with a wave of her hand, and changes the Viper's paint color. Max refills a beer keg, and later tries to heal Michael. Michael gets drunk, causing his senses to become hyper-sensitive.

Adam Rodriguez and Nick Wechsler hang out on the set of Roswell's *series finale, "Graduation Day"* (Photo by Christina Radish)

When being healed, Michael levitates. Also, green lightning flashes occur just under his skin. These are later seen in Liz during "Ch-Ch-Changes."

SODA MOMENT: Max mentions avoiding "New Year's Rockin' Eve." He's referring to the infamous show and countdown in New York hosted by Dick Clark. Also . . . just for fun, Jane looks at Jim Valenti and asks, "Who's that Guy Lombardo over there?" Born in Canada, Guy Lombardo was a popular band leader who was known for his New Year's Eve musical program and popularized "Auld Lang Syne" as a New Year's Eve song. The program ran from 1929 to 1976. Dick Clark began his show in 1972.

COOL FACT: "A Tale of Two Parties" is the first and only episode written by *Roswell High* authors Melinda Metz and Laura J. Burns. The title is taken from the novel "A Tale of Two Cities" by Charles Dickens. The novel touches on social dissatisfaction and corrupt politics in France and England leading up to the French Revolution.

MUSIC: Mr. Parker (John Doe) sings "Totally Yours" by The John Doe Thing. "Get This Party Started" by Toby Mac plays when Maria, Max and Michael arrive at the frat party. "Wear Me Down" by Treble Charger is in the background as the jocks carry Max on their shoulders. Jet Set Satellite's song "Baby, Cool Your Jets" is on while Michael is drinking. At Kyle and Isabel's party, "The Life" by Mystic is the song playing when Kyle sees Isabel in slow motion. Later, during the kiss, we hear "Underdog (Save Me)" by Turin Brakes. The song playing at "Enigma" is "Smile Fades Fast" by the Boo Radleys. Finally, Michael and Maria enter the Crashdown the next morning singing "Alive" by P.O.D.

3.11 I Married an Alien

ORIGINAL AIR DATE: January 29, 2002
WRITTEN BY: Ronald D. Moore
DIRECTED BY: Patrick Norris

GUEST CAST: John Doe (Geoff Parker), Garrett M. Brown (Philip Evans), Susan Barnes (Social Worker), Kristoffer Polaha (Eric Hughes)

Isabel imagines what her life with Jesse would be like if it were a sitcom. Jesse's college buddy, Eric, writes a story that threatens to expose the truth about the alien teens.

Welcome to the world of *Roswell*, circa 1960, with a laugh track and alien wackiness

Adam Rodriguez at Bogart Backstage (Photo by Christina Radish)

galore. It was bound to happen, considering all the allusions to *Bewitched* and *I Dream of Jeannie* in previous episodes. The two main storylines in this episode may weave in and out of each other, but are very different in tone. The moral of the story is obvious: real life is not as simple as a sitcom. Things do not get wrapped up in half an hour. (An interesting moral considering it's a fictional television show that is delivering the message!)

The sitcom concept enters Isabel's mind as Michael watches an episode of *Bewitched* ("Long Live the Queen"). Immediately we are taken into that world through the delightful opening credits that mimic the classic animated style of *Bewitched*. Look closely and you'll see that the credits are copywritten to Isabel J. Imagination, Inc. While it may not have been intentional, the fact that you can see the strings holding up various floating objects only adds to the kitschy atmosphere. Jesse captures the essence of Darren, constantly stressing that someone will discover Isabel's alien background. Brendan and Jason are the only actors who seem a bit more awkward acting in the "sitcom" style, and it shows. The most impressive part of the cross-over is Katherine Heigl. Not only does she capture the physicality of Samantha's character, but her voice is dead on.

The main concept involves reality vs. fantasy. In the fantasy, everything is amusing, and nothing is a major concern. In reality Isabel is dealing with very real concerns. Eric (nicely played by Kristoffer Polaha) is ambitious enough to put his friendship on the line for a story. And what is refreshing is that he puts two and two together so fast. His investigation causes Jesse to start questioning the "odd" occurrences that he's been trying to ignore. Combining the two concepts could have been messy, but instead it is well done with fast, smooth transitions. One of the better transitional moments involves Max, Isabel, and Michael standing in a hokey spaceship, then cuts to the three of them in the car dealing with their present emergency.

While the whole cross-over concept works well, the episode's strength lies in revealing more about Jesse. We see him drinking, then later find out his past isn't so lily-white after all. We also get a taste of his temper when he confronts Eric. Considering in the past he's come off as a bit of an underdog, I'm glad to finally learn more about him. While the focus in this episode may have been on Isabel, Jesse stands out.

If you have ever seen *Bewitched*, you will get a kick out of this episode. If you haven't, you'll still appreciate the cute moments. If you hated *Bewitched*, you can still enjoy the tension created in the present-day storyline. Essentially, this episode has a little something in it for everyone.

FLASH: Max declaring that the world revolves around Michael, and Michael agreeing.

IRKS: Okay, having Michael use his powers to move the nearby bushes aside is one thing. Having him bend trees so close to the fairway? Odds are Eric wouldn't have been the only one to see it. Also, why does Eric steal the file when he could just copy down the information? Stealing seems drastic. It's rather bizarre to see Jesse take Eric's bottle up to his mouth as though to open it with his teeth, only to have him toss it to Eric unopened.

ALIENISMS: In the reality sequence: Isabel fixes Kyle's carburetor. Michael and Max change the colors of paint on Isabel's walls. Later, as they argue, they turn the television on and off with their powers until Michael eventually fries it. Michael makes bushes and trees bend so he can see the golf green in the distance. Michael also causes Eric's laptop to crash. Apparently, when Michael was six, he levitated a kitchen table. In the fantasy sequence: Isabel uses her powers to clean the dishes, to make French toast (which she is unable to do in reality), to clean the apartment with a flick of her wrist, to make a side table disappear and pull Jesse's bed to hers, to change a meat cleaver into a bouquet of daisies and finally to turn Eric into a bird. Max turns Eric into a dog, then back to his human form.

SODA MOMENT: While there are a few, two that stand out are as follows: Isabel throws the line "psychic like Carrie?" at Jesse. She is referring to the Stephen King title character played by Sissy Spacek in the 1976 Brian De Palma film. Teased brutally by her classmates, Carrie unleashes her psychic telekinetic powers at the prom leading to deadly results. Later, when Isabel turns Eric into a parrot, the bird says "Damn it Jim, I'm a reporter not a parrot." Loyal *Star Trek* fans out there will know what this means. Doctor 'Bones' McCoy's classic line was, "Damn it, Jim. I'm a doctor not a (fill-in-the-blank)." Some of those fill-in-the-blank words have been: engineer, bricklayer, escalator, aerobics instructor, and coal miner.

COOL FACT: Michael compares the character of Samantha to a "modern day Athena." In Greek mythology, there were many aspects to Athena. She was considered the Goddess of Wisdom as well as a warrior who protected civilized life. She also protected the artesian and agricultural communities. She is one of three virgin goddesses, and was fiercely proud of her chastity. She was one of Zeus's favorite children. A virginal warrior Goddess and domesticated married witch? Not sure where Michael is going with this one.

MUSIC: "Gonna Make You Sweat (Everybody Dance Now)" by C & C Music Factory is the first song on the CD Eric puts on as Isabel goes to bed. Following that is "I Touch Myself" by the Divinyls as Eric and Jesse bond over beer. As Max and Isabel discuss telling Jesse about their secret at the Crashdown, "Do It All Over Again" by Spiritualized is playing. Finally, "Chains" by Mercury Rev plays when Michael, Isabel, Jesse, and Eric discuss what happens on the golf course.

3.12 Ch-Ch-Changes

ORIGINAL AIR DATE: February 5, 2002
WRITTEN BY: Gretchen J. Berg, Aaron Harberts
DIRECTED BY: Paul Shapiro

GUEST CAST: John Doe (Geoff Parker), Michael Chieffo (Mr. Seligman), Meredith Scott Lynn (Dominique Lazar), Hal Ozsan (unknown), Aki Aleong (unknown), Michael Medico (George Winkler), Ryan Ford (Busboy), Joseph Williams (Singer)

Liz begins to experience physical changes that seem suspiciously alien, while Maria gets discovered by a talent scout and offered a record deal.

So far season three has had some okay episodes, and some good episodes. A lot of them have been on the lighter side, lacking that intensity we love from "285 South" or "The End of the World." But then "Ch-Ch-Changes" comes along and we are once more reminded of the coolness of *Roswell.* It's nice to see Mr. Seligman's science lecture once more related to the episode: a lesson in the genetic changes in fruit flies. The tension in this episode is wonderful as we deal with the concept of change on physical, emotional, and relationship levels.

Maria comes to her personal realization in "Behind the Music" because Billy Darden has arrived in town. Liz, on the other hand, realizes her relationship with Max may be harmful to her when she undergoes some painful physical changes. Shiri does a great job depicting how Liz moves from flu-like symptoms to more serious ones like hearing loss and hallucinations. When illness overcomes us, our bodies can feel like separate entities, betraying us by causing pain or worse. Liz's doctor makes reference to STDs, which is an appropriate comparison considering she does "catch" this from a loved one.

Her physical changes lead to an emotional revelation. Like Michael in "Behind the

Music," Liz is no longer able to contain her emotions, which leads to an explosive burst of energy. The whole Tess situation has never really come up after season two, which is perplexing. Now we see that Liz is trying to bury the past. Many doctors would argue that emotional suppression leads to illness, and in this episode, as soon as the release occurs, Liz seems to heal. Like Maria, she has to step into her own power to try to find answers to the ever popular question "Who am I?" While Max struggles to take control of the situation and fails, Liz succeeds.

Maria fails to see that her impulsive actions with Michael could lead him to a different conclusion than her own. A break-up is hard enough without throwing sex into the mix. Caught up in her record deal, Maria also fails to see beyond Liz's attitude to recognize that something is seriously wrong. Maria eventually sees the harsh reality of the situation through Michael. Michael also takes the role of "voice of reason" when it comes to Max. As Kyle later notes, Max isn't listening to Liz, and that is what could kill her. Max and Maria learn from their impulsive behavior, even if the results are less than ideal.

The Buddhist and the Bad Boy are the heroes of this episode. Kyle brings sensitivity and humor to the scene as he supports Liz, while Michael uses intelligence and maturity to deal with Max and Maria. While the balcony scene brings lumps to our throats, the episode still rocks.

FLASH: Kyle's reaction to Maria and Jim's version of "Paradise by the Dashboard Light" is precious, but Liz closing the window is heartwrenching.

IRKS: Will somebody please tell me why Liz hasn't explained the whole "Future Max" episode to Max? She's devastated that he slept with Tess, but Max believed that she had slept with Kyle. She has to take that into consideration. It's not fair to put all of the blame on Max. Perhaps that is why Liz represses her anger about the situation for so long. Also, if Michael's apartment door is unlocked (which it seems to be) why does Maria wait outside his apartment for two hours? Sure, they broke up, but they're still friends. And it would be a quick and easy excuse for Liz if she just tells the Harvard man she has the flu when she starts to freak out.

DOUBLE TAKE: Maria's hair is contained while she has her conversation with Jim in the Crashdown. Moments later when talking to Michael in the kitchen, it has winged out significantly.

ALIENISMS: Liz melts a plate with her hand, hallucinates that she has no face (which looks suspiciously like an alien shape), loses her hearing at points with bizarre visual effects, causes a car radio to pulse with electricity, sets a book on fire, and her skin pulses with green electricity. Finally, she makes the healing stones explode. Max puts a fire out and attempts to heal Liz.

SODA MOMENT: When Jim gives Maria her cut of the profits, she tells him it's "all for the love of the Loaf." She is referring to the singer Meat Loaf, whose song they cover at Cow Patty's. Later, she tells Liz she is going to invite Dominique to her "all-you-can-eat-crow-buffet." The expression "to eat crow" means to reluctantly admit defeat and admit one's mistake.

COOL FACT: "Ch-Ch-Changes" has also been an episode title for *Dawson's Creek*. The *Dawson's* episode had a similar storyline as Andie's mental illness leads to her leaving town. Liz may not have a mental illness, but she does follow the same path.

MUSIC: Majandra Delfino and Bill Sadler do a cover of Meat Loaf's "Paradise by the Dashboard Light" as the episode opens. "Strange Condition" by Pete Yorn plays when Maria sorts through clothing and talks to Liz about her upcoming recording. Majandra Delfino sings an acoustic version of her song "Behavior" in the studio. Jude's "Everything I Own" plays when Maria talks to both Jim and Michael in the Crashdown. Later, we hear the remix version of Majandra's song "Behavior." "The Door" by Turin Brakes is on while Liz and Kyle talk in the car after the healing attempt. Finally, "More Than Us" by Travis is the song playing when Liz is on the bus.

3.13 Panacea

ORIGINAL AIR DATE: February 12, 2002
WRITTEN BY: Russell Friend, Garrett Lerner
DIRECTED BY: Rodney Charters

GUEST CAST: Clayne Crawford (Billy Darden), Meredith Scott Lynn (Dominique Lazar), Jason Peck (Sheriff Hanson), Freda Foh Shen (Dean Hackett), Ashley Johnson (Eileen Burrows), Martin Starr (Monk), Morgan Fairchild (Meris Wheeler), Jack Donner (Clayton Wheeler), Karl Wiedergott (Scientist)
  Michael discovers Meta-Chem has been gathering information on him and the other aliens. Liz adjusts to life at boarding school. Maria records her demo in New York.

Panacea: a noun meaning universal remedy. With so few episodes left, why the writers chose to take this route baffles me. I want to like this episode, but I feel as though it's in need of its own panacea.

Liz makes her way to the Winnaman Academy in order to pull her life together. The powers, which seem to show up only when Liz talks with Max, are no longer an issue. Having Liz explore her new powers could have been a great storyline. Liz soon befriends her room-mate, Eileen, by "being herself," which consists of recounting various illegal endeavors and breaking curfew to drink in the school speakeasy. Why are we even in Vermont? It seems the whole point of this segment is to show us that Liz is finally embracing her rebellious side and leaving behind the responsible girl she once was. While learning to be less uptight is part of Liz's greater character arc, the time frame and situation where it occurs feels contrived.

Maria is recording a demo for the record company, and already she's being treated like a major star. Meredith Scott Lynn does a fabulous job as the manipulative talent scout, carefully choosing her words so Maria will go along with her. It's true that many young people get suckered into the business with promises, then later realize the dream isn't quite what they thought, but while it's nice to see that Maria holds on to her integrity, we see her do that last episode. Also, she doesn't seem to be taking school very seriously if she can go to Vermont to catch up with Liz without any ramifications. And how is it she is able to get into the Academy so late at night? There is a curfew, after all. Even stranger, Liz asks Maria to stay for awhile. Stay where? In the attic?

Michael has some nice moments, as does Jim. The best part of this episode is seeing Jim in uniform once more, although the whole Meta-Chem storyline is contrived and doesn't work. While it's a nice touch to show how Max's past actions have caught up to him over the years, the whole concept seems absurd. If Meris had Michael's picture since Max healed the children in season two, why does she wait so long to see if Michael is the healer? Morgan Fairchild is a fine actress, but she stands out like a sore thumb on *Roswell*. I feel as though I'm watching an episode of *Falcon Crest*, especially when she keeps repeating "*Heal him.*" It's the little things, too, like having open beakers with unnamed colored liquids hanging around the lab just waiting to crash to the ground for more effect, or Michael's emancipated minor file (stolen by Eric in "I Married An Alien") lying around the lab with the rest of the evidence.

The ending has a great cliffhanger, but the rest of the episode really doesn't mesh, giving us confusing time lines and a rather scattered plot.

FLASH: Michael and Jim's conversation right after Jim is hired by Meta-Chem.

IRKS: See above. Also, Liz says she and Eileen have the whole place figured out, yet she's only been there for two weeks.

DOUBLE TAKE: After Monk is shot, Michael moves his body and Monk's arm slides in the blood, but the blood does not move. Also, Max unbuttons part of Jim's shirt to heal him. In the final shot of Max and Jim looking at Meris, Jim's shirt is buttoned.

ALIENISMS: Michael's blood helps to sustain Clayton Wheeler for a short time. Michael uses his powers to break into the lab. Liz makes a phone receiver melt. Max throws two guards back, heals Jim, then later heals Clayton Wheeler. When Max's body falls, flames spread across the floor.

SODA MOMENT: Monk's last name is "Pyle." Perhaps he is a distant relative of Gomer Pyle (played by Jim Nabors), who was a loveable but dimwitted character on *The Andy Griffith Show*. The spin-off dedicated to the character (*Gomer Pyle U.S.M.C.*) began in 1964.

COOL FACT: Recognize Liz's roommate Eileen? Ashley Johnson once played young Chrissy Seaver on the 1980's television series *Growing Pains*, which also gave Leonardo DiCaprio his start.

MUSIC: When Liz arrives at Winnaman Academy, Mozart's "Piano Concerto No. 21" is playing. "Have A Nice Day" by the Stereophonics plays when Liz and Eileen first talk. During Maria's voice-over about New York, the song is "Are You Gonna Move It For Me?" by the Donnas. Finally we hear Majandra Delfino's "Behavior" remix once more in the studio when Dominique first meets Billy.

3.14 Chant Down Babylon

ORIGINAL AIR DATE: February 26, 2002
WRITTEN BY: Ronald D. Moore
DIRECTED BY: Lawrence Trilling

GUEST CAST: Ashley Johnson (Eileen Burrows), Morgan Fairchild (Meris Wheeler), Jack Donner (Clayton Wheeler), Paul Fitzgerald (Paul)

Clayton Wheeler and Max struggle internally to take over Clayton's new body. Liz struggles with the news of Max's death. After being shot, Isabel struggles to survive.

"Chant Down Babylon" starts off where "Panacea" leaves off, and is definitely more satisfying than its predecessor. There are some interesting references in this episode, beginning with the title.

The ancient city of Babylon was praised by the Greek historian Herodotus for its architecture and general aesthetics. Its hanging gardens were one of the seven ancient wonders of the world. "Babylon" itself means "The Gate of God" in ancient Greek. And yet, for people of the Jewish faith, Babylon was a place of exile for many of their race from 597 to 538 B.C. While a certain despair came with the exile, it is said that a bond was formed among the Jews as they remade themselves, purifying their practices in the hopes of once more gaining Yahweh's blessings. The New Testament paints a different picture of Babylon: "And the woman was clothed in purple and scarlet . . . having in her hand a gold cup full of abominations and of the unclean things of her immortality. And upon her forehead a name was written, a mystery, 'Babylon the great, the mother of harlots and of the abominations of the earth.' And I saw the woman drunk with the blood of the saints, and with the blood of the witnesses of Jesus." Following that, an angel explains her presence: "And the woman whom you saw is the great city, which reigns over the kings of the earth." In essence, Babylon is painted as a land of corruption which houses the sinful, and represents the evils of wealth and material worship. Bob Marley's song references the same evils when he sings of the city.

Also referenced is Diogenes of Sinope (c.320 B.C.), who was known for his contempt for corruption in society. A naturalist, Diogenes had no dependence on luxuries, and was part of the Cynics, a Greek philosophical school that believed in a simplistic lifestyle. As stated by Paul in "Chant Down Babylon," Diogenes was searching for an honest man. Paul speaks of Jesse being that man. His words ring true when he speaks of the other men in the Valenti house: they are not honest. Neither is Isabel. This episode represents a loss of innocence on Jesse's part, seeing as he, too, has involuntarily become part of the alien conspiracy. Having Jesse discover Isabel's secret in a violent setting is not only compelling dramatically but emotionally, considering he is torn between his relief and his obvious confusion about the situation.

Personal struggle is a major issue in "Chant Down Babylon" as the safe world everyone strives for comes to pieces. Max's struggle is internal as he battles for possession of his body. Clayton is the man whose dreams and aspirations of youth crumble in front of his face. Liz's reaction to the news about Max is both realistic and sad as she suppresses her pain with alcohol. Isabel's near-fatal experience causes a multitude of reactions, and Jesse's struggle is also portrayed realistically, avoiding heavy dramatics. As Jesse and Isabel fiddle with their wedding rings, neither one knows where their relationship can go. Michael has a lovely scene, sharing with Isabel his fears of being alone. The most powerful aspect of this episode involves Isabel's shooting and the way the men rally to save her.

Much has crumbled in this episode leaving the characters in the ashes of old, preparing to rebuild. "Chant Down Babylon" is definitely the remedy for "Panacea."

FLASH: Kyle's touching attempt to heal Isabel. Beautiful.

IRKS: I am left with a question about alien mortality after this episode that is never answered. By infusing his soul into another man's body, Max manages to turn that man into himself and possess that body. That would suggest that Max is in some ways immortal, whereas with Isabel, it's suggested that she is somewhere on the brink of dying. Also, the whole slow motion fall to the earth is pretty cheesy, detracting from the drama of the moment. Liz's decision to go with Max and Maria at the end once again makes me question why they bother with the Vermont storyline. And, does anyone else go to this school? Sure, people are on break, but I can't believe Liz is the only one staying there. No one appears to be on the streets, either. And doesn't anyone notice that Liz leaves town at the same time a person is murdered in the library?

DOUBLE TAKE: When Jesse and Michael are in the garden, Paul joins them, leaving the gate wide open. Later, the gate looks mostly closed. Paul leaves, closing the gate, and moments later the gate is wide open again.

ALIENISMS: Isabel and Michael force open a door, as well as hurtle two guards over a limo. When shot, Isabel's hands emit a strange red electricity and sparks, which appear almost robotic. Michael changes a spiky plant to flowers as a demonstration for Jesse. Liz blasts open the wall in the attic, has flashes when she touches Clayton/Max, sends jolts through Clayton/Max outside, then later throws him backwards. Clayton/Max has flashes of Liz, creates a shield for Liz to land on, and physically morphs from Clayton to Max after the crash.

MUSIC: "Save Yourself" by Sense Field plays when Liz sits in the garden and Maria tells her Max is dead, then at the end when Max, Maria, and Liz walk away from the school. Maria puts on Bob Marley's "Chant Down Babylon" when Liz goes to shower.

3.15 Who Died and Made You King?

ORIGINAL AIR DATE: April 23, 2002
WRITTEN BY: Gretchen J. Berg, and Aaron Harberts
DIRECTED BY: Peter B. Ellis

GUEST CAST: John Doe (Geoff Parker), Garrett M. Brown (Philip Evans), Yorgo Constantine (Agent Burns), Harry Groener (Dr. Burton Weiss), Man in Black (Douglas Owen McDonald), Waiter (James Oberlander)

When the Royal Seal of Antar proclaims Michael the new leader, all hell breaks loose. Jesse sees a therapist as he tries to deal with his newfound knowledge about the aliens.

After almost two months of intense waiting, the return of *Roswell* was highly anticipated. There is a reference made in "Who Died and Made You King?" to the preparation of the Italian rice dish, risotto. The preparation of the dish symbolizes the two main storylines in this tense, long awaited episode.

Cooking risotto requires patience as well as time. First, the rice goes into a large pot containing a small amount of heated oil. Next, you need to stir and coat the rice with the oil. Then, you pour one ladleful of stock into the pot. Once the liquid has been absorbed by the rice, the next ladleful goes in. This process continues until the rice is soft and sticky. It is also imperative to stir the mixture frequently as it cooks. The actual process can take anywhere from 20 to 40 minutes, depending on the ingredients used.

So, how does this apply to "Who Died and Made You King?" The tension between Michael and Max has been growing slowly since season one. It's been obvious from the start that Michael likes to act while Max prefers to wait. At the start of this season, there's a role reversal with Max acting impulsively and Michael offering rational advice. Max's death causes them to revert back to their original behaviors: Max did not want to be the leader, while Michael craved it. With each argument Michael and Max have had over the seasons, more fuel is added to the fire. This episode brings the tension to a head, causing Michael and Max to literally fight over the crown. It's as though Michael is rejecting his human side that he embraced readily at the end of season two. A risotto builds up as the rice expands, eventually unable to absorb any more liquid. As Michael's arrogance leads to violence, he becomes physically unable to contain his anger any longer.

In Jesse's situation, the risotto analogy relates to his loss of innocence. Jesse's suspicions begin slowly, until he is driven to follow Isabel to Meta-Chem. After discovering her secret, Jesse becomes part of a conspiracy he has no desire to join. His "broth" is circumstance, which keeps piling on him until he has no choice but to become part of the alien madness, saturated by the conspiracy. In "Chant Down Babylon," Jesse's friend Paul reminds Jesse that he is an honest man. In this episode, Jesse tries to stick by his morals, knowing how lies eventually backfire. When Jesse watches the cooking show, looking at the rice in the pan as the chef describes the rice absorbing the liquid, the moment is even more intense considering what Jesse now associates with the frying pan. This is a pivotal episode for the character of Jesse: an apex for his seasonal arc.

Everyone has a nice moment in this episode as the characters come to terms with past events. Liz and Max try to find some sense of normalcy again as Jesse and Isabel struggle with their marriage. Past issues arise with the resurgence of the Special Unit and photos of various victims from the past seasons. All in all, "Who Died and Made You King?" is well done.

FLASH: Kyle's statue of Buddha at the garage.

IRKS: Nice to see the FBI haven't learned the fine art of disguise. They continue to stand out like a sore thumb, both physically and through their incompetent behavior. Not only that, but they store all of their alien information in an empty warehouse with no one guarding it. Where's Jim Valenti in all of this? He would be a helpful hand. And Dr. Weiss needs to seriously consider getting some more lamps in his office. Also, it's a little ignorant of Jesse to be so surprised that Agent Burns bugged his briefcase.

DOUBLE TAKE: At the restaurant, when Isabel talks to her father about Liz, her napkin is pointing up on the table. Moments later, it's flat on the table. Also, when Michael shows Max the seal on his chest, the close-up has the apex of the "V" pointing to Michael's right. When the camera moves back, the apex points to the left. Finally, we discover the healing power is unique to Max, and yet Michael heals River Dog's ankle in "Into the Woods."

ALIENISMS: Isabel waves her hand to fix her hair, make-up, and nail-polish, then reverses the effect. Jesse dreams that Isabel's kiss puts him in a strange alien sac. Isabel later burns the files, incinerates a body, operates a crane and car compactor, and melts a gun into a frying pan. Michael sports the Royal Seal, heals his own hand, hurls Jesse into the wall and pushes him towards the ceiling, then attempts to blast Max. Max heats an instant dinner, loses his ability to heal and create a shield, throws Michael into the wall, shatters glass that blinds Michael, then takes the Seal with his hand.

SODA MOMENT: Maria describes Michael's bizarre behavior as "desert wandering Anne Heche times 1,000." Actress Anne Heche, known for her relationship with comedienne Ellen

DeGeneres, was hospitalized after she wandered into a Cantua Creek, California, home apparently wearing only a bra, shorts, and tennis shoes in August 2000. Anne and Ellen had just ended their three-and-a-half year relationship. Apparently Anne told the family that she was the daughter of God, and her name was Celestia. God had spoken to her and told her that her work on Earth was done and she had to go out into the desert to catch a spaceship back to her home planet. Between Michael's fairly recent break-up with Maria, and his very bizarre attitude, Maria's comment works. (Though Anne wasn't homicidal.)

MUSIC: "The Middle" by Jimmy Eat World plays as Max asks out Liz in the Crashdown. Later, when Michael kicks Maria out of the Jetta, "Evolution Revolution Love" by Tricky is playing. The final song, "Paint the Silence" by South, is on when Isabel and Jesse are in the junkyard, and then back at their trashed apartment.

3.16 Crash

ORIGINAL AIR DATE: April 30, 2002
WRITTEN BY: David Simkins
DIRECTED BY: Patrick Norris

GUEST CAST: John Doe (Geoff Parker), Mary Ellen Trainor (Diane Evans), Garrett M. Brown (Philip Evans), Woody Brown (Major Carlson), Samantha Shelton (Connie Griffin), Larry Poindexter (Colonel Griffin), Paul Shultze (Hitman), Lamont Thompson (Guard), Brien Blakely (Reporter), Stephen Rockwell (Scientist)

Michael helps a young cadet rescue her father after a suspicious military plane crash. Mr. and Mrs. Evans question Isabel and Jesse.

Another possible title for "Crash" could be "Michael Redeems Himself After Acting Horribly in the Last Episode." The *Roswell* series begins by referencing the '47 crash, so it seems rather appropriate that we will end the series with one.

Michael's stubbornness at the beginning of this episode is understandable considering everyone is angry about his behavior in "Who Died and Made You King?" Max returns to his safe, cautious self after stealing the Seal back, while Michael regresses right back into the character he was in season one — a defensive loner. And yet, Michael manages to connect with yet another military officer in this episode, just as he did with Hal in "Summer of '47." Unfortunately the father/daughter military story really doesn't serve the overall storyline.

Isabel continues to struggle when it comes to her marriage and her family. With Jesse out of town with Philip, it's a perfect opportunity for Diane to coax information out of Isabel.

Mr. Evans's investigation is another loose thread that needs to be tied up in the next two episodes, and with such a cliffhanger ending, there's no doubt that the situation is coming to a head. The crash aside, there are a couple of cute moments, including Liz's X-rated game of footsie with Max and Kyle's tattoo suggestion for Michael. Seeing the team back in action and not worrying about questions is a nice touch as well.

I feel like Geoff Parker does at the beginning of this episode: enthusiastic about the potential of what is ahead, only to be left disappointed. "Crash" veers off track as soon as the two aircraft collide, taking us on the military track rather than the extraterrestrial one.

FLASH: Max and Michael dressed as "aliens" with their helium-enhanced voices.

IRKS: Michael picks up a black cone that he insists is alien, but in the final two episodes, the cone serves no purpose whatsoever. Connie's car flips over even though there is no incline from the highway to the dirt shoulder. Not only that, but wouldn't a military cadet have sense enough to at least try to get herself out of the car? And Maria's pretty quick to forgive Michael, especially since he claimed he was being himself when he told her the humans were better off dead. The camera has a blinking red light: why wouldn't Isabel see that when she turns out her lights to go to bed?

DOUBLE TAKE: Major Carlson shoots the hitman square in the forehead, and when he takes off the bag, the hitman's head is straight before falling to one side. Why, then, is the bullet wound on the left side of his head? Major Carlson is on the right side of his body. It would be impossible for him to make that shot from the way he was aiming.

ALIENISMS: The UFO causes Michael's bike to die. Michael pulls the door off Connie's car, causes the hitman's gun to fly into the wall, and morphs the alien mask to look like the hitman. Max creates a shield to obscure the hitman's view, and spins him around twice as part of their "torture." He later changes the van from silver to white. Someone uses alien powers to bind the hitman to the chair. Upset, Isabel causes items in her room to spin around in a mini tornado, then returns everything to its place with a wave of her hand.

COOL FACT: Connie refers to Michael as a "friendly." The military definition of "friendly" is a contact person who has be positively identified as someone who is not an enemy.

MUSIC: "Someday, Someway" by Marshall Crenshaw plays during Liz's podiatrist discussion, and as Michael enters with the boxes. The song playing during Jesse and Mr. Evans's discussion in the hotel is "The Devil and the Deep Blue Sea." We hear "21 Things I Want in a

Lover" by Alanis Morissette when Maria waits on Major Carlson and the hitman. Finally, Isabel causes her mini-tornado to "Brothers and Sisters" by Coldplay.

3.17 Four Aliens and a Baby

ORIGINAL AIR DATE: May 7, 2002
WRITTEN BY: Russel Friend, Garrett Lerner
DIRECTED BY: William Sadler

GUEST CAST: Emilie de Ravin (Tess Harding), Mary Ellen Trainor (Diane Evans), Woody Brown (Major Carlson), Garrett M. Brown (Philip Evans), Bart McCarthy (Colonel Thompson), Gunther Jensen (Air Force Officer), Adrianna Banovich (Reporter), Chris Butler (Scientist #1), Gary Riotto (Scientist #2), Jonathan Fraser (M.P.)

Tess and her baby hide with the Roswell gang while the military searches for her. Mr. and Mrs. Evans confront Isabel about the tape.

Talk about killing two birds with one stone! "Four Aliens and a Baby" brings two major issues to the forefront during a high pressure situation. William Sadler does a great job in his directing debut, giving this episode a slightly darker slant as the team fights against the ticking clock to save Max's son.

The search for Max's son has been a dominant theme throughout the season. After his resurrection, Max chooses to live for the moment rather than obsess about the past. As the classic saying goes, "It will come when you least expect it," and without warning, Tess arrives with baby Zan. While we get some closure with Tess, the interesting part involves Zan's genetic condition. By giving his son the chance to be "normal," Max lives out his dream vicariously through Zan. After all, how many times have we heard Max say he wished he was human and could live like everyone else? Tess is afforded the opportunity to right her wrongs, which requires a bit of suspension of disbelief, yet is justifiable. Kivar had betrayed her the way she betrayed everyone else. While everyone has different arguments against Tess, Kyle's words and Liz's merciful action seem to affect her the most. The whole situation also allows for closure for both Max and Liz, thus dealing with the major kink in their relationship.

While the Tess story element is intense, it all happens rather fast. The same thing goes with Mr. and Mrs. Evans and their confrontation with Isabel and Max. While the situation is a compelling time to reveal the truth, we don't ever truly get the opportunity to explore the Evanses' reaction to it. The best we get is a moment with Diane clutching onto Philip. Still, the scene offers some interesting moments, including Isabel's facial expression after watching the tape.

There is no doubt that "Four Aliens and a Baby" is one of the darker *Roswell* episodes. The opening sequence at the base and the trashed Valenti homestead with streaks of blood have a definite *X-Files* vibe. The ominous "chopper" sounds along with flashes of the search-lights throughout the episode add to the intensity, as does the military pursuit. It's the first time that the team really feels "trapped," which works very well. The vote at Jesse and Isabel's has a morbidity to it, as does Tess's final decision. Baby Zan's cries after the explosion add to the devastating effect.

There's not much to say without spoiling it further. Max has some beautiful scenes with Zan, and the baby's spaceship rattle is poignant. While "Four Aliens and A Baby" seems to wrap up too easily, it's on the whole an interesting and necessary episode.

FLASH: Liz blasting Tess in Michael's apartment.

IRKS: While it could have taken away from the intensity of this episode, I feel there was a missed opportunity here. The Tess storyline could have overlapped with "Crash," giving that episode more weight. And Mr. Evans may have had a week to deal with the truth, but his conversation with Max in the kitchen suggests he's pretty comfortable with the new circumstances, which is a bit odd. Also, how does Liz get Tess out to the air force base without being stopped? Earlier Michael, Max, and Tess couldn't go anywhere in Roswell without armed guards surrounding them, so why don't any security vehicles stop Liz?

DOUBLE TAKE: At Michael's apartment, the chopper lights fill the room from what appears to be the ceiling. Max, Tess, and Michael all look to the ceiling rather than the window.

ALIENISMS: Tess uses her powers to massacre 16 people, to blast a hole in Kyle's room, to mindwarp two guards, to melt a fence, and finally to cause a massive explosion. Max makes his door close, then uses his abilities to implant a memory in Zan's head. Michael causes a military jeep to explode. Liz blasts Tess twice in Michael's apartment.

COOL FACT: On the show *Angel*, Darla gives birth to Angel's son as she sacrifices herself to save her child, just as Tess does. Coincidentally, the baby used to play Zan (the actors are actually a set of triplets) was the same one used to play baby Connor. The child of vampires, then the child of half-breed aliens . . . that's one mixed-up kid!

MUSIC: "Destiny" by Zero 7 plays while Max and Liz make out, as well as after Jesse and Isabel start arguing. When Liz and Maria talk about Tess in the Crashdown, "Red" by Elbow is on. Max says goodbye to Zan to "Nullarbor Song" by Kasey Chambers.

3.18 Graduation

ORIGINAL AIR DATE: May 14, 2002
WRITTEN BY: Jason Katims, Ronald D. Moore
DIRECTED BY: Allison Liddi-Brown

GUEST CAST: John Doe (Geoff Parker), Diane Evans (Mary Ellen Trainor), Philip Evans (Garrett M. Brown), Winnie Holzman (Madame Vivian), Taylor Young (Hannah Mills), Barry Livingston (Bryce McCain), Bob Morrisey (Principal), Brian Evers (General Wallace)

As graduation approaches, Liz begins to experience psychic flashes showing vivid premonitions of a grisly future. The military closes in on the aliens.

"I can't believe it's all ending this way," Isabel says out in the desert, and I have to agree with her. After three years of struggling for the ratings, the little show with big potential finally comes to a close. "What happens now, Max?" is replaced with a new declaration, one of independence from destiny and past hierarchies. The desert location where the Royal Four were born is now a different sort of launch site as the writers tie up the series. In an interview with Kenn Gold, Jason Katims said this episode took a "nostalgic" turn, and "[the episode is] sort of a love song to the show itself, to how we started."

One of those nostalgic elements include framing the episode with Liz's journal voice-over. Liz's flashes are also back, only this time when she makes out with Max (or touches someone else), she sees images of the future. Maria consults Madame Vivian once more regarding her future with Michael. The last time we saw the fortune teller was in "The End of the World" when Liz altered her future with Max. It may have taken 34 episodes to get back on track, but it was worth it. We also get to see Jim holding that golden badge once more, as well as witness again the complete incompetence of the FBI. The story also begins and ends with a potential shooting, both involving Liz. Ah, those *Roswell* memories.

With Liz stepping into the space Tess has left behind, all bets are off. For the first time it truly feels as though the aliens and humans are linked, a new team out to do good, while evading the law, as Liz tells us. Liz ran from Max because he had a destiny, and now it seems that she is tied up in it. In the last episode, Maria tells Liz she has to make a choice — either forgive Max or leave him. In "Graduation," Liz relays the same message to Maria — figure out what you want, and go for it. As the guest speaker gives his speech to the graduating students, he once more reiterates the show's original theme regarding teenage alienation. Max follows with his "coming out" speech, encouraging the students to be themselves no matter what others may think. His words, combined with Liz's advice, really hit home. Leaving high school is, for many, leaving normal. While Liz and the gang are in a more extreme situation

Shiri Appleby on the set of Roswell's *finale, "Graduation Day"*
(Photo by Christina Radish)

than most students heading off to college, the advice still rings true.

Max speaks of the "long, hard road" the teens have traveled, and we're reminded of just how adventurous a journey it's been when we see Geoff Parker reviewing Liz's story. It has been an ever-changing road: sometimes a joyous one, sometimes disappointing, sometimes thrilling. It has undoubtedly been a memorable road. Much had to be resolved in a short time, and the episode may not be perfect, but thankfully Jason Katims and Ron Moore have come through for the fans, giving us the chance to experience adventure, sorrow, and joy with the characters we have come to know and love. As the bumper sticker says: "Thank you for visiting Roswell!" I would like to say "Thank you, *Roswell*, for having us along for the ride."

FLASH: The wedding.

IRKS: I'm sorry that we don't get any goodbyes with Jim except for Kyle's. It's also a little odd that the principal wouldn't dispute Max taking over the podium. Max speaks of the feeling he got from helping Mrs. Mills, and yet she is the one who points the finger at him and Liz, albeit under duress. Maria seems to do a 180 in this episode by suddenly wanting to pursue a relationship with Michael. Why the change of heart? Finally, we've waited three long years to see Max and Liz consummate their relationship on the show — and nothing. What a disappointment!

DOUBLE TAKE: At the beginning of the episode, Kyle opens the Crashdown menu while talking with Liz. Seconds later, he opens it up again.

ALIENISMS: Liz has psychic flashes involving Mrs. Mills' potential death, her acceptance to Northwestern University, then later sees Isabel, Michael, Max, and herself shot. Max makes a gun fly out of the mugger's hand, sets off a car alarm, changes a written speech into a warning message, then makes the lights go out in the gym leaving only a spotlight. Michael blasts a ceramic statue out of anger, then creates a blinding light in the gym.

SODA MOMENT: Max makes a reference about Superman turning a piece of coal into a diamond. The moment occurs in *Superman* III. Knowing his high-school crush Lana Lang had to pawn her diamond engagement ring, Superman takes a piece of coal and creates a new diamond for her. Later, as Clark Kent, he gives her the ring courtesy of Superman. Considering the heavy competition from the series *Smallville* was one of the reasons *Roswell* was eventually cancelled, the reference was a sad reminder.

COOL FACT: The fans of *Roswell* continue to work hard to raise money for charity even though the show's fate has long since been sealed. Rumors of a movie spin-off continue to keep the fans hopeful, while reruns of the show will be broadcast by the Sci-Fi channel in the U.S.

MUSIC: "Somehow, Someday" by Ryan Adams plays while Liz and Max discuss their future plans in the Crashdown. Liz and Maria discuss her premonitions to "Here We Go Again" by Riddlin' Kids. Later, "Deep Love" by Mandalay is the make-out music for Liz and Max when she gets her first flash of their impending deaths. Frou Frou's song "Breathe In" is playing when Liz and Max make-out in her bed, and Liz sees Bryce in her vision. Finally, "Shining Light" by Ash fills the air as the group drive off on a new adventure.

Bibliography

THE ROSWELL INCIDENT

"This is something . . ." Marcel, Jesse Jr., "The Roswell Incident," *International* UFO *Museum and Research Center.* Online.

"Well, they're not . . ." Joyce, Frank, "The Roswell Incident," *International* UFO *Museum and Research Center.* Online.

THE POD SQUAD
JASON BEHR

"I don't know what . . ." Justin, Neal, "Jason Behr is from Here and There." *Star Tribune.* April 11, 2000.

"I got out of school . . ." "Jason Behr on AOL Live!" AOL *Live.* Online. April 17, 2000.

"It was great because . . ." Hensley, Dennis, "Behring It All." *Teen Movieline Magazine.* July 2000.

"I was always an outsider . . ." Moore, Richard, "Leaving Normal." *Xposé Magazine.* January 2000.

". . . is such an important . . ." "Jason Behr on AOL Live!" AOL *Live.* Online. February 19, 2001.

"Dawson's Creek was . . ." Moore, "Leaving Normal."

"When I was starting out . . ." Hensley, "Behring It All."

"I related to Max's search . . ." Hensley, "Behring It All."

"There are a lot . . ." Justin, "Jason Behr is from Here and There."

"First, let me say . . ." *Starlog.* November 1999.

"I found Jason . . ." Salva, Victor, "An Interview with Victor Salva, the director of *Rites of*

Passage." *Wolfe Video Web site.* Online. March 17, 2002.

"I actually got . . ." Behr, Jason, *The Rosie O'Donnell Show*, December 2001.

". . . our eyes started . . ." Hensley, "Behring It All."

"He's a professional . . ." Justin, "Jason Behr is from Here and There."

"Maybe that's why . . ." Justin, "Jason Behr is from Here and There."

"For people to tell you . . ." "Roswell Star Behr Mulls Movies." *SciFi Wire.* Online. March 13, 2000.

KATHERINE HEIGL

" . . . organ donation is . . ." Moran, W. Reed and Stephen A. Shoop, M.D., "Katherine Heigl says Families should discuss Organ Donation." *Spotlight Health.* May 16, 2002.

"[to] take us away . . ." Bryson, Jodi and Susan Miller, "Heavenly Creatures." *Teen Magazine.* November 2000.

"[Acting is] like . . ." Spelling, Ian, "Acting Alien: An Interview with Katherine Heigl." *Sci-Fi TV Magazine.* April 2000.

"Eventually the director . . ." Bell, Chris, "Close Encounter." FHM *Magazine.* October 2000.

"I was a good . . ." *Iannios Broutman Public Relations Biography for Katherine Heigl.*

"This is what . . ." Spelling, "Acting Alien."

"Katie Heigl's character . . ." *Starlog.* November 1999.

". . . just because she . . ." Heigl, Katherine, Internet chat. AOL/TV *Guide Online.* May 12, 2000.

"She's the girl . . ." Spelling, "Acting Alien."

"When I started . . ." Spelling, "Acting Alien."

"That makes up . . ." Spelling, "Acting Alien."

". . . she would get into it . . ." Spelling, "Acting Alien."

"It's a different story . . ." Beck, Marilyn and Stacey Jenel Smith, *San Francisco Chronicle.* November 30, 2001.

"It takes a lot . . ." Heigl, Internet Chat.

"Whenever I'm watching . . ." Heigl, Internet Chat.

BRENDAN FEHR

"I like math . . ." Rammairone, Nerina, "Faces & Places: Man of the Hour." US *Magazine.* March 2000.

"I was a smartass . . ." "Cutie Close Encounter." MXG *Magazine.* Feb/Mar 2000.

"In Winnipeg . . ." "Q & A with Brendan Fehr." FHM *Magazine.* July/August, 2001.

"When Metallica . . ." "Q & A with Brendan Fehr."

"He had just . . ." Spaner, David, "No! — Fehr: BC's Brendan Fehr stays clear of sex, drugs and alcohol." *The Province.* May 2000.

"It was going . . ." Wallenfels, Jessica, "Roswell." *Ultimate* TV. Online. October 1999.

"Anthony said in . . ." Fehr, Brendan, Interview with Vicki Gabereau. *The Vicki Gabereau Show.* Vancouver. October, 1999.

". . . his least favorite . . ." Wallenfels, "Roswell."

"Acting's not fun . . ." Wallenfels, "Roswell."

"Brendan Fehr has . . ." *Starlog Magazine*, November 1999.

"I didn't like . . ." St. Germain, Pat, "Fehr & Square." *Winnipeg Sun.* January 12, 2000.

"When I moved . . ." Coble, Leesa, "Guy We Love." JUMP *Magazine.* March, 2000.

". . . never been drunk . . ." Socol, Gary, "Brendan Interview." *Movieline* magazine. March, 2000.

"that's just common sense . . ." Spaner, "No!"

". . . our sense of humor . . ." Wallenfels, "Roswell."

"I signed with Roswell . . ." Gross, Edward, "Roswell: Producer Jason Katims," *Fandom.com.* Online. April 24, 2000.

"[Brendan's] one of . . ." Oswald, Brad, "No Longer Alien." *Winnipeg Free Press.* January 15, 2000.

". . . a good, character driven . . ." Celebrity section, *L.A. Daily News.* September 10, 2001.

"The person I want . . ." Oswald, "No Longer Alien."

". . . personal growth . . ." St. Germain, "Fehr & Square."

"Don't let yourselves . . ." Fehr, Brendan, "Passions Focus & Importance." *Brendan-Fehr.com. Message board.* Online. January, 2000.

THE CRASHDOWN WAITRESSES
SHIRI APPLEBY

"I just wanted . . ." Rudolph, Amanda, "Backstage Pass: Shiri In Bliss." *Seventeen Magazine.* February 2000.

"I wanted to . . ." Conroy, Tom, "Coming Up Next: Shiri Appleby." *Rolling Stone Magazine.* September 1999.

"I decided I was . . ." Beebe, David, "Roswell's Shiri Appleby." *Venice Magazine.* October 2001.

"A friend of mine . . ." Rudolph, "Backstage Pass."

"A.J. had worked with . . ." *Starlog Magazine.* November 1999.

". . . because I wasn't . . ." Florence, Bill, "Down-to-Earth Shiri Appleby educates 'Roswell's' Alienated Liz Parker." *Starlog Magazine.* December 2000.

"[Jason Katims] really is . . ." Moore, Richard, "Leaving Normal."

"I had my schoolbooks . . ." Schatz Rosenthal, Sharon, "Star Crossed Lover." WHAT *Magazine.* December 2001.

"I just hung up . . ." Rudolph, "Backstage Pass."

"In the first season . . ." Beebe, "Roswell's Shiri Appleby."

". . . incredibly touched . . ." Appleby, Shiri, TV *Guide* AOL *Live Chat Transcript.* Online. October 16, 2001.

"You just wanna . . ." Moore, "Leaving Normal."

"While I was reading . . ." *Teen Movieline Magazine.* Spring 2001.

"the most positively . . ." Appleby, Shiri, "Alien Love Story." *ETOnline.com.* Online. November 8, 2001.

"This kind of stuff . . ." Beebe, "Roswell's Shiri Appleby."

"People think I'm . . ." Schaltz, Rosenthal, "Star Crossed Lover."

"I don't feel . . ." Appleby, TV *Guide* AOL *Live Chat Transcript.*

MAJANDRA DELFINO

"[I] was told . . ." Delfino, Majandra, TV *Guide Online.* February 29, 2000.

"He was just . . ." Delfino, Majandra, "Majandra answers more Fan Questions from Fan Forum," Crashdown.com. Online. November 14, 2001.

"I guess when . . ." Lumpkin, Jenni and Kathy Wyman, "Majandra Delfino," *efanguide.com.* Online. May 7, 2000.

"I guess when . . ." "You're on the Roswell Set!" *Entertainment Teen Magazine.* May 2000.

"In the tenth grade . . ." Lumpkin and Wyman, "Majandra Delfino."

"When I read the script . . ." Martindale, David, "Meet Majandra Delfino." *The Fort Worth Star-Telegram.* May 9, 2000.

" . . . when you go in to test . . ." Radish, Christina, "Delfino's Delight." *Filmstew.com.* Online. 2001.

" . . . my character's crazy . . ." Radish, "Delfino's Delight."

". . . never been more . . ." Delfino, "Majandra answers."

"Napkins . . ." Delfino, "Majandra answers."

"When I wrote . . ." Delfino, "Majandra answers."

"The whole point of . . ." Radish, "Delfino's Delight."

"Find a good . . ." Delfino, Majandra, "Star Boards — Majandra Delfino." Eonline.com. Online. 2001.

". . . she always has . . ." "Majandra Revealed." MXG *Magazine.* June/July 2000.

"It is a joy . . ." Delfino, "Majandra answers."

"Shiri is kind of like . . ." Delfino, TV *Guide Online.*

"Children are our angels . . ." Meister, Hillary, "The Roswell Connection." *Route99Live.com.* Online. 2001.

"Probably married and . . ." Lumpkin and Wyman, "Majandra Delfino."

THE SUPPORTING CAST
WILLIAM SADLER

"I loved that place . . ." Sadler, William, "William Sadler: The Early Years." *William Sadler Wild on the Web.* Online.

"In a way, I feel . . ." Spelling, Ian, "The Law in Roswell." *Starlog Magazine.* March 2000.

"My friend and I . . ." "Aliens Won't Elude Roswell Sheriff." *SciFi Wire.* Online. February 1, 2000.

"It was more fun . . ." Sadler, "William Sadler: The Early Years."

"My father insisted . . ." Sadler, "William Sadler: The Early Years."

"Playing one of the . . ." Sadler, William, "Welcome to the Theatre, Mr. Sadler!" *William Sadler Wild on the Web.* Online.

"I knew I would . . ." Sadler, "Welcome to the Theatre, Mr. Sadler!"

"The film scared me . . ." Spelling, "The Law in Roswell."

"We didn't know . . ." Spelling, "The Law in Roswell."

"We didn't know whether . . ." Carter, Chelsea, "The Age: William Sadler goes from Big Screen to Small." Associated Press. November 19, 2000.

"I really admire . . ." "TV. 2000 Roswell — Get to Know the Cast Behind this Teen Alien Nation." *"16" Magazine.* February 2000.

"I sometimes wonder . . ." Carter, "The Age."

"I've seen it . . ." Sadler, William, AT&T WorldNet Community. Online chat. October 29, 2001.

NICK WECHSLER

"I saw a play . . ." Wechsler, Nick. *efanguide.com.* Online chat. August 13, 2000.

"She taught me . . ." "T.V. 2000 Roswell."

"I didn't go through . . ." Wechsler, *efanguide.com.*

". . . the one who . . ." "Team Knight Rider press kit." *Team Knight Rider.com.* Online. 1997.

"I had to get . . ." Carter, Chelsea, "Five Questions with Nick Wechsler." *Yahoo.com.* Online. January 31, 2001.

"He's so damned . . ." Wechsler, Nick, *React.com.* Online chat. February 2000.

"It's kind of strange . . ." Carter, "Five Questions with Nick Wechsler."

"I know I'll be . . ." Carter, "Five Questions with Nick Wechsler."

"He's got these . . ." Wallenfels, Jessica, "Roswell." *Ultimate* TV. Online. October 1999.

"Pretending . . ." Wechsler, *React.com*.

"[Nick's] very gifted . . ." Spelling, Ian, "The Law in Roswell."

"My favorite thing . . ." Wechsler, *efanguide.com*.

COLIN HANKS

"For me, it's always . . ." Pierce, Scott D., "Tom Hanks' Son says he Became an Actor because it was 'All I'm really good at.'" *Deseret News*. March 2000.

"I'm pretty outgoing . . ." "You're on the Roswell Set!" *Entertainment Teen Magazine*. May 2000.

"[My father] stayed . . ." Pierce, "Tom Hanks' Son."

"People are always so . . ." Higgons, Jenny, "Rocket Man," *Gist.com*. Online. November 2000.

"The pilot . . ." Pierce, "Tom Hanks' Son."

"I went through . . ." Carter, Chelsea, "Five Questions with Colin Hanks: Standing on his own feet," Associated Press. March 8, 2000.

" . . . just because a kid . . ." Higgons, "Rocket Man."

"I'm just happy . . ." Pierce, "Tom Hanks' Son."

"Two weeks later . . ." Pickle, Betsy, "What's in a Name?" Scripps Howard News Service. January 2002.

"And to be honest . . ." Guthmann, Edward, "In his father's footsteps: Colin Hanks moves out from the shadow of his famous dad." *San Francisco Chronicle*. January 12, 2002.

ADAM RODRIGUEZ

" . . . strong, with . . ." Sanchez, Joy, "Behind the Badge." *Latina Magazine*. May 1998.

"My payback for . . ." Sibbald, Vanessa, "Adam Rodriguez has 'Soul.'" *Zap2it*. Online. April 17, 2001.

" . . . I had to go in . . ." Sibbald, "Adam Rodriguez has 'Soul.'"

"I get to do . . ." Sibbald, "Adam Rodriguez has 'Soul.'"

"I think that . . ." Spelling, Ian, "I Married an Alien." *Cult Times*. Special Edition #20, Christmas 2001.

"I had to learn . . ." "Rodriguez Reveals Roswell Details." *SciFi Wire*. Online. November 13, 2001.

"I'd like to bring . . ." Spelling, "I Married an Alien."

EMILIE DE RAVIN

"I'm very into . . ." Higgons, Jenny, "True Grit." *Gist.com*. Online. April 2001.

"When I read . . ." Spelling, Ian, "Going Ravin Mad!" *Xposé Magazine*. January 2001.

"We get along . . ." Florence, Bill, "The Fourth Alien." *Starlog Magazine*. June 2001.

"Those two guys . . ." Florence, "The Fourth Alien."

"At first I got . . ." "Sci-Fi Babes: Emilie De Ravin." FHM *Magazine*. July/August 2001.

" . . . I haven't had any . . ." Spelling, "Going Ravin Mad!"

"I was online . . ." Spelling, "Going Ravin Mad!"

"It's a wonderful way . . ." Higgons, "True Grit."

"I want to pursue . . ." Florence, "The Fourth Alien."

THE ROSWELL FAN PHENOMENON
THE ALIENS HAVE LANDED

" . . . if you want . . ." Katims, Jason, "The Roswell Press Tour transcript." *Crashdown.com*. Online. July 1999.

"My biggest goal . . ." Nazzaro, Joe, "Roswell High: Educating Aliens." TV *Zone Magazine*. April 2000.

" . . . the Isabel character . . ." Amy, "An Interview with Roswell's Kevin Kelly Brown." *Popgurls.com*. Online.

"If you don't . . ." Nazzaro, "Roswell High: Educating Aliens."

"You cast for . . ." "The Cast of Roswell, Outsiders for the Millennium." *Space.com's Guide to the Series*. October 5, 1999.

". . . skewed too young . . ." Jackson, Terry, "WB Matches Teens, Aliens in Roswell." *Miami Herald*. July 24, 1999.

" . . . I think . . ." Nutter, David. "The Roswell Press Tour transcript."

"I think that Roswell is going . . ." Spelling, Ian, "New Frontiers." *Starburst Magazine*. February 2000.

"I think that Roswell is going to be . . ." Gross, Edward, "Jonathan Frakes on Relaunching Roswell." *Cinescape Magazine*. April 3, 2000.

"We're hopeful, but . . ." "Roswell Heads for Cliffhanger," *SciFi.com*. Online. February 28, 2000.

". . . the top-ranked . . ." Strachan, Alex, "Roswell a Surprise on TV and Online." *Vancouver Sun*. March 6, 2000.

TABASCO TO THE RESCUE

"But it doesn't mean anything . . ." Kelly Brown, Kevin, "Letter from Kevin Brown to Roswell
   Fans." *Crashdown.com*. Online, March 2000.

TABASCO TO THE RESCUE — AGAIN!

"[The show] evolved in all . . ." "Roswell Talk, Jonathan Frakes." *Cinescape Magazine*. July
   2000.

" . . . the character interaction . . ." McCarthy, Mandy, "Save Our Roswell." *Zap2it*. Online.
   April 10, 2001.

"There are many reasons . . ." McCarthy, "Save Our Roswell."

"The fact that [Buffy] . . ." O'Hare, Kate, "Roswell Faces Departure." *Zap2it*. Online. May
   8, 2001.

"We're in a good . . ." Wolfe, Ron, "Roswell Rolls On." *Zap2it*. Online. June 2001.

" . . . when Jason [Katims] offered . . ." Bergman, Kristi, "Crashdown Interview with Melinda
   Metz and Laura Burns." *Crashdown.com*. Online. October 2001.

". . . all the production . . ." Bergman, "Crashdown Interview."

"WHAT HAPPENS NOW, MAX?"

"What [UPN] wants . . ." Wanda, "Wanda Welcomes the Lovely Ladies of Roswell for a Live,
   Out-of-This-World Chat!" *E!Online*. Online. November 9, 2001.

" . . . we were prepared . . ." "Roswell Happy with UPN." *SciFi Wire*. Online. October 23, 2001.

"When we first started . . ." "Behr Bears Roswell." *SciFi Wire*. Online. December 18, 2001.

"I'd never do . . ." Sibbald, Vanessa, "Roswell's Fehr Swears Off TV Acting." *Zap2it*. Online.
   November 2001.

" . . . several of the stars . . ." Jay, Kimber, "Scoops & Spoilers." *Teenmag.com*. December 2001.

". . . sort of a love . . ." Gold, Kenn, "Fan Forum/Crashdown's Interview with Jason Katims."
   Crashdown.com. Online. March 20, 2002.

"I also worked . . ." Gold, Kenn, "Fan Forum/Crashdown's Interview with Jason Katims."
   Crashdown.com. Online. March 20, 2002.

SEASON TWO
MEET THE DUPES — COOL FACT

"It just looks funny . . ." "Q & A with Brendan Fehr." FHM *Magazine*. July/August 2001.

SEASON THREE
CHANT DOWN BABYLON

"And the woman was . . ." Revelations 17:4-6. *New Testament.* The Gideons International. 1985.

"And the woman whom . . ." "Revelations 17:18." *New Testament.* The Gideons International. 1985.

GRADUATION

". . . [the episode is] sort . . ." Gold, Kenn, "Fan Forum/Crashdown's Interview With Jason Katims." *Crashdown.com.* Online. March 20, 2002.

EPISODE GUIDE

"14 Days in October: The Cuban Missile Crisis." *ThinkQuest.* Online. February 14, 2002.

"The Age of Majority." *Tangled Moon Coven.* Online. February 10, 2002.

Allingham, Philip V. "A Synopsis of Dickens' A Tale of Two Cities." *The Victorian Web.* Online. May 28, 2002.

"The Andy Griffith Show." *TV Land.* Online. February 16, 2002.

Armstrong, Mark. "Anne Heche Hospitalized." *E! Online News.* Online. June 2, 2002.

"Article on Show from Parents Council." *Crashdown November* 2001 *archives.* Online. May 22, 2002.

Attenborough, Richard. "A Brief History of Mohandas K. Gandhi." *Engaged Buddhist-Dharma.* Online. February 3, 2002.

Beck, Sanderson. "Ethics of Hindu Philosophy." *Literary Works of Sanderson Beck.* Online. February 3, 2002.

Brackett, Leigh and Lawrence Kasdan. "The Empire Strikes Back." *Sci-Fi Scripts.* Online. February 13, 2002.

Brumbaugh, Robert S. "Diogenes of Sinope . . ." *The Wild Bohemian.* Online. May 31, 2002.

"Buffy The Vampire Slayer — Episode Guide." TV *Tome.* Online. February 19, 2002.

C-Span.org. Online. February 13, 2002.

Carlin, Gerry and Evans, Mair. "Notes on James Joyce's Ulysses." *University of Wolverhampton, U.K.* Personal Web Pages. Online. February 4, 2002.

"Chaka Khan Biography." *The Chaka Khan Official Web Site.* Online. February 10, 2002.

"Chaplain serves as coordinator of Native American Spirituality." *North Carolina Department of Correction News — July* 1999. Online. February 6, 2002.

Cook, Anthony, Christopher Hansen, and Melanie Wang. "The History of the Observatory." *The Griffith Observatory Home Page.* Online. February 20, 2002.

"Cyclotron." *Physics.about.com.* Online. February 13, 2002.

"DEFCON — Defense Condition." *Federation of American Scientists.* Online. May 24, 2002.

"Deputy Dawg." *Yesterdayland.* Online. February 15, 2002.

"Dick Clark's New Year's Rockin' Eve." *Dick Clark Productions.* Online. May 28, 2002.

Dirks, Tim. "Bonnie and Clyde." *Greatest Films.* Online. May 15, 2002.

Doak, Michael. "Native American Spirituality." *Religious Movements Page, University of Virginia.* Online. February 6, 2002.

"English as a Second Language." *About Homework help.* Online. May 28, 2002.

"Favorite McCoy Lines." *The Trek* BBS. Online. May 28, 2002.

Flaspoehler Jr., Edward P. *The Constellation Aries — The Ram.* The American Association of Amateur Astronomers. February 12, 2002.

"Food as a Drug." *Zone Perfect.* Online. May 22, 2002.

Frost, Robert. "Stopping By The Woods On a Snowy Evening." *Jollyroger.com.* Online. February 20, 2002.

George, Roy. "The Encyclopedia of the Goddess Athena." *The Shrine of the Goddess Athena.* Online. May 28, 2002.

Goodman, David H. "'Dad' — Episode description." *Welcome to Angel's Acolyte.* Online. June 3, 2002.

"Guy Lombardo." *Infoplease.* Online. May 28, 2002.

Harte, Holly. "The Texas Healing Women Trilogy." *Holly Harte.* Online. February 4, 2002.

"Heckle and Jeckle." *Yesterdayland.* Online. February 22, 2002.

Hooker, Richard. "Exile 597–538 B.C." *The Hebrews: A Learning Module.* Online. May 31, 2002.

"Israel." *The Internet Ancient History Sourcebook.* Online. May 31, 2002.

"It's the Eye Of The Tiger . . ." *Dooyoo.* Online. May 17, 2002.

"James Joyce's Ulysses." "Culture Shock Literature." *PBS.org.* Online. February 4, 2002.

Kingsbury, Linda, Dr. "Spirit Herbs for Awareness." *Spirit Herbs.* Online. February 10, 2002.

"Knives and Scissors — Not a good gift." ABC*'s for* ABC*'s* . Online. February 16, 2002.

Kooper, Rob. "Virtual Reality Exposure Therapy." *Graphics Visualization and Usability Center.* Online. February 22, 2002.

Krystek, Lee. "Amazing Mazes." *Museum of Unnatural Mystery.* Online. February 12, 2002.

"La Jolla home." *La Jolla.* Online. May 23, 2002.

"Long Live the Queen." *Bewitched.net.* Online. May 28, 2002.

"Machu Picchu, Home of the Ancients." *Machu-Picchu, Peru.* Online. February 6, 2002.

Mair, Evan, M.D. "Medical Encyclopedia — Cranial MRI." *Medline Plus Health Information.* Online. February 5, 2002.

"Making Hubble Work." *The Hubble Project.* Online. February 12, 2002.

Malaiya, Yashwant. "Gandhi's Religious Background." *Colorado State University*. Online. February 3, 2002.

Mankiewicz, Tom (final revision). "Superman — Shooting script." *Sci-Fi Scripts*. Online. February 13, 2002.

McCabe, Joseph. "Babylon and Its People." *The Story of Religious Controversy*. Online. May 31, 2002.

"Mescalero Apache Tribe." *NewMexico.org*. Online. February 4, 2002.

"Miko Hughes." *LonoMyth's Kid Actor Spotlight*. Online. February 16, 2002.

"Military Terminology." *Military Lexicon*. Online. June 2, 2002.

Mitchell, Robert. "International UFO Congress." *International UFO Congress*. Online. February 9, 2002.

"Population and Welfare." *Statistics Sweden*. Online. February 20, 2002.

Quinion, Michael, "Frick and Frack." Q and A Section. *World Wide Words*. Online. February 8, 2002.

Reader's Digest Travel Guide to North America. The Reader's Digest Association. 1996.

"Roswell Frequently Asked Questions." *Roswell Convention and Visitors Bureau*. Online. February 9, 2002.

Shakespeare, William. *Hamlet*.

Tate, Scott. "Virtual Reality: A Historical Perspective." *Virginia Polytechnical Institute and State University*. Online. February 22, 2002.

"Virtual Reality: History." Cyberia. *The National Center for Supercomputing Applications*. University of Illinois. Online. February 22, 2002.

"Voodoo History." *Vudutuu.com*. Online. February 6, 2002.

"Welcome to John Gray's Universe." *Marsvenus.com*. Online. February 9, 2002.

Welcome Wagon Canada. Online. February 12, 2002.

"Who are Mutt and Jeff?" *Ask Yahoo!* Online. February 18, 2002.

Yee, Matthew. "Charles Dederich, founder of cult-like religious group Synanon, dies at 83." The Associated Press. *Recovery Watch*. Online. February 8, 2002.

ADDITIONAL SOURCES

Appleby, Shiri and Ellen Lieberman (editor). "Roswell Rescuer." *Teen Magazine*. May 2000.

"The Art of Being . . . Brendan Fehr." *TheWB.com*. Online. 2001.

"Bad Boys We Love — Brendan Fehr." TV *Guide Ultimate Cable*. April 29, 2000.

Beebe, David, "Katherine Heigl." *Venice Magazine*. December 1998.

"Behr Essentials." *Dreamwatch Magazine*. April 2000.

"Behring It All Again!" *Teenmovieline.com*. Online. July 2000.

Blood Brother. Online.

Boyle, Fionna. Brendan's Biography. *Crashdown*. Online.

Brady, James. "In Step With Katherine Heigl." *Parade Magazine — The Philadelphia Inquirer*. February 13, 2000.

Braxton, Greg. "Frakes to Guide *Roswell* Toward Older Generation." *L.A. Times*. April 2000.

"Brendan Fehr Chat Transcript." *React.com*. Online. 1999.

Brendan's Interview. MXG *Magazine*. January 2000.

Bury, Martine. *Cosmo Girl Magazine*. October/November 1999.

Calderone, Samantha. *Meet the Stars of Roswell*. New York: Scholastic Books, 2000.

Carter, Chelsea J. "Jason Behr Blasts Off!" Associated Press. March 6, 2000.

Colin Hanks Interview. *Entertainment Teen*. May 2000.

"Colin Hanks is his Own Person." *Lifestyle, Philippine Daily Inquirer*. April 16, 2000.

Conroy, Tom. "Shiri Appleby article." *Rolling Stone Magazine*. September 1999.

Cooney Carrillo, Jenny. "Tom's Boy Colin." *TV Week*. Australia. May 27–June 2, 2000.

Majandra Delfino interview on 102.7 KIIS FM, Los Angeles. February 29, 2000.

——. Interview. TV *Guide on* AOL. Online. March 2000.

Dianne Farr article. *Daily Variety*. March 23, 2000.

"Diversity on Roswell." *Roswell: Space.com's Guide to the Series*. Online. October 5, 1999.

Duffy-Stone, Heather. "Brendan Fehr: alien among us." *React.com*. Online. January 16, 2000.

Emilie de Ravin Online. Online.

"E.T. Does It." *People Magazine*. December 13, 1999.

Feldman, Len P. "Jason Behr Copes with Teenage Alienation." *Gist.com*. Online. April, 2000.

"Frakes Sees Roswell Pickup." *SciFi.com*. Online. February 17, 2000.

Giltz, Michael. "TV's Five Freshest Faces." *New York Post*. January, 2000.

Gross, Edward. "Roswell: The Behr Necessities." *Fandom.com*. Online. April 10, 2000.

Guss, Daniel. "Home Theater: Bachelor Party." *Movieline Magazine*. April 2000.

Heigl, Katherine and Nancy Heigl. In-Studio Guests. *Crossing Over with John Edward*. June 25, 2001.

Herrera Mulligan, Michelle. "The Bright Pack." *Latina Magazine*. November 1999.

Hewett, Simone. "Jason's new world as a secret . . . ALIEN." *Sunday Telegraph* TV *Guide*. Australia. March 11, 2000.

Huff, Richard. "'Roswell': A Fehr Appreciation." *New York Daily News*. May 8, 2000.

——. "Series Fans Speak Out." *New York Daily News*. March 21, 2000.

The Internet Movie Database. Online.

"Jason Behr, Extraterrestrial — The *Roswell* Hottie's E.T. Obsession Saves the Day."

"Jason Behr — Out of this World Actor." *J-14 Magazine*. January, 2000.

Jason Behr Unlimited. Online.

"Jason Behr's Career about to Take Off!" *Washington Times*. February 2000.

"Jason Felt Like an Alien in High School." *J-14 Magazine.* April 2000.

Jekielek Insprucker, Mary. "Meet Roswell's Shiri Appleby!" 16 *Magazine.* March 2000.

Kaplan, Don. "Hanks A Million." *New York Post.* May 26, 1999.

Katherine Heigl Online.

Laudadio, Marisa. "Actress Profiles." *Teen Magazine.* January, 2000.

Lee, Patrick. "What Planet is Jason Katims From?" *SciFi.com Weekly.* Online. March 2000.

Levesque, John. "Doubtful At First, Heigl Now a Believer in Roswell." *Seattle Post-Intelligencer.* May 2000.

Lishings, Linda. "The Nutter Files." *TheWB.com.* Online. January 2000.

"Living on a Fault Line." *N.Z. Herald.* February 19, 2000.

"Mad Max and Brendan?" *ComingSoon Net.* Online. November 22, 2001.

Mandy. "Brendan Fehr Sizzles in Interview." *UltimateTV.* Online. January 12, 2000.

Mason, Dave. "Aliens Among Humans." *Ventura County Star.* March 2000.

McLatchie, Heather. "The 'Roswell' File." *ChickClick.com.* Online. July 2000.

Metz, Melinda. *Roswell High.* New York: Pocket Books, 2000.

Moore, Jim. "Earth to Aliens: It's a New Millenium, so Give Us a Call." *Seattle Post-Intelligencer.* January 1, 2000.

Moore, Richard. "Alien Love! Jason Behr Talks Roswell." *Xposé Magazine.* January 2000.

Muse, Heather (introduction) and Amanda Rudolph (interview). "Shiri In Bliss." *Seventeen Magazine.* January 2000.

Musto, Michael. "Shiri Appleby." *Interview Magazine.* December, 1999.

The Nick Wechsler Fan Base. Online.

Nick Wechsler. KLUC radio interview. Las Vegas. May 1, 2000.

"Nutter Leaving Roswell?" *SciFi.com News Wire.* Online. February 7, 2000.

O'Hare, Kate. "Other Worlds." *Tribune.* March 2000.

Oz Crash Festival. Online.

"Plot Thickens on Roswell." *Pittsburgh Post-Gazette.* April 21, 2000.

Pond, Steve. "Secrets & Fries." *TV Guide.* February 5-11, 2000.

Roberts, Robin. "Vancouver Actor A Model E.T." *TV Week.* November, 1999.

Roche, Eddie. "Roswell Star Reveals Paper Cut Drama." *TV Guide.* May 23, 2000.

Rochlin, Margy. "Running a Network Like a '30s Film Studio." *New York Times.* December 12, 1999.

Rohan, Virginia. "Earth to WB." *The Record* (Bergen County, NJ). May 10, 2000.

Romine, Damon. "The Aliens are Among Us!" *Soap Opera Update.* February 1, 2000.

"Roswell Actors Ponder Their Fate." *TVGuide.com.* Online. April 17, 2000.

"Roswell Close Encounters — for authorized eyes only." *Entertainment Teen Magazine.* January, 2000.

Roswell High. Online.

"Roswell Rocks with Humanity." *Gannett News Service*. February 2000.

Rudolph, Amanda. "Sizzling Sixteen 2000." *E! Online*. Online. January 7, 2000.

Ryon, Ruth. "Sunset Strip Area is now Alien Territory." *L.A. Times*. March 9, 2000.

Shaw, Kristen. "20 Things You Never Knew about Roswell." *Twist Magazine*. January 2000.

Shiri Online.

Socol, Gary. "Jason Behr Thinks Starring on 'Roswell' is Out of this World." *New York Times Special Features*. December 10, 1999.

——. "What on Earth? It's Not Easy Being A Hunted Alien . . . But She Deals." *Chicago Tribune*. December 28, 1999.

Spelling, Ian. "The Kids are ET." *Cult Times*. January 2000.

St. Germain, Pat. "X-Files Jr." *Winnipeg Sun*. October 7, 1999.

"Star Chat — Julie Benz." *Teen Celebrity*. February, 2000.

Starr, Michael. "Can Hot Sauce Save This Show?" *New York Post*. April 7, 2000.

"The 25 Hottest Stars Under 25." *Teen People*. June/July 2000.

Topping, Keith. *Roswell High Times*. U.K.: Virgin Books, 2001.

Transcript of the WB 20 Cast Interview. March 30, 2000.

"Various Awards involving Roswell." *Crashdown.com*. Online. March 21, 2000.

Vitrano, Alyssa. "Who Says Roswell Rocks?" *YM Magazine*. March 2000.

Webroswell.com. Online.

Weeks, Janet. "X-Rocker John Doe Finds a New Beat on Roswell." *TV Guide Ultimate Cable Magazine*. February 5–11, 2000.

Weinstein, Farrah. "Katherine Heigl." *New York Post*. February 6, 2000.

Zitz, Michael. "Majandra Delfino Wants Out of Roswell." *The Free Lance-Star*. February 14, 2002.